Rober

February 1977

Paris

A THEORY OF CONFLICT

A THEORY
OF CONFLICT

BRIAN CROZIER

HAMISH HAMILTON
LONDON

First published in Great Britain 1974
by Hamish Hamilton Ltd
90 Great Russell Street London WC1

Copyright © 1974 by Brian Crozier

SBN 241 02458 7

This book is dedicated to the victims of

Revolution

the world over

Printed in Great Britain by
Western Printing Services Ltd, Bristol

CONTENTS

Author's Note

By kind permission of the Chairman and Council of the Institute for the Study of Conflict, this book contains certain passages drawn from my own contributions to ISC publications. The views expressed, however, are my own: they do not commit either the Institute or its Council, still less individual members of the latter.

INTRODUCTION

This is a work of political and moral philosophy. I am concerned almost exclusively with *revolutionary* conflict: international challenges to the authority of the State. Is the State necessary? I argue that it is. Why, then, is rebellion against it inevitable (as I also argue)?

Part I is concerned with the fundamentals of conflict: the necessity of the State and the causes of rebellion. Part II looks at the State in greater detail, since this is what the rebel wishes to destroy or bring down. I trace and interpret the history of the State, and of theories of the State, from earliest times. But since the questions I raise are not only fundamental and timeless but also of the most urgent topical interest, I turn next to contemporary events and problems. I try, however, to write of these matters as though already benefiting from historical perspective. I describe, therefore, in broad but selective terms, the state of the world in the 1970s and how it came to be what it is, attempting (in a manner that cannot, fortunately for the writer, be disproved in the immediate future) to see it as a later historian might.

I conclude that in our time, the alternatives to pluralism are the authoritarian way and the totalist (which I suggest as a less cumbrous substitute for totalitarian); and that in western Europe especially, the dangers of the totalist alternative (and the lesser danger of the authoritarian one) are enormously increased by the preponderant military power and forward policy of the Soviet Union, and by the gradual abandonment by the United States of its world role.

After dealing with the specific revolutionary challenges of our time, I turn to the capacity of existing States to contain, suppress or divert revolutionary challenges, and dwell upon methods of prevention and repression.

At this point, I return to history and philosophy, in parts IV and V. Past and present examples of revolutions are considered, and judged by the light of their leaders' stated aims and claims.

The moral and practical problems involved in the containment of dissent are then examined: and I turn at the end to suggestions of a suitable polity for the technological age, or post-industrial society.

Since the purpose of this note is to inform and forewarn, it is only fair for me to mention my underlying assumptions. My 'axioms', in the Spinozan sense, concern the nature of the human animal (that is, of Man; which, if the feminists will forgive me, or even if they will not, includes Woman). They are these:

—Man is innately envious and aggressive.
—His nature is not subject to change (except perhaps through bio-chemical means still insufficiently tested).
—His behaviour, however, is susceptible to change, either for the better or for the worse. (Indeed, behavioural change can be in-duced, for instance through brain surgery.)
—He has an overwhelming need of order.
—Human progress is dependent upon free inquiry.

Traditionally, it has no more been required of a philosopher (whether amateur or professional) than of a geometrician, that he should adduce proof for his axioms, since by definition the latter are self-evident. The trouble with my set of 'axioms', however, is that many people will not accept them as self-evident. (Hence my inverted commas.) If the truth of my five assertions is accepted, the inevitability of conflict will be readily perceived, and the implications of this inevitability are further explored in Chapter 1, and indeed throughout the book. Not all will accept the assertions, however, and I therefore offer a summary defence of them:

1. *Man is innately envious and aggressive.* The concept of the 'noble savage', popularised though not invented by Rousseau, has been completely exploded by the findings of modern anthropology and ethology. The persistence of the myth, which lies at the base of much socialist thinking and of modern educational theories, reflects the prevalence of naïvety and the readiness of men to accept flattering self-portraits.

To take a less flattering view is not to take a wholly negative one. Both aggression and envy may perform socially useful functions. Aggressiveness has been defined as 'the competition of beings without which natural selection could not take place'.[1] As such, it does not necessarily entail violence. One authority sees aggression (including violent aggression) as important to the survival of the species.[2] Even

[1] Robert Ardrey, *The Socialist Contract* (Fontana edition, 1972), p. 257.
[2] Konrad Lorenz, 'Ritualised Fighting' in *The Natural History of Aggression*

Freud, who began by denying the existence of a separate instinct of aggression, concluded in the end that 'the tendency to aggression is an innate, independent, instinctual disposition in man.'[3]

Of envy, it could be said that we are all surrounded by evidences that it is of the nature of Man. Less research has been done in this field than in that of aggression, but much ground was covered by Professor Helmut Schoeck of Mainz in a powerful, difficult but rewarding work, *Envy: A Theory of Social Behaviour*.[4] A sociologist, Schoeck based his theory largely upon contemporary anthropological research —a fact that prompted Lord Halsbury to comment: 'If the egalitarians would talk less and read more anthropological literature, they might have a better appreciation of the social dynamite they are playing with.'

Unfortunately, egalitarians, idealists and do-gooders are generally reluctant to concede the existence of envy, let alone study its manifestations. Although Schoeck worked independently from Ardrey and along different disciplinary lines, he reached much the same conclusions in his view that society is made possible by the instinct to cast out the stranger or refuse him admittance, while making the necessary social compromises to stay within the group. This is Ardrey's 'territorial imperative'[5] in different words. It leads Schoeck, however, to conclude that without envy, society would not be possible: fearing the envy of others, the individual tends to conform lest he be made an outcast.

Socially useful though both envy and aggression can be, it seems equally clear that in widely varying circumstances, they can also be causes of revolutionary conflict. In exacerbated form, envy lies at the core of the revolutionary psychology; and aggression channels it into violent forms.

2. *Man's nature is not subject to change.* Such, at least, is the evidence of history. Having said this, I add immediately that on a point so fundamental, history proves nothing. To say this is not to accept Henry Ford's terse and celebrated dismissal of history as 'bunk'. But the fact remains that historical experience, extending at the most over 10,000 years or so, represents a drop in the ocean of Man's existence.

(Institute of Biology, Academic Press, London and New York), p. 39. See also the same author's *On Aggression* (Methuen, 1972 impression).

[3] The words are those of Derek Freeman, of the Australian National University, in the Institute of Biology symposium quoted in the preceding footnote.

[4] Secker & Warburg (London), 1969. The implications of Schoeck's work were considered, and his conclusions sharpened, in an unpublished and privately circulated precis and commentary by Lord Halsbury, FRS, from which I quote above.

[5] See the best-selling work of that name (1967; Fontana edition, 1972).

We do not yet know for certain whether the nature of Man has always been the same. Nor can we be certain that it will never change in the future. All we can say is that there is absolutely no evidence to suggest that Man's nature is changing for the better, or at all. Hitler's genocide of the Jews, Stalin's great terror, or the tribal massacres of Burundi yield not at all in horror to the monstrous deeds of Tamerlane or Ghengis Khan.

What is perhaps more relevant to this book is that none of the social and political theories predicated on the perfectibility of Man has been validated by events. This is as true of the experiments of Robert Owen and other Utopians, as of the more gigantic and enduring non-Utopias, such as the Soviet Union and the Chinese People's Republic. It should never be forgotten that Lenin was convinced his Revolution would create a new type of man—*Homo Sovieticus*—whose behaviour would be motivated by social, not personal, considerations. His theory of the 'withering away of the State' rested upon this flimsy foundation of optimism. *Homo Sovieticus*, being a new species, would not need the coercive apparatus of a central authority: the State would become unnecessary. Instead, the State has never ceased to strengthen itself in the Soviet system, and repression is a way of life, more than 55 years after the Revolution that was to make it unnecessary.

If the evidence of countless visitors to the Chinese People's Republic is admitted—as I think it must, on the main point at issue—the Chinese form of totalism has been a good deal more successful than the Soviet in producing mass uniformity of demeanour: all visitors have commented on the endless sea of smiling faces mirroring an apparently permanent euphoria. But there is also evidence that the smiles and the happiness are no more than skin-deep. When Mao Tse-tung relaxed censorship and other controls in 1957, in the so-called 'Hundred Flowers' phase, the authorities were astonished at the volume and bitterness of the complaints released; and soon clamped down again.

Despite the Soviet and Chinese experiences, I should hesitate to conclude that social and political 'engineering' will *never* alter the nature of Man. But the proposition does seem to me highly improbable. In Sweden in recent years, the socialist State has had some success in producing a majority of people apparently happy with a declining measure of liberty.[6] On the other hand, Sweden has one of the highest suicide rates in the world, and one suspects that given an

[6] Roland Huntford brilliantly dissects the Swedish experiment in *The New Totalitarians* (Allen Lane, London, 1972).

appropriate change of government, and a chance to breathe more freely, it would not be long before the floodgates of pent-up resentment were opened wide.

What of biology? Clearly, this is a field in which, as distinct from politics, I have no more than a layman's knowledge. But what is known to me of the 'new biology' strongly suggests that the prospects for changing human nature stand much higher than ever before (I had almost written 'are much brighter'; but who can say that the powers of the new biology, manipulated by the morally defective men of today, would be used for any cause of which a higher morality would approve?). Ever since James D. Watson and Francis Crick of Cambridge discovered the double helix in 1953, Man has held, at least potentially, the power to change himself. DNA, or deoxyribonucleic acid, with its double-helical shape, is claimed to be 'the master molecule of life' (as *Time* magazine put it in one of its better cover stories on 19th April 1971). Men like Robert Sinsheimer of Caltech—the California Institute of Technology—Arthur Kornberg of Stanford and others have tested some of the implications of the Watson-Crick discovery. Sinsheimer is optimistic enough to say: 'For the first time in all time, a living creature understands its origin and can undertake to design its future.'

If Sinsheimer's optimism is not misplaced, the implications could be shattering, and quite possibly horrific. It may well be, as Arthur Koestler asserts,[7] that at some distant moment in prehistory, something went wrong with 'the circuitry of [Man's] most precious and delicate instrument—the central nervous system', causing us to be permanently flawed. Will the new biology prove capable of undoing an evolutionary mistake of half a million years ago? Or will the new biologists confine themselves to the removal of defective genes in the congenitally malformed or handicapped, or to the production of a *Homo futurus*, robot-like and divided into functional categories, on the style of the ant-heap or *Brave New World*, working hard, fighting, or droning in the permanent search for pleasure, because his preconditioned genes tell him this is what he *wants* to do, ordering him by the same token to be content with his lot?

I have no idea whether these questions will ever become more than hypothetical, and still less what the answers will be if they do. In the here-and-now, my second 'axiom' stands: Man's nature *is* unchanging.

3. *Man's behaviour is susceptible to change, either for the better or for the worse.* At first sight, this third assertion may seem to contradict the second. Have I not just pointed out that Hitler behaved no better than

[7] In *The Ghost in the Machine* (Hutchinson, London, 1967), pp. 267 et seq.

Genghis Khan? But the contradiction is only apparent. There are innumerable examples to prove that over measurable periods, the behaviour of men, either as individuals or in groups, may change sensibly, even dramatically. The Germans of the Weimar Republic did not, in the mass, behave as did the Germans of Hitler's Reich, only a few years later. The Chinese under Chiang Kai-shek's Republic behaved very differently from those—many of them the same people —under Mao's People's Republic. For that matter, the same ethnic group can behave quite differently in different places at the same time, as any visitors to Hong Kong, Taiwan and communist China will testify. It is hard to see in the bustling, smiling Japanese of today the brutal conquerors of Tojo's militarist Japan. The English in the eighteenth century worked children to death and hanged or deported petty thieves (to the greater benefit of the new Australian nation). In the second half of the twentieth, they are miserable if all children (except those battered to death) are not pampered and distressed if anybody gets punished at all.

Is the point made? It is an important one, for if Man is not perfectible, as I assert, then we may have to make do with improving his behaviour and trying to keep it improved as long as possible, for fear that if the conditions that made the improvement possible are allowed to deteriorate, his essential nature will reassert itself and there will be a relapse into savagery. The need for vigilance on this score was only too apparent in the 1970s.

In this context, it is well to pay attention to the startling difference between the behaviour of men as individuals and that of the same men in a crowd. If Paul MacLean, of the American National Institute of Mental Health, is right in his illuminating theory of the evolutionary brain, much of the work and many of the hopes of the sociologists and socialists, and even of traditional moralists and theologians, are shown to be misplaced or futile. The brain of Man, says MacLean, consists of three parts, of which two are animal and only one is truly human.[8] The earliest and most central area is the reptilian brain, concerned with 'instinctually determined functions such as establishing territory, finding shelter, hunting, homing, mating, breeding, forming social hierarchies, selecting leaders, and the like'. Around this rudimentary mental mechanism a more sophisticated 'primitive cortex', common to all mammals, has wrapped itself. To the primitive

---

[8] See Ardrey, *The Social Contract*, pp. 353 et seq., commenting on various articles by Paul D. MacLean. See also Koestler, *op. cit.*, Part III, 16, 'The Three Brains'.

cortex, mammals, including Man, owe their sense of smell, certain capacities to learn from experience, the knack of adapting old ways to new circumstances, and a range of emotions.

The third and highest brain, the neo-cortex, appeared in the apes and monkeys and is therefore, strictly speaking, as animal as the other two in origin. But the evolutionary mutation that created Man, a mere half-million years ago, gifted him with an explosively expanded neo-cortex, granting Man his unique capacity for precise communication, for reasoning and logic, for aesthetic appreciation and all the other characteristics that distinguish him from even the highest of the other mammals.

It is our tragedy to have three brains cohabiting within the same cranial box. When Man behaves like an animal, as alas he does so frequently, this is literally true, for at that point one or both of the earlier animal brains takes over. The mob, as Ardrey percipiently puts it, reverts to the reptilian brain, reacting to 'shouts, rhythms, loaded words, gestures to rival the upraised tail, the hot symbol of a cross, a swastika, a dummy hanged in effigy. A mob transcends its leaders, becomes a single wild happy thing satisfying identity, stimulation, the following response, xenophobia, australopithecine joys of the hunt and the kill, a thing that through delirious social self-approval discards all neo-cortical inhibitions. . . . To regard it as a storm of disorder is . . . incorrect, for a mob is as orderly a human phenomenon as one will ever encounter: let a single voice of rational dissent be raised within it, and observe what happens to the dissenter.'

Arthur Koestler has had the characteristic boldness to point out that the transcendental social tendencies of human beings, often praised because they do indeed transcend the selfish and individual level, are far more destructive than the self-assertive tendencies of individuals: '. . . the crimes of violence committed for selfish, personal motives are historically insignificant compared to those committed *ad majorem gloriam Dei*, out of a self-sacrificing devotion to a flag, a leader, a religious faith or a political conviction.'[9]

And the distinguished British psychiatrist, Anthony Storr, writes with the disillusionment of experience that '. . . although we may recoil in horror when we read in newspaper or history book of the atrocities committed by man upon man, we know in our hearts that each one of us harbours within him those same savage impulses which lead to murder, to torture and war.'[10]

[9] *Op. cit.*, p. 234.
[10] Introduction to *Human Aggression* (Allen Lane, London), 1968.

When we talk about improving human behaviour, then, what we are really talking about (in much the same way as Molière's character was when he learned with delight that he had been speaking prose all his life without knowing it) is improving the capacity of the neo-cortex to keep the reptilian stem and ganglions under better control.[11]

4. *Man has an overwhelming need of order*. This proposition is often disputed by those who are aware that order, divorced from law, is the antithesis of freedom. There is some justice in this objection, and only those playing semantic games with the word 'freedom' would contest that freedom is impossible except within a framework of law as well as order. But I am postulating a *need*, not advocating a goal. Man appears to have an instinctive dread of chaos and anarchy, and turns to those promising order to escape from the dangers of uncontrolled violence. This tendency is not necessarily good, however, for in the (reptilian?) mass, men will readily turn to a Hitler, a Stalin or a Mao, for relief from the horrors of chaos.

Alone, the individual is vulnerable. He is also lonely. To overcome his loneliness, he seeks a mate and the company of other fellow-beings. For defence or mutual advantage a group is formed. Leaders emerge; a system evolves. Always the trend is *towards* order. Within the group, tribe or nation, conformity is, in general, expected. But when authority breaks down, rebellion lurks, and rebels seek chaos: the breakdown of society. Yet this drive towards chaos or anarchy is deceptively temporary, for one of two things then happens: either authority is reasserted, and in a harsher form than previously; or the rebels, having won, impose their own new order, invariably harsher (though perhaps after a period of euphoric freedom) than the order that has been undermined and overthrown. These are laws of conflict.

And yet, a remarkable range of freedom and of individual choice is possible, as modern pluralist societies have shown. The problem is to preserve enough order to guarantee the exercise of freedom while protecting conformists and indeed all members of a society from its abuse.

5. *Human progress is dependent upon free inquiry*. In the eyes of Western liberals (in the English sense of that ambiguous word), this last proposition would probably be accepted—still—as the most axiomatic of my 'axioms'. But I wrote that sentence with signal lack

---

[11] It is interesting, though not decisively significant, to note that the authors of a symposium, *The Challenge of Violence* (ed. Derek Richter, Ardua Press, 1972), showed no awareness of this dimension of the problem they were considering—a comment, perhaps, on the isolation of academic disciplines.

of confidence. For all over the Western world in recent years, freedom of inquiry and debate has been eroded, not least in the universities, where it ought to be safest. Free inquiry into the connection, if any, between race and intelligence, for instance, not merely has been discouraged but has become physically dangerous, as shown by the beating up of Professor Eysenck by a gang of political thugs from Birmingham University in a crowded hall at the London School of Economics and Political Science. Moreover, the attackers went unpunished by their university authorities, although their identities were known. In many universities, notoriously in Paris and Bremen, the Marxisation of faculties has meant that teachers who do not happen to be Marxists are subjected to intimidatory pressures. Clearly, the semantic sticking point in my fifth 'axiom' is 'progress'. To the traditional liberal, progress means one thing, to the Marxists and other extremists, it means another, in which free inquiry has no place. It is indeed a sobering thought that the number of States in which free inquiry is legally or administratively permitted is very small, and shrinking.

Even totalist States, however, are prepared to practise, if not expressly to admit, the principle of free inquiry in certain fields, especially in science. Even there, the freedom may at times be circumscribed. For years, Stalin gave a place of honour in Soviet scientific circles to a quack geneticist named Lysenko because his experiments appeared to confirm the view that acquired characteristics could be transmitted by heredity: in other words, that *Homo Sovieticus* was a scientific possibility. Colleagues who pointed out the errors in Lysenko's methods and conclusions were disgraced. The dethronement of Stalin (after his death) by Khrushchev permitted Lysenko to be discredited, although the optimistic doctrine that a new kind of man could be created by socialism and communism was not discarded.

In China, it is worth noting, scientists, and especially nuclear scientists, suffered considerably less than other citizens from the barbarous depredations and pressures of the Red Guards during the Great Proletarian Cultural Revolution (which started in April 1966 and went on for about four years). But the distinguishing characteristic of the Cultural Revolution was the extent to which the principle of 'better red than expert' was applied. Those who were merely expert—that is, good at their jobs—but suspected of being lukewarm or cool towards the doctrines of Chairman Mao—were sent to till the fields, leaving the work to be done by incompetents who were unstinting in their praise and zeal. The fact remains that when it is vitally important for communist regimes to produce difficult things—especially in the fields of advanced weaponry and space—governments will leave the scientists alone. That is, when their interests would be disserved by interference, they will apply the principle of free inquiry.

But in other fields, totalist and even authoritarian governments suppress free inquiry. This is particularly true of philosophy, history, politics and sociology. In totalist countries, the only philosophy that can be granted the seal of truth is the prevailing State philosophy. All others can be presented, if at all, only through the distorting lenses of the approved outlook. This is even truer of political inquiry than of more general speculation. As for sociology, which Marx and Engels are generally credited with having invented, it consists of studying non-Marxist societies and finding 'evidence' to justify the Marxian-critique of capitalism, colonialism or whatever needs to be demolished. There can be no true need of sociology in, say, the Soviet Union, for by definition there are no social contradictions to be studied.

There is a true contradiction, however, between my fifth 'axiom' and my fourth, which I touched upon in the last paragraph of my explanation of the fourth. Total freedom is impossible, except for the strongest, and total order excludes freedom of any kind. Authoritarian societies, nowadays, are generally willing to allow freedom of religion and conscience (reluctantly, in a Catholic country like Spain), freedom of economic competition and of the banking system, freedom of travel, and unrestrained freedom of scientific inquiry. They draw the line, however, with varying degrees of severity, at politics and political philosophy, and at free collective bargaining between labour and bosses. Since the possibility of opting out of politics is the feature that most clearly distinguishes authoritarian from totalist regimes, the citizens suffer considerably less from repression in such countries than in, say, Communist ones or in Nazi Germany. But the intellectuals do, and so do the trade unionists. Whether intellectuals and trade unionists should be required to pay a price for the order that makes the prosperity of countries like Spain or Greece possible, is a matter for debate. That order is worth *some* price is evident to all—even to intellectuals or trade unionists. Not all peoples are equipped by their history to provide the framework for freedom within order. It is, I think, undeniably easier to enforce order than to permit freedom within limits. Some peoples learn the art; others fail or fall short of full success: none should feel complacent. At all events, the sophisticated necessity for freedom of inquiry—a product of the expanded neo-cortex if ever there was one—and the primitive need for order imposed by the central brain core, are an inherent cause of conflict—*because* they co-exist and compete for attention.

All that follows rests upon these five propositions.

Acknowledgment

This book was conceived and written in more than usual isolation. However, Professor Maurice Cranston kindly agreed to read and comment on the entire text. I owe much to his friendly but severe criticism, which resulted in many changes. He is, of course, in no way responsible for the final product, and least of all for those passages which, in my perverseness, I left as they were.

PART I

The Fundamentals
of Conflict

THE NECESSITY OF THE STATE

The ground covered in this chapter

Necessity of the State; inevitability of rebellion—aggression and envy constants in man's psychology—normality of war: peace the rare exception—man obstinately unequal in intelligence and character— force of the State necessary to prevent individual violence and protect the weak—problem of the brutal State—where rebellion may be morally justified—total oppressiveness guarantees failure of rebellion —outlets for dissent in liberal societies—excessive weakness provokes rebellion—minor and major rebellion—minor rebellion endemic in all States—major rebellion not necessarily violent—right of the State to self-defence—any State better than no State, but individual States not necessarily inviolable—regimes as custodians of State power—the State normally does defend itself; some exceptions—conditions that may justify rebellion—when rebellion is wrong—violent revolution rarely justified: onus on revolutionaries—removal of a tyrant

THE STATE is necessary; but rebellion against it is inevitable. The whole theory of conflict lies in the two clauses of this paradox.

Both halves of it, however, call for explanation. First, *why* is the State necessary? Could men not, as the Anarchists propose, manage their own affairs without the elaborate, expensive and—as they see it —inevitably oppressive apparatus of the State to hinder, stifle or merely regulate their lives? Was Lenin right, not to predict (since his predictions have not come true) the withering away of the State but to sense that this, at heart, was what his revolutionary followers really wanted?

The answer is inherent in the nature of the human animal. Not that the scientists and philosophers have ever displayed unanimity on this fundamental point. Is Man an angel fallen from grace but capable of redemption? Does the burden of original sin sit crushingly on his shoulders, and for all time? Is he, on the contrary, a blameless savage in the state of nature, essentially good, and therefore best left free to work out his individual and collective destiny?

I have already stated which side I take in the argument. In this context, history supplements everyday observation. It is not to deny the nobler traits of the creature, which are many, to note that *aggression* and *envy* are constants of his psychology. The small boy who hits his smaller brother over the head because he covets a toy (even though he may own a better one) is true to a nature over which, at a tender age, he has no control. With luck and parental or pedagogic patience, he will be trained, not necessarily out of his innate aggression and envy, but out of the habit of using violence to achieve his ends. The contagion of good example will help, but appears not to suffice; the discipline of an organisation and a hierarchy, of punishment tempered by justice and if possible by mercy, seems also to be needed.

As it is with the individual, so it is with the species. Peaceable tribes exist but are rare. To the extent that they are fortunately isolated from contact, and therefore from conflict, with more aggressive tribes, they may even survive. (Their contribution to human progress, incidentally, will tend to be slender, for aggression and ambition are indissolubly linked. But it does not follow that only the aggressive are inventive, or else Attila and Tamerlane might have been among the benefactors, instead of scourges, of mankind.) But aggressive tribes predominate, if not at the beginning, then in the end, since by the aggressive assertion of their envy, they will expand their dominion at the expense of weaker units.

The occasional periods of comparative peace that are known to the historians appear in the main to have been the consequence of warlike exhaustion. The notion that peace is the normal state of international relations appears to be no more than an idealistic fantasy. War is normal, peace the exception. It is indeed more than probable that such periods of peace as have been recorded are known as such only because of our imperfect knowledge of events in remoter areas at times of primitive communication. At all events, there has been virtually no peace, everywhere on earth at the same time, at any time since the twentieth century began.[1]

---

[1] In an interesting monograph, *Conflict in the Twentieth Century* (Institute for Strategic Studies, Adelphi Papers No. 48, June 1968), David Wood lists 128 'conflicts' in the seventy years between 1898 and 1968. Other writers have arrived at widely diverging totals; however, such differences appear to be the result of differing definitions of 'conflict'. Wood's definition confines the term to situations involving regular armed forces only—thus excluding, for instance, civil riots in which only the police or para-military security forces are involved. In the

Aggression and envy, then, are prevalent. Nor is there any reason to suppose that they will ever be eradicated from the human character. To be sure, that possibility cannot be entirely excluded, but we can accept it only as a hypothesis. The researches of contemporary biology and psychology raise expectations of genetic 'engineering' that may or may not be fulfilled, and that may, if successful, create as many problems as they solve. But this is in the realm of speculation. The political philosopher of the eighth decade must deal with the world as it is, not as it may become.

Man, moreover, is obstinately unequal. Not only are there meek and satisfied tribes; there are meek and unacquisitive individuals. In the mythical 'state of nature', their lot is an unenviable one. They had better hold their peace, for the bully or the strongman will not be stilled. If lucky, they will live out lives of subservience; if unlucky, of brutal servitude. The bully will form a gang and impose his will. The tyrant will satisfy his whims, however cruel. The strongman may also be just, but his will, too, will require obedience, and therefore enforcement.

Nor is intelligence at all uniformly distributed. Some are bright, more are dull; at either extreme are the geniuses and the subnormal. Aggression and envy are not necessarily exerted through brute force: low cunning sometimes suffices; the wiles and deceptions of the politician may take the place of weapons. Or the force of authority and character may yield a consensual power, maintained thereafter by eloquence or organisation.

In this jungle, the weak need to be protected from the predatory strong, and the dull have to be cushioned against the acquisitiveness of the enterprising few. That is why, in the last resort, the State is not merely necessary but morally justified. Indeed the few anarchies of which we have a record soon degenerate into frightful tyrannies.

At this point, another apparent paradox emerges: for *force is necessary to avoid violence*. In other words, the necessary force of the State replaces the uncontrolled violence of the strongest. Today's revolutionaries contend that the violence with which they challenge authority is in reality a counter-violence, made necessary by the reactionary violence of the State. But the argument (to which we shall return) is sophistical: force and violence must be distinguished. The State, too, may be guilty of unnecessary or abusive violence, as with the torture of suspects, or terror bombing in war. Ideally, the force of

major wars during this period, civil and military deaths totalled more than 62 million.

the State should not be used but be held in reserve. But sooner or later there will be instances of last resort: the police will be compelled to use force, the armed forces to intervene with their powerful weapons. If discipline breaks down or a war escalates, the force may degenerate into violence, but at all times the two need to be distinguished. Similarly, in private life, the father's or mother's power to chastise is perhaps better held in reserve: known to be available rather than used. But there will come a time when chastisement is inevitable; and the distinction will remain, between the parent who uses force with restraint, and the brute who batters babies to death.

In the State, the alternative to the force of authority is the terrorism of the gangster, whether his motive is criminal profit or the achievement of political power. The bullet, the bomb and the torture rack may be alternatives to the rule of law; which in turn needs the backing of enforcement, and therefore (in the background) the bullet, the bomb and even, in some States, the torture rack.

If all States were good and all dissidents evil, the moral problems implicit in conflict would be agreeably simplified. But there are good States and bad. What if a State is brutal, corrupt and oppressive? What if it is unjust and arbitrary? What if it is manifestly illegitimate? In such cases, is the force with which the State maintains its power a necessary force? Is the force with which the dissident seeks to overthrow it still a reprehensible violence? We shall return to these inescapable and sometimes anguishing questions. At this stage, let me say only that at times and in definable circumstances, rebellion against the State (in the form of a hated regime) is not merely inevitable but morally defensible. The issue, however, is the necessity of the State, and it is unaffected by the character of any regime that may happen to be in power. Revolutionaries who overthrow a hated tyranny, or merely an inefficient and bumbling democracy, will set up their own State as soon as they get a chance. A monarchy may yield to a republic, a democracy to a dictatorship. A State may be unitary, federal or confederal: it will still be a State, whether relatively free or oppressively autocratic.

Indeed, so few and transient are the instances in which the State has ceased to exist where it previously and subsequently did, that one is tempted to say that the State is not merely necessary but *inevitable*. A philosophical doubt may hang over this question. But for all practical purposes, the proposition is true: the State *is* inevitable.

In that sense, it is the immovable object in a famous hypothetical situation. But here the second clause in my initial paradox obtrudes.

Rebellion against the State, I postulated, is also inevitable. Is the rebel, then, the irresistible force in collision with the immovable object?

The metaphor is tempting, but necessarily imperfect. The rebel is an irresistible force only where the State is weak; where it is strong, it is the State that is the immovable object. When conflict, endemic and latent, breaks out into violence, it becomes a test of power, in which the justice of the rebels' cause, or of the State's existence, becomes of less importance than the means at the disposal of the protagonists. The form the rebellion will take, and its intensity, depend upon the strength of the State and the degree of its oppressiveness.

The latter is important. Inevitably, the State—even if relatively liberal—is restrictive; and Man, inescapably an individual (though gregarious) and ultimately isolated within his lonely psyche, can never totally accept the restrictiveness of the State. The degree of his rebellion, however, is dependent upon the character of the central power. Total oppressiveness, while it does not entirely rule out attempted rebellion, virtually guarantees its failure. The history of twentieth century autocracies illustrates the proposition. Stalin, during his twenty-four years of power, ruled by terror and sent millions to their deaths, often on patently untrue charges of conspiracy; and died in his bed of old age. Hitler, popularly regarded as the worst tyrant of the century, narrowly escaped death in the bomb plot of 20 July 1944. Since 1917, the history of communist tyrannies has been punctuated by palace revolts, some of which (e.g. the one that unseated Khrushchev in 1964) were successful. But success has never meant more than the replacement of one set of Communists by another, never the overthrow of the regime. It does not follow that no communist regime will ever be overthrown; but it does suggest that the repressive techniques of communist autocracies are more efficient than any others.

At the other end of the scale, parliamentary democracies or liberal presidential ones may guard against rebellion by providing outlets for normal political dissent, such as a free press and freedom of speech, an unfettered and elected assembly, the right to demonstrate peacefully and to strike for better pay or conditions. In modern industrial societies, however, such rights and freedoms, though necessary, may be insufficient unless supplemented by stable and expanding economies, educational systems geared to employment outlets and reasonable access to cheap housing. Inflation, unemployment, depressions or fluctuations of boom and recession, the frustrated aspirations of university graduates—all these may be contributory causes of rebellion.

Then again, while political freedoms may be a useful safety valve, excessive freedom is dangerous to the State. The absence or abdication of authority provokes rebellion by making it too easy and therefore too tempting. The aim of the rebel is indeed to provoke the breakdown of the State, that is, at least initially, to exploit and exacerbate that sectional strife and political instability which the Greeks called *stasis*, taking advantage of the resultant paralysis of authority that will give him his chance to take over. But rulers who have lost the will to rule, or who have allowed their authority to be flouted to excess, are meeting the rebels half way.

Inevitable though rebellion is, it is not necessarily violent. We shall return to the distinction between violent and non-violent rebellion, but at this stage, it is perhaps more useful to distinguish between *minor* and *major* rebellion. Here, a law may be stated: *minor rebellion is constant, in all States without exception*. There is perhaps no better place for an example than Britain, arguably the least violent, and among the most law-abiding, of modern nations.[2] Even in Britain, individual citizens, even normally law-abiding ones, often assert their independence of the State by evading or avoiding income-tax, by infringing parking regulations and in countless other relatively unimportant ways. There is little point in pursuing to logical conclusions any argument over the extent to which such infringements of the Law constitute rebellion against the State. In most cases, there is no question of a conspiracy, and certainly no intent to bring down the State. But by such acts, citizens demonstrate, constantly and in all States, that they contest the right of the central authority, however constituted, say, to deprive them of a portion of the money they had earned or of space for their private vehicles.

Nor is the phenomenon confined to democratic countries. Objectively, the daring or foolhardy individuals who remedy the deficiencies of the planned economy in Russia by procuring and selling materials or services in short supply—in other words, who practise private enterprise—are indulging in minor rebellion against the State. The penalties, however, are less minor than elsewhere. For the Soviet State labels such activities 'economic crimes' and punishes them by lengthy terms of imprisonment, or even death.

Clearly, *major* rebellion is more rare than *minor*; but it, too, is

[2] In *Protest and the Urban Guerrilla* (London, 1973), Richard Clutterbuck draws attention to the astonishing fact that in the fifty years between 1919 and 1972, no one was killed in England, Scotland and Wales in political demonstrations, riots and strikes. The facts are elaborated on p. 3.

endemic in human societies. In distinction to minor rebellion, major rebellion aims at weakening and ultimately overthrowing the central authority; or at least, at forcing the State to concede reforms or remedy grievances. But major rebellion is not necessarily violent. Peaceful demonstrations have often been effective in persuading authority to take note of a grievance and remedy it. In India, Gandhi's prolonged campaigns of civil disobedience, resting at least theoretically upon 'soul-force' (*satyagraha*), were not violent uprisings, even though the master's followers did not always live up to his 'non-violent' aspirations. But they certainly constituted a major rebellion against the State authority of the British Raj.

Faced, then with endemic rebellion, whether minor or major, what is the State to do? First, as a general law, *the State* (as an abstract concept) *has the right to defend itself*; this right indeed is inherent in the necessity of the State. For if a thing is necessary it is entitled to protection against those who seek to destroy it. The State, however, is not an abstraction: it is a man-made set of bodies, comprising in general a government, an assembly (whether elected or nominated), a body of laws, administrative institutions and a machinery of enforcement. And there are good States and bad, legitimate and illegitimate, popular and unpopular. When we say that 'the State is necessary', we mean no more than *a* State, some State or other, is needed; indeed, we postulate no more than that any State is better than no State. But it does not follow that any *particular* State is inviolable. When a regime is overthrown, the country in which the event takes place is not necessarily deprived of a State for more than a few hours, if at all, especially in the case of a successful military *coup d'état*. Rebellion, then, does not necessarily, or indeed usually, signify the end of the State, even when it is successful. It is therefore not incompatible with the necessity of the State.

In matters of rebellion and conflict, a regime in power should be thought of essentially as the custodian of State power. The Chinese concept of 'the Mandate of Heaven' fits the case. The Prince or Emperor ruled with Heaven's Mandate; but the Mandate could be withdrawn as well as conferred. If the Emperor was held to have lost the Mandate of Heaven, by ill-rule, his subjects were within their rights in rising against him. If successful, the rebel leader would claim that the Mandate had been transferred to him.

The Emperor however, does not necessarily recognise that he has lost the divine sanction. As a general rule, though not as an invariable law, he will use force to defend himself. In other words, *the State will normally defend itself, whatever its degree of legitimacy, or of public acceptance.* In Cuba, the dictator Fulgencio Batista defended his Republic until the discredit into which it had fallen persuaded him to flee the country, so that the then rebel, Fidel Castro, marched into Havana unopposed. But there are exceptions. A monarch, for instance, may abdicate or flee to avoid bloodshed or because the looming conflict has caused him to lose his nerve. Although Alfonso XIII of Spain was in no way compelled to quit in 1931, he lost his nerve and went into exile, though he never abdicated, thus paving the way for the proclamation of the Spanish Second Republic, while leaving the country, at least in the eyes of the monarchists, still legally a monarchy.

Although the State has the right to defend itself—and will normally do so anyway, even if the right is contested—*the citizen or subject, too, has the right, in certain circumstances, to rebel against it or to disobey its laws.* It is, of course, a moral, not a legal right; and a conditional, not an absolute one. Let us spell out some of the conditions or circumstances that may justify rebellion, or at any rate make it inevitable:

When it is clear beyond doubt that the State is not going to do anything to remedy evident injustices or anomalies. There can be no doubt, for instance, that the Stormont regime in Ulster involved a permanent injustice to the Catholic minority in that province, who were deprived of all political power not so much by the Constitutional provisions of 1920 as by the sectarian interpretation of them by the Protestant majority. Given the history of Anglo-Irish relations, some kind of rebellion was therefore inevitable.

When it is manifest that the State is unnecessarily repressive; in other words, when the degree of force used to maintain law and order (or, as some may prefer to call it, civil peace) is obviously greater than is strictly needed. Paradoxically, however, and as we have seen, though rebellion against a brutal State may be morally justified, it is far from inevitable, and usually unsuccessful. 'Papa Doc' Duvalier's *tontons macoutes* in Haiti did not entirely prevent rebellion, but they did ensure that it failed every time. The thwarted Hungarian revolt in 1956 was not a conspiracy against the brutal Rakosy regime, but a comparatively rare example of a spontaneous uprising, which was duly crushed by Soviet tanks.

When there is no outlet for normal dissent, in speech, the press, parliament or the street or factory floor. But again, the justness of the rebel cause is no guarantee of success.

We have tried to clarify the circumstances that may justify a rebellion or make it inevitable. An even more difficult question is: When is it *wrong* to rebel? The difficulty is inherent in the nature of violent political action. Is revolutionary violence ever, even in the long run, justified?

There is, in my view, no moral justification for the armed rebellion of a group or movement against a system clearly acceptable to the overwhelming majority of the population. It follows, however, that there must be some machinery whereby public opinion can be ascertained. The absence of rebellion in a totalitarian State does not signify the assent, except in the most passive sense, of the majority. Instead, it reflects the power and efficiency of the repressive apparatus. In a democratic country, with freedom of speech, assembly and the press, the alienation of a substantial part of the population would be necessary before revolutionary violence could be justified. (It is, however, one of the purposes of revolutionary violence to *create* the conditions of alienation; as we shall see in subsequent chapters.)

Nor is mere dissatisfaction of the political 'outs' with the rule of the 'ins', in itself a justification of violent action, especially when there are constitutional provisions, normally observed, for the alternation of parties in power through electoral processes in conditions guaranteeing freedom of choice. But here as elsewhere circumstances alter cases. The 'ins' may be unnecessarily oppressive of the 'outs'. Or the 'outs' may feel, perhaps with justification, that the system condemns them to perpetual opposition. A democratic system may be said to function when parties or coalitions do, in fact, alternate in power. The democratic system of the Federal Republic of Germany may be said to have proved its credentials when Willy Brandt and his Socialist party were elected to office in 1969, displacing the ruling Christian Democrats and their allies who had monopolised power ever since a West German State emerged from the ruins of the Second World War. By this token, the democratic systems of a number of countries—including Japan, India and Malaysia—remained untested as late as 1974. The alternation of ruling parties, however, presupposes a degree of consensus about the nature of the system and constitution that is never easy to achieve. In Japan, where the Liberal Democratic Party under one name or another had been in power continuously since 1949, the Socialist opposition, divided and at times demoralised, has often clamoured its complaint against 'the tyranny of the majority'. Although such frustrations are the stuff of rebellion, however, it did not follow that rebellion was inevitable, for the overwhelming majority of the population, including the opposition, taken as individuals, shared in the general and astonishing rise in prosperity made possible by the industry and ingenuity of the Japanese people, and evidently favoured by the political power of the ruling party.

A priori, then, in my eyes at least, violent revolution is rarely justified; although a swift and successful *coup d'état*, removing a notorious tyrant from the scene, may often be justified. The trouble with revolutionary violence is that it tends to be protracted. And historical experience suggests that the destruction and loss of life caused by the act of revolution tends to be so sweeping that it may be years before the country recovers to the point reached before the revolution—so many years, indeed, that it could well be argued that more subtle and peaceful means could have achieved reform in a comparable time-span.

Hence the onus is surely on the revolutionaries to convince the people that what they offer is going to be better—considering all things, including the certainty of death and destruction—than what might be achieved without violence. Unfortunately, revolutionaries are reluctant by nature to persuade by reasoned argument. They prefer to offer 'proof' the hard way, through fire, explosion, the sword and the bullet. Ordinary people suffer the consequences; and, hypothetically, enjoy the benefits, if there are any, and if they survive.

TWO

THE CAUSES OF REBELLION

The ground covered in this chapter

*Rebellion and conflict never spontaneous—rebellion favoured by con-
ditions but not caused by them—cause lies in rebel's mind—tolerated
and 'intolerable' conditions—Che Guevara's Bolivian error—examples
of rebellions: Algeria, Portuguese Africa, Britain's Angry Brigade—
importance of social change—the Uruguayan example—a biochemical
factor?—rebellion and criminality—the monstrous rebels: Hitler,
Lenin, Mao, Stalin—frustration and intolerance—sources of frustration: education, poverty, nepotism, unemployment, land-hunger,
injustice, nationalism, ideology—problems of affluence—problems of
underdevelopment—religion and conflict—new sources of conflict:
population explosion, acceleration of technological change—television
and mass communications—imitative terrorism—television as an
exacerbating factor*

REBELLION CANNOT be considered in isolation from the rebel. As
a writer once put it, 'it takes a rebel to rebel'. Thus baldly stated, the
proposition seems trite, but the nature of rebellion and of revolutionary conflict cannot be understood unless its deeper implications
are grasped. The point is that rebellion and conflict, in the sense in
which this book uses these terms, are *never* spontaneous. A rebellion
happens when somebody, somewhere, decides that he is in conflict
with the society in which he lives, or with the government in power,
and goes into rebellion. It is not necessarily the consequence of prevailing social, economic or political conditions.

The proposition is therefore more important than it seems at first
glance, and raises fundamental issues. It contradicts Marxist assumptions about the importance of economic factors and the historical
inevitability of the class struggle. More importantly, it flies in the face
of conventional wisdom among the majority of contemporary sociologists who seek the origins of conflict in the study of social conditions.

13

To say this is not to deny the importance of social—and indeed of economic and political—conditions. Without the 'right' conditions, a rebellion is unlikely to begin, or if it begins, to take root. But the social environment, in itself, is not the cause of the rebellion, even if it is its essential background. A rebellion begins when somebody feels strongly enough about it to *do* something: in other words, to rebel. What goes on in the mind of the potential rebel leader is more important than what surrounds him.

The truth of this proposition lies in the observable fact that the silent majority is almost infinitely tolerant; or, if that word is considered excessively complimentary, apathetic. Conditions that are tolerated by many people over a long period may be intolerable to a few over a relatively short period. The key to rebellion lies not in the objective phenomena but in the subjective reaction to them. Such is the diversity of human nature, of metabolism, of cultural levels and of environment and history that the range of responses to external stimuli is infinite. Transplanted to the Tropics, the Eskimo suffers intensely from the heat; but no more than the Ghanaian jet-propelled to the Arctic will suffer from the cold.

Similarly, whole peoples will put up with poverty, hunger, exploitation and injustice if that is all they have ever known. It was one of the major errors of psychology of the Argentine–Cuban revolutionary, Che Guevara, to ignore this simple truth when he tried to stir the Bolivian Indians to revolt. He and his imported followers found the living conditions of the locals on the high Andean plateau intolerable; but the locals themselves were apathetic about their lot and saw no very good reason to take up arms at the behest of these foreigners whose language they did not understand and who did not speak their own.

In 1954, before the Algerian revolution began, perhaps a million Algerian Muslims were actively in favour of dependence on France in that they had a personal stake in the survival of the French connection; perhaps a million more were undecided; and the remaining majority of the population, desperately poor, cared only for the daily struggle to eat and live. But nine Algerians (now known as 'the nine immortals') decided that the French connection was intolerable and plotted to sever it. Eight years later, after a bloody conflict marked by tortures, massacres, terrorism and set battles, they had their way: Algeria was independent.

Similarly, many Portuguese Africans—probably the great majority of the population in Mozambique, Angola and Portuguese Guinea—

are content with the Portuguese connection. Many serve in the Portuguese forces helping to put down rebellions initiated some years earlier by groups of men who had decided they could no longer tolerate the Portuguese connection.

More striking still—almost a *reductio ad absurdum*—is the case of the Angry Brigade, an anarchist group in England. During more than three years (1968–71), the Angry Brigade exploded bombs (notably in the homes of two government ministers) and indulged in other acts of violence. Some of the members were sentenced to terms of imprisonment, and others acquitted, in late 1972 after the longest trial to date in British legal history. The point, however, is that at the height of their activity, the group numbered no more than about twenty young people. It was their peculiarity that they found British society intolerable. Yet the 55 million or so others who shared that society with the Angry ones found it, by and large, acceptable. (Even if all other revolutionary groups in the country were deducted from the total population, it would not reduce the figure of the relatively content majority to anything approaching 54 million.

To say, then, that social conditions are intolerable merely begs the question: To whom?

More important than the conditions at any given time is the trend. Are conditions improving, deteriorating, or stagnant? Is something being done to redress grievances, or is the government indifferent or incompetent, or both? It is generally agreed that social change— whether for better or for worse—is more conducive to revolt than a static condition of misery. As Alexis de Tocqueville remarked in a much-quoted passage, the French Revolution came not when conditions were at their worst but when they had been steadily improving. The stagnant society lives in apathy or despair. The experience of change is novel and intoxicating. If things can change, then there seems no reason why they should not change faster. In our own century, Adlai Stevenson called it 'the revolution of rising expectations'. Conversely, change for the worse after a period of comparative prosperity is also perilous. Uruguay had been one of the relatively few contented countries in Latin America. It was a welfare State and had a democratic way of life. Falling world markets for wool and meat— the country's principal exports—started a period of economic decline. In the decade after 1960, the income of the average Uruguayan dropped by more than 10 per cent. Strikes and official mismanagement compounded the *malaise*. A group of middle-class youths decided that they had had enough. Calling themselves the Tupamaros—after a legendary Inca hero of the resistance to the Spaniards, named Tupac Amaru—they turned to rebellion. In 1965, when they signed their first manifesto, it is doubtful whether there were fifty of them, in a population of about 2½ million. Yet between 1968 and 1971, their numbers grown to perhaps 3,000, they almost paralysed the administration, terrorising, kidnapping and robbing banks at will, either immune from arrest or if arrested able to escape with obvious police complicities.[1] In Uruguay, it was a case of falling expectations. But it could have been the other way round: it is *movement* that is fatal.

If the proper study of rebellions is that of rebels, then the scientific study of conflict is in its infancy. What is there in the rebel that makes him intolerant of conditions that others tolerate? Is rebellion, in some degree, a biochemical phenomenon? Is there an 'X-factor' in rebels? Is rebellion, like blue babies and possibly criminality, a matter of chromosomes? I do not pretend to know. Nor do I believe anybody else does. Quite a lot is known about the biochemistry of the criminal, and while it would be foolish to identify the criminal and the revolutionary, it is a matter of record that the process of insurgency involves the perpetration of common law crimes, such as bank hold-ups, robberies with violence, torture, murder and kidnapping for ransom. Does the profession of a political motive turn a criminal into a 'respectable' revolutionary? Certainly all outbreaks of revolutionary violence attract men who were already living a life of crime or would have turned to 'straight' crime if the chance of joining a revolutionary group had not come their way. Such men, in other words, chose to commit their crimes within a revolutionary group instead of as members of a criminal gang. It seems at least a reasonable working hypothesis that if the criminal's chromosomes are arranged in a special way, the rebel's may also be. But the answers to such questions will have to wait on the day when governments with the raw material—in the form of revolutionary detainees—may find it of interest to subject their charges to biochemical examination.

The question is not without practical interest, although the application of any discoveries that might be made would not necessarily be enlightened. The patient efforts of Douglas Hyde,[2] who carried the courage of his conviction to the extent of sharing prison cells with

---

[1] See Robert Moss, *Uruguay: Terrorism versus Democracy* (*Conflict Studies* No. 14, Institute for the Study of Conflict, London, Aug. 1971).

[2] A former British Communist, author of *I Believed* (London, 1950) and other works.

detainees for months on end, have shown beyond doubt that in certain conditions some detainees, including revolutionary leaders, can be rehabilitated—that is, brought back to normal and useful civilian occupations. In other words, that the rebel can be cured.

Would early detection help to divert the rebel's intolerance to more fruitful pursuits than revolutionary violence? Or would governments armed with the knowledge merely liquidate the potential rebel (or criminal), or reduce him, by biochemical means, to the status of a vegetable?

Whatever it is that makes a rebel what he is, is clearly possessed in *varying* degrees by rebels. In some there is what might be called a hypertrophy of the rebellious factor. The outcome is a Hitler, a Lenin, a Mao, a Stalin. In private life, these men, with the possible exception of Stalin, were kind and honest. It was in their public lives that they were monsters. None had the slightest compunction about sending thousands or millions to their deaths to further their concept of historical destiny. To preserve mankind from such people might be considered a worthy object of scientific inquiry.

Excluding biology, a study of many revolts, rebellions, revolutions, conspiracies, mass uprisings, suggests that the one factor common to all rebels, revolutionaries and political conspirators everywhere is *frustration*. I use the loaded term in a morally neutral sense, to connote a state of mind, and my intent is not necessarily pejorative. To be frustrated is to be denied something one wishes to have, or believes oneself entitled to have, regardless of the thing desired, or of the objective validity of the claim. Rebellion begins when the frustration becomes intolerable. Intolerable, that is, to the rebel; for the phenomenon is subjective, not objective. The distinguishing characteristic of the rebel is that his 'frustration threshold' is lower than the ordinary person's. But all rebels do not have the same frustration threshold. What is tolerable to one potential rebel for ten years may be intolerable to another for more than five.

Initially, as we have seen, rebels are normally (and probably invariably) in a minority, the conditions which they find intolerable having been tolerated, until the time of their rebellion, by the great majority. The success of their rebellion therefore, will depend on their success in persuading (or forcing) others to *share their refusal to tolerate* (these words too, like 'frustration', being used in a morally neutral sense, implying no value-judgment either on the rebel's cause or on his character).

The frustrations that may (in certain people) cause rebellion, stem from a diversity of sources so great that it is impossible to list them all. But the most important sources seem to me to fall under the following subject-headings: education; poverty; nepotism; unemployment; land hunger; injustice; nationalism; and ideology.

There is no special significance in the order chosen; moreover, there is inevitably some overlapping. Let us take *education* first. It is possible to feel frustrated because one has been denied educational opportunities open to others; or because the nature of the education offered seems irrelevant to current problems, or for a variety of other reasons. The first of these is comparatively rare nowadays, and perhaps always was. Most rebellions have been started by people of the educated middle class, and this was as true of anti-colonial revolts as of most contemporary attempts at 'social' revolution. True, a number of the original leaders of the Algerian revolution were of working class or peasant origin; and so are most of the leaders of the Irish Republican Army. But these are exceptions. The Asian and African leaders of revolts against the rule of the Americans (in the Philippines), the British, French and Dutch, were products of good Western schools who felt the more keenly the inequality of the opportunities open to them, or to their fellow countrymen, under imperial systems.

The rebels of the late 1960s and early 1970s are mostly of the professional middle class, and their grievances tend to be unspecific: it is a case, rather, of a sweeping rejection of the whole system—or their concept of it. Many of the students who rebelled against their places of learning, often causing extensive damage, especially in 1968 (the year of the New Left), were in reality protesting against the nature of the society that created their universities rather than against the universities themselves. True, there were protests and demonstrations against specific courses, on the ground of their supposed 'irrelevance', or with the object of forcing the governing bodies to concede student representation, or (in American colleges) to force faculties to admit unqualified black students, or to introduce courses on Marxism–Leninism. But, often as not, these were not the real issues. Even Vietnam, the rallying cry of protesters in the 1960s, was just the convenient cause that happened to be at hand. What the protesters really wanted was to do their bit to bring the system to a halt, before making common cause with the workers and overturning society. And after that. . . . After that, revolutionary objectives dissolved into vagueness.

Poverty and *underprivilege* are a powerful spur to rebellion, not necessarily by those who are themselves poor and underprivileged, in societies where there are glaring contrasts of wealth and opportunity.

The communist-led Huk rebels in the Philippines would never have gained the momentum that was theirs if the peasants of central Luzon had not suffered from the curses of poverty, absentee landlordism and usury. The Black Power movement thrived, for a while, in the United States, upon the despair of migrant Negro communities who felt themselves excluded from the expanding technological revolution.

Nepotism, though less important than some other factors, should also be mentioned. It is a facet of human nature that nepotism, or favouritism, is rarely resented by those whom it benefits. It is a different matter when a man's chances of promotion are overlooked in favour of the claims of men of lesser merit, but who happen to have the right friends in high places. Not that nepotism is necessarily a bad thing. But when it is rampant, it is likely to be a symptom of a corrupt society or administration, in which injustices are multiple and the chances of reform, remote. The rebel frustrated by nepotism turns easily to plotting.

What of *unemployment*? Until the late 1960s, unemployment in industrial societies was traditionally regarded as a symptom and product of economic sluggishness. It was thought bound to be accompanied by deflation and low interest rates. In modern economic history, unemployment was typical of the great depression of the 1930s. To eradicate it became the State policy of most advanced countries, and full employment became a standard aspiration of enlightened governments. Most of them achieved their objectives, though usually at the price of sustained inflation. And then, in the late 1960s and early 1970s, some countries, most notably the United States and Britain, began to experience an unusual combination: high unemployment *and* inflation.

The economists were nonplussed, but their puzzlement need not detain us here. Our concern is with a possible cause of unrest, and this was one. Almost certainly its origin lay in the inevitable tensions of the technological revolution. As first America, then other industrialised countries, entered what a distinguished American academic has called 'the technetronic age'—the age of electronics, automation and computers—workers of many kinds were declared redundant. Through no fault of their own, they found themselves, as it were, outside the economy, or marginal to it. In many cases, it was a crisis of readjustment, susceptible of cure by retraining for other jobs. But in many more cases, the trouble lay deeper. A new, dispossessed urban proletariat, often coloured, was not merely unemployed but quite possibly, in the technetronic age, *unemployable*.

There was little sign, as these words were written, of a solution to this grave social problem, or even that a serious effort was being made to understand it and remedy it. In Britain, the hardships of the new unemployables were cushioned, to some extent, by the Welfare State. In America, welfare varied from State to State, inexistent in some, generous in others. That this was a new and potentially explosive source of conflict was evident.

But there was another kind of unemployment, long familiar to certain underdeveloped countries and now spreading to the affluent ones: the unemployment, or ill-chosen employment, of intellectuals. Traditionally, the universities of the Third World had tended to over-produce lawyers (whose distraction was politics) and doctors (who tended to work in the cities and avoid the countryside) and under-produce the people most needed to foster economic development, such as engineers and agronomists. The frustrations of intellectuals in the advanced countries were different in kind. They were the product of the 'explosion' of higher education. The notion that virtually everybody is entitled to higher education is a comparatively recent one. In the recent past, access to the universities was regarded as the privilege of wealth or the reward of special merit. To ensure that young people of intellectual attainment should not be deprived of a place in the university system by the accident of poor birth or lowly station was a noble objective. But to go still further, and decree that virtually everyone, regardless of merit, should have access, was a misguided exercise in egalitarian democracy.

The consequences were predictable. In America, academic standards were lowered and many courses were introduced for the benefit of those who, though not studious, wanted something to show for their attendance at college: such as Square-Dancing and Basket-Weaving. Lower degrees having been devalued, it became increasingly necessary for those who had the brains and the seriousness of purpose to go on to get a doctorate. Hence many young people do not emerge to face the realities of life until they are thirty or more.

In France, where standards were kept high, classes became impossibly overcrowded and the failure rate at finals rose dramatically. In Britain, there was certainly some lowering of standards (though possibly less than in the USA), but the greatest problem soon became the employment of young graduates. For some years, industry and commerce absorbed the new wave of graduates, products of the new universities, the sons and daughters of parents whose education had stopped short of higher studies. Then a sales resistance set in on the employers' side. The value of degrees, especially Arts degrees, *per se*, was called in question. Too many of the young people were enrolling for degree courses in Politics and Social Sciences. Surrounded, as it were, by the raw materials of their study—life itself, Khrushchev would have said—they liked not what they saw, and set about changing it, sometimes with violence, often with shouting, always at the expense of civilised behaviour. (One excepts, even in those fields, the thousands who wanted only to learn and graduate; but the proportion of extremists among budding sociologists was strikingly higher than among, say, novice medical doctors and fledgling lawyers.)

I have mentioned *land hunger*, and this, clearly, is a problem of stagnant, under-developed or traditional societies. Not all such societies, however, count land hunger among their problems. Thailand, for instance, even before the American connection ushered in the boom of development in the 1960s, had plenty of land for everybody although each of the adjectives in the first sentence of this paragraph was applicable. So had Burma. But in more overcrowded countries— in China before the communist revolution, in India and Pakistan (and what later became Bangladesh), in parts of the Philippines, in Mexico before the revolution of 1910, to name a few cases—land hunger was a factor of high revolutionary potential.

The Communists, in particular, promised land for the peasants and the chance of revenge on the landlords. The second of these promises was a promise kept in blood in China and North Vietnam; the first, as in Russia in Stalin's day, was cruelly denied. First the land was given to the landless; then later, it was taken back by the merger of individual plots into collectives.

Land reform has been tried in many countries. Inertia, corruption and the political 'pull' of landlords have proved powerful obstacles. In very few places has reform worked. The only two that were wholly successful were Japan and Taiwan; in each, land reform—the redistribution of land, with proper, phased compensation for the dispossessed—probably averted a revolution. In India, where the dead weight of the caste system as well as the accompanying evils of inherited debt and usury, and of absentee landlordism, exacerbated the problem, little had been done by the early 1970s, and the violent excesses of the Naxalites[3] testified to the revolutionary dynamic of the land issue.

A much broader source of revolutionary frustrations is the sense of

[3] Maoist extremists, named after the Naxalbari area of West Bengal, where a peasant revolt was launched in 1967.

injustice, whether it is felt by a group or by an individual. In the great days of empire, the discrimination encountered by intelligent young black and brown men at Western, especially British, universities was a powerful factor in their later dissidence. Unhelpful landladies at innumerable bed-sits, permanently anonymous and unaccountable, have much to answer for, in the eyes of history! Since perfect justice for all without distinction seems a remote ideal, and since the *sense* of injustice can be subjective as well as real, here is a blanket source of rebellion that will probably never be eliminated.

Let me illustrate the dual nature of the problem. The Basques, that nation of uncertain linguistic origin, straddling the Franco-Spanish border at the Western end, are gifted and successful people. In the late 1960s, however, a small minority among the Spanish Basques felt so deep a sense of injustice at the fact that the Basque provinces were ruled centrally from Madrid, that they formed a clandestine terrorist group named Basque Homeland and Liberty (*Euzkadi ta Azkatasuna*) to prove their case with bombs and bullets. Now, the fact that the Basque provinces were not sovereign was a reality; but only a minority felt that this constituted an injustice. And among these, a smaller minority still felt strongly enough to turn to violence. Once again, it took rebels to rebel.

The sense of injustice, ethnic and cultural in the case of the Basques, may be felt equally on racial and religious grounds, and doubtless on others. The sense of cultural injustice can take a variety of forms, of which the linguistic is by far the most widespread. The Irish, the Welsh, the East Bengalis, the Flemings of Belgium and the Catalans of Spain and France, however disparate, share with countless other cultural minorities the possession of a language that is not, or was not, accepted officially in the land of their birth as an equal with the dominant tongue.

Religion, too, continues to be a powerful source of conflict. Although the great wars of religion lie in the past, discrimination or persecution on religious grounds is far from dead. Persecution is not too strong a word for the treatment of Christian churches in the Soviet Union. In South Vietnam, the Buddhist community felt a sense of discrimination on the part of the ruling Ngo Dinh family, with its Catholic bias, and protested against it, both by mass demonstrations and processions and by the self-immolation of bonzes, whose blazing example was imitated elsewhere by individuals who did not share their religion. In Northern Ireland, the Catholic minority can scarcely claim to be persecuted on religious grounds, but the political deprivation of the Catholics as a community, together with the further coincidence that they were more likely to be poor than the Protestants, was a strong cause of the wave of violence of the late 1960s and early 1970s.

I come to *nationalism*. Between this source of conflict, and various others, there is inevitably some overlapping. One may choose to define the Basque problem as an ethnic or cultural one, or one of nationalism. One may regard the Ulster problem as a religious, socio-political or nationalistic one. The trouble is that no one has ever succeeded in defining a 'nation' to the universal satisfaction. In Britain, ball games between Wales and England, or England and Scotland, are termed 'international'. The Union of Soviet Socialist Republics consist of fifteen constituent republics, within whose vast borders live a far greater number of 'nationalities'. There is no end to the anomalies and ambiguities of nationalism, not the least of which is that the dependent territories of the European powers in Africa, most of which gained national independence in the 1950s and 1960s, were in no sense nations. Once again, we are in the realm of the sub-jective. Apart from a minority of nationalists, most Scots are quite content to be British subjects, as indeed are the Welsh; but the Irish, by and large, always had less reason to be content with the English connection and have nursed a sense of injustice at their subjection (as they see it) by the British. This feeling has frequently given birth to violence.

A similar, though not identical, feeling caused the Ibos of Nigeria to rise against central rule and try to set up a separate State, which their rebel leaders named Biafra. The central government contested this claim, which the rebels were forced to surrender after the shedding of much blood.

Often irrational, but invariably felt, when present, with the deepest intensity, nationalism remains one of the most powerful forces in politics and one of the most potent sources of frustration turning into rebellion; in other words, of conflict.

I have left *ideology* to the last, but it is not the least of our contem-porary plagues. It is important, however, to explain what one means by ideology, for it means different things to different people and in different places. In Germany, for instance, it is sometimes held to be synonymous with what, in English (or Greek) one would call a national 'ethos'—a strong if nebulous combination of prevailing emotions, attitudes and ideas, characteristic of a nation at a certain period of its history. The English connotation of ideology is more precise, but I shall not take it for granted. In the context of this book,

I define ideology as a system of ideas and arguments, held to have the
force of absolute truth, usually but not invariably attributable to one
or more authors whose works are quoted as authorities and used, in
effect, as intellectual courts of appeal.

This definition has, I submit, the merit of greater precision than that
given by a contributor to a useful little symposium: 'Generally,
Ideology is a mode of social thought whose content includes significant
programmatic elements which are intended to influence the political
activity of a large body of people.'[4] True, the author goes on to draw
attention to another aspect of ideology which seems to me to lie at the
heart of the matter, when he points out that in one formulation,
'Ideology deprives both intellectual criticism and traditional political
study of any relevance. This Ideology is a sort of super-principle which
diminishes all claims of practice and thought.' It is in this sense that
I use the word.

In an increasingly irreligious age, ideology has taken the place of
religion. Like religion, ideology has its prophets, its holy texts, its
established churches, its schisms and its sects. It has, too, its heretics,
who may be banished, tortured or killed for their deviations or dis-
beliefs. Although many countries, especially among the newer ones,
have their State ideologies (e.g. Burmese socialism, or Arab socialism,
or the 'personalism' of the Diem regime in Vietnam), by far the most
important of the contemporary ideologies is Marxism–Leninism. It is
the State religion in the Soviet Union, throughout eastern Europe, in
China, North Vietnam, North Korea and Cuba. Nor is this fact in
the least affected by the circumstance that Peking and Moscow dispute
with each other the claim to be the centre of the cult. The Christian
religion, too, has many churches and Rome has its rivals. Moreover,
not only is the Marxist–Leninist non-religion established in the
countries named, but it is the secular faith of Communist Parties
everywhere, whatever version of the doctrine each may accept, and
of countless factions and groups, many of which dilute or flavour the
given gospel with touches of Maoism, Guevarism, Castrism or
Titoism.

Once established, Marxism–Leninism is a device for the enforcement of conformity and obedience among subjects. For intolerance is
the distinguishing mark of ideology. By definition, the absolute truth
does not admit of competition. But in its unestablished phase, ideology
is equally intolerant. Ideologically motivated terrorists, or mere

---

[4] H(enry) D(rucker) in Maurice Cranston, ed., *A Glossary of Political Terms*
(Background Books, Bodley Head, 1966), p. 45.

protesters, claim the right to remove, or bully and intimidate, individuals or groups that do not share their convictions. In contemporary society, therefore, ideology is a particularly virulent source of conflict. The ideological revolutionary's special frustration is that the majority of the people do not share his views.

The new sources of conflict

With some exceptions, the sources of conflict we have been considering have been constant throughout human history. Some of the problems of education, land hunger, poverty, nepotism, injustice and nationalism have always been with us. Ideology, in the sense in which I have used the term, is new, or at any rate a phenomenon of the twentieth century. Yet the special kind of intolerance, fanaticism and proselytising zeal it breeds is not unfamiliar in history. It is closely akin, indeed, to the zealotry of religious fanatics in the days of the Church's power. Those who spread Islam or Christianity by the sword, forcibly converting infidel or heathen, were closely akin, in their faith in revelation and their assertion of special righteousness, to the zealots of Marxism–Leninism or Maoism. And there was little difference in kind between the torture and burning of heretics, and the torture and liquidation or banishment of political dissenters.

The special problems of contemporary education and adjustment to technological change are, however, really new—that is, they did not exist, or hardly at all, as social problems, before the end of the Second World War. Moreover, as they appear, so they multiply, for biological as well as technological reasons. If one were asked, therefore, to give generic names for the new sources of conflict in the contemporary world, one would offer: *the population explosion;* and *the acceleration of technological change.*

Even if there were no new technology, the 'biological time-bomb' would still have been exploding among us. In fact, it would have exploded much sooner, for the countries that suffer most from exploding birth-rates and the greatest pressures on scarce resources are the relatively poor and backward ones, such as India, China and Indonesia. But such is the relentless logic of geometrical progression that even the populations of advanced countries with widely practised birth control, are increasing too fast for comfort. Before the war, Britain's population was about 46 million; by 1973, it had reached 55½ million. During that time, the population of the United States rose from 137 million to more than 203 million. The pre-war statistics for China (admittedly unreliable) recorded a population of 420 million; it is widely thought to have exceeded 732 million by 1973.[5] The point is that everywhere there are more and more people, eating more, consuming more, competing ever more fiercely for classroom space, for housing, for parking and driving space. If social problems are bad, the birth explosion makes them worse. If they were manageable, they become unmanageable.

The acceleration of technological change is another cause of social tension. The German physicist Max Born wrote in 1968:

> The fears generated by political and military events, together with the complete breakdown in ethics—all of which I have witnessed in my lifetime—are not symptoms of a temporary weakness in the social order, but an inevitable consequence of the dominance of the natural sciences.[6]

In traditional societies, the sense of permanence, durability and stability is profound. Whether the prevailing attitude was satisfaction or resignation, the anti-revolutionary effect was the same. That is why change, when it does come, is so inflammatory; and especially rapid change. Even in our industrial societies at earlier stages of their development, in the last twenty years of the nineteenth or the first three decades of the twentieth, the pace of change, though remarkable, was bearable. 'Good' manufactures were built to last. Now obsolescence, though not necessarily 'built in' in the sense of a deliberate policy-choice, comes with each new model of a car, each new delivery of Hi-Fi equipment and each new passenger airliner. The consumer hardly has time to boast of his new acquisition before he starts casting envious eyes at those who bought a few months later than he did. The advertising pressures reach out at him or her from the hoardings, the newspapers or television. He is constantly tempted to satisfy his wants, often either imaginary or induced in him by relentless publicity. But no sooner has he yielded than he is made discontented by visions of the newest and best.

Moreover, the computer replaces the human employee (with, in the early stages, highly unsatisfactory results), thus creating unemployment and adding a further frustration to the modern citizen's already impressive collection: that of having nobody to complain to if his bank balance comes out wrong or his gas bill is patently absurd. The

---

[5] All these figures are approximate.
[6] Quoted by Hans Josef Horchem in *West Germany: 'The Long March through the Institutions'* (*Conflict Studies* No. 33, Feb. 1973).

contribution of accelerated technology to the dehumanisation of life, and to its store of conflicts, is thus enormous, and growing fast.

Among the marvels of the technological age, those that are the most relevant to any study of conflict are: *television* and *mass communications*. It is not part of my purpose to give a balanced consideration to either, beyond conceding that there are many good aspects, as well as some bad, about both. It is useful, when the system works, to be able to make quick telephone calls across national boundaries; and it can be thrilling to watch the Olympic Games or soccer internationals in the comfort of your own armchair. Both of television and of mass communications, it could be said that they are rather like the tongues in Aesop's fable: they can be used for bad purposes as well as good.

I first became aware of this simple truth in the early 1950s after the French film *Rififi* had attracted international attention. Its central theme was an ingenious jewel robbery, in which the robbers drilled through the ceiling above the target shop, catching the plaster in an unfurled umbrella. The point is that within a few months, the crime was imitated in perhaps half a dozen cities, including two as far apart as Melbourne and Buenos Aires.

So it is with television, radio and international wire services. A diplomat is kidnapped by Uruguayan or Guatemalan terrorists, and in no time, there is a wave of such abductions in other countries. An airliner is hijacked for ransom or against impossible political demands; and soon, the sport of political hijacking becomes fashionable among 'urban guerrilla' groups.

The rapidity of jet travel and its enormous spread, have been obvious aids to international terrorists. A young fanatic can be in Tokyo one day, yet commit an outrage in Rome the next. Moreover, the extraordinary escalation of jet travel offers unprecedented opportunities for concealment.

Likewise, an invaluable adjunct to international plotting is the advent of self-dialling long-distance telephone systems. A group in Munich can concert operations with accomplices in Paris. Hence a proliferation of conspiracies across the borders. Hence, too, the rapid standardisation of the technology of terrorism. An inventive terrorist who has perfected a technique, or, say, miniaturised an explosive device, does not keep the knowledge to himself, but passes it on to the ideologically like-minded in some other country. Typically, a Japanese group can machine-gun air travellers in an Israeli airport on behalf of Palestine extremists (the Lod massacre, 30 May 1972).

The role of television in such events is inevitably controversial. I am not in this context referring to the quality of the reporting, but to factors inherent in the nature of the medium. Two characteristics, in particular, virtually ensure that television reporting of situations of revolutionary conflict shall be one-sided and misleading.

By its nature, television reporting of news events is *evanescent* and *exclusive*. In other words, in television the image and sound (as in radio, the sound alone) are fleeting. The viewer cannot 'turn back' the programme in time to correct or confirm his impressions. The printed word—as in newspapers—lacks this serious disadvantage. It is possible to *think* one has seen something when one only thought one saw it. However, so great is the power of such dicta as 'seeing is believing', or 'I have seen it with my own eyes', or 'the camera cannot lie', that the average viewer, having learnt his news by sight of the little screen, is more likely to believe he is in the possession of the truth than if he had read the same information in his daily newspapers. Indeed the popular wisdom about newspapers tends to be in the opposite direction, as in the familiar admonishment, 'You can't believe everything you read in the papers'. Self-delusion is therefore more likely with the TV news than with the printed word.

Television news, then, is evanescent but convincing. Its impact is far greater, far more dramatic, than that of pictures in a newspaper or magazine. Moreover, it is normally exclusive of rival accounts, if only by virtue of the limitations of the optic nerve. Just as the ears cannot give equal attention to two competing speeches, so the eyes cannot satisfactorily take in more than one projected image.

To be given a choice of programmes is thus often an illusory benefit. I cannot speak for other countries, but I have noticed that in England, the competitive news programmes sometimes coincide. Since one cannot watch both at once, even if more than one set is available, the viewer is denied the advantage of comparing different accounts of the same events; whereas the newspaper reader can compare *The Times* with the *Daily Telegraph*, or on the Eastern seaboard of the United States, the *New York Times* with the *Washington Post*. (Some readers would say that the latter choice is no choice, but this complaint, which I have heard, does not affect the argument.)

But in addition to the physical limitations of the medium, there is a more disquieting factor still, which is inherent in the nature not of television but of war itself, and especially of revolutionary war. It is in the nature of war that the reporter does not, except in the rarest of cases, gain access to the enemy side. Normally, therefore, he reports only what his own side is doing at first hand. In conventional wars, it is normal for the governments of protagonist States to institute censorship of the press on grounds of national security. Even in democratic countries, this temporary curtailment of liberty is generally accepted as in the national interest, on the understanding that it is indeed temporary and that full freedom of the press will be restored once hostilities are over.

Revolutionary war, however, has raised new problems. The phenomenon itself is new, and we shall be returning to it in these pages. Let me simply say at this stage that the techniques of revolutionary war were elaborated in the 1930s, 1940s and 1950s in China and Vietnam; and that it is the most total form of warfare yet devised, transcending the strictly military field and impinging on psychology, social organisation and politics. Those who resort to people's revolutionary war, in fact, aim at the complete destruction of the enemy's administration, the undermining of the society in which both operate, the shattering of the enemy's will to resist—and, more importantly perhaps, of the people's resistance or indifference to the revolutionary movement. In such a war, gains or losses in territory are *relatively* unimportant, but the psychological aspect has a special importance. What matters is less whether the enemies of the revolutionaries are, objectively, winning or losing, as whether they *think* they are. If they think they are losing, or if public opinion at home ceases to support the armed forces, or if the government loses its nerve, or if it begins to be thought that the war is too expensive and cannot be won—in any of these cases, the revolutionaries are, in fact, winning, whatever the situation on the battlefield.

This is why television was overwhelmingly important during the second Indochina War. This was, in fact, the first war in history to be fought on the television screens, the first to be enacted in every home of the people of one of the contending parties. The effect was shattering. Mothers saw their sons being killed or flying off on missions from which they might never return. Brutalities and atrocities, whether intentional or accidental, on the American and South Vietnamese side, were duly recorded. Feeding off this powerful material, the protest movement gathered strength, further sapping public and official morale and adding greatly to the difficulties of the Administration. The grand climax of this television war came with the Têt offensive launched by the North Vietnamese and Vietcong forces at the time of the Vietnamese lunar new year early in 1968. Militarily, the Têt offensive was a devastating defeat for the communist side. Psychologically however, it was accepted as a defeat by the American public;

and the psychological aspect, since this was a revolutionary war, was more important than the military. A spectacular political casualty was President Johnson, who announced his decision not to run for a second term in the world's most powerful elective office.

Clearly it would be an exaggeration to ascribe the withdrawal of the President of the United States solely to the impact of television reporting; but there is no doubt that it played a part, and that the new phenomenon of television emerged for the first time as a factor in the outcome of an armed conflict. It has been observed that if the First World War had been covered on television and without censorship, and if the families of the British tommies had watched as 20,000 of them were being slaughtered every *day* on the muddy fields of Flanders, the war might have ended sooner than it did, as a consequence of a British decision to lay down arms.

Certainly during the first Indochina war, when the peninsula was under French rule, the defending forces did not labour under a comparable handicap. Not only was there no television, but the French, although they never proclaimed a state of war, did impose censorship, at any rate of press cables (by an anomaly which some correspondents turned to temporary advantage, there was no censorship of outgoing mail). Indeed, with admirable economy of official effort, the same army officer was both the military spokesman and the chief censor; so that foreign correspondents were first told what they could say, then required to submit their dispatches for the same man to check whether they had exceeded his brief. (All this did not, incidentally, save the French from ultimate defeat, but it is arguable that the collapse of morale which led the French to the conference table would have taken place much earlier if the war had been covered, as the second Indochina war was, on television and without any censorship at all.)

And now, after this lengthy but necessary digression, I come to the real point of the argument: *the television coverage of revolutionary wars —that is of such situations as Vietnam and Ulster—is invariably one-sided and detrimental to the official side in the conflict.* The reason for this is twofold. On the one hand, in revolutionary wars as fought hitherto, correspondents have access, as they have not in conventional wars, to the enemy, who is able to argue his case and even, in rare cases, take reporters on conducted tours of 'liberated zones'. However, I have yet to hear of a case where the revolutionary or terrorist side invites the press to witness the disembowelling or massacre of civilians (as in Vietnam), or the beating up or tarring and feathering of selected victims (as in Northern Ireland). In Vietnam, for instance, the whole world saw a South Vietnamese police chief personally shooting a Vietcong prisoner. But Western viewers and readers were spared the spectacle of communist execution squads shooting several thousand people on their black lists and burying them in mass graves, sometimes while still alive, in Hué and other towns temporarily under communist control during the Têt offensive (1968). Thus, 'atrocities' on the government side were shown, but not those on the revolutionary side.

Television therefore takes its place as a major new factor in contemporary situations of conflict. I shall leave to a later chapter the problem of whether television should remain unfettered; and if not, what limitations should be imposed on it.

PART II

The State
as Fact and Theory

FROM PREHISTORY TO J. S. MILL

The ground covered in this chapter

States and theories of the State—Egypt, Sumer and China—Greek city States—Plato's gloomy Utopia—Aristotle on rebellion, democracy and tyranny—the Roman Republic—the early Emperors—Christian theorists of the State: St. Augustine, St. Thomas Aquinas, Luther—Machiavelli and scepticism—Bodin—Hobbes and authoritarian government—Rousseau and his influence—prophets of liberalism: Locke and Mill

DOES THE State exist for the people, or the people for the State? The controversy implicit in this dual question has bedevilled the contending political theories of the past two centuries.

Yet for thousands of years, the question hardly ever arose, as an object of philosophical inquiry. There were States long before speculation about the State began, and indeed long before the word 'State' existed. If the principal attribute of the State is sovereignty—that is, enforced authority within more or less defined boundaries—then sovereign States existed before the concept of sovereignty had been discussed; and indeed before the human race had invented writing. Archaeology has unearthed the story of Predynastic Egypt, though not its details. There as elsewhere, stronger tribes expanded at the expense of weaker ones. As in more recent times, strength was synonymous with skill in the manufacture of weapons. Those with the skill and the weapons conquered those inferior and without. The god of the stronger became the symbol of conquering sovereignty and the conquered were forced to worship the totems of the conquerors. Thus by 4,300 B.C. the uraeus serpent had become the unifying totem of the kingdom of Lower Egypt; and the vulture, of Upper Egypt. When the first Pharaoh—whom legend calls Menes—unified the two kingdoms under his rule, he wore a double crown bearing both a vulture and a serpent. It was the south that had conquered the north and the unity thus achieved was precarious. Every now and then the northern tribes revolted, reasserting their sovereignty, and at such times Egypt reverted to two kingdoms—that is, two States.

Ancient Sumer, that rival cradle of civilisation, also worshipped local gods, each of whom presided over a city-State ruled in its name by an *ishak* or tenant farmer. Skilled in agriculture and the arts of war, versed in astronomy and mathematics, the Sumerians were the first to codify a system of civil laws: a relatively sophisticated exercise in State sovereignty.

The Chinese peasantry under the Western Chou dynasty (1,000–950 B.C.) deferred to the sovereignty of the princes by tilling land for them. Some centuries later, Confucius's posthumous disciple Mencius (Meng K'o) urged China's feudal princes to adopt the people's welfare as the objective and condition of their royal authority. There, too, practice predated theory. The ruthless Emperor Ch'in united China by force, using cavalry with devastating effect. Then came the philosophers, Han Fei-tzu and Li Ssu (who died in 233 and 208 respectively) to justify the use of force to unify the warring States in a legalistic doctrine. Their fellow-scholars included more than 400 freer souls whom the Emperor had put to death for their inquisitive dissidence. The sovereignty of Ch'in was bloody as well as absolute.

There are interesting parallels between ancient China and ancient Greece, the more interesting in that there was no known intercourse between them. In both countries, a philosophical golden age occurred in the fifth and fourth centuries B.C. There were remarkable similarities in the ideas that emerged in both. But geography dictated profound differences as well. Roaming at will over the vast expanse of northern China, Emperor Ch'in enforced unity by the sword. The Greeks, confined to their narrow and rugged peninsula, with tribal groups separated from each other by mountains, never progressed beyond the city-State. They were, perhaps, no more warlike than the Chinese, but the Greek wars, though frequent, did not in the end create a nation. Even the Spartans, though victorious in the Great Peloponnesian War (431 to 421 and 414 to 404), refrained from annexing Athens.

The Greeks, however, were unique in that it was they who first experimented with self-government. Between 900 and 600 B.C., the tribal monarchies had yielded to the rule of the aristocrats, or oligarchs. But in the last 150 years to the fifth century, tyrannies had sprung up in most areas, ambitious men seizing the opportunities offered by discontent in a situation in which the oligarchs denied political

equality to the landless traders and manufacturers, and the rich
exploited the peasants, often reducing them to slavery by forcing them
into debts which they could not repay.

Then came 'democracy'; which should, at least initially, be given
quotation-marks, for it is notorious that the Greeks used the word,
which they coined, in quite a different sense from today's. (Indeed,
Greek roots often belong to the category of linguistic traps known as
false friends. 'Tyranny' is another, for to the Greeks the 'tyrant' was
merely one who usurped power and not necessarily a man who exercised power tyrannically.) The democracy of the ancient Greeks
merely extended political rights to landless freemen, thus breaching,
for the first time, the monopoly of the oligarchs. But the unfree
remained far more numerous in the polis or city-State than those with
rights. Sensibly enough, in the circumstances of the day, children,
women and slaves were excluded from participation in the political
process. The great Athenian leader, Pericles, moreover restricted
citizenship to those whose mothers and fathers were pure Athenians.
For all that, the experiment was a great step forward. But it should
always be kept in proportion: at the height of its power and brilliance,
the Athenian city-State had no more than 60,000 citizens—that is,
adult males with political rights. A political community of that
size could govern itself directly in a way that is impossible in the popu-
lous nation-States of the twentieth century. (We shall turn later
to our contemporary theorising about 'participatory' democracy.) In
a sense, democracy was born in ancient Greece; and died there,
too.

Meditating upon these circumstances, Plato produced the first, and
surely one of the gloomiest, of the political Utopias, in his dialogue
The Republic. Born in 428 or 427—that is, about the time Pericles
died—Plato had shed his political ambition with the passing of his
mentor Socrates, condemned to drink hemlock on charges of dis-
respect for the gods of the city and of leading youth astray by his
teaching. It is hard, however, to know how much of The Republic is
Socrates and how much Plato, since the younger man wrote custom-
arily in the form of dialogues in which the leading speaker is always
Socrates. The most likely interpretation is that this was simply a
literary device and that the master-ideas were Plato's.

At all events, The Republic stands as the first prototype of the totalist
State. As such, it has been described as the precursor or even the
inspirer of the Hitlerian or Stalinian States. But this is surely carrying
the argument too far; for my part, I prefer to regard The Republic as a

first illustration of the proposition that the philosophical idealist is more likely to deprive his fellow-men of freedom than the realistic and sceptical observer.

In Kallipolis, Plato's 'Fair City' and ideal commonwealth, wives were to be held in common, and children too, so that 'the parent should not know its own offspring nor the child its parent'. Curiously, in the light of this apparent bondage, girls were to be given the same training as boys, on the principle of equal work for (although he does not put it this way) equal pay. Those not equal to the high standards of fitness should not be treated medically, but allowed to die (it will be seen that Plato would have been intolerant of the wastefulness of the Welfare State). There was to be a ruling élite, consisting of philosophers and described as the Guardians, assisted by soldiers called Auxiliaries. By virtue of a 'Noble Lie', the whole population would be conditioned to suppose that all this, including the predominance of the Guardians, was preordained, so that if the wrong people attempted to do the jobs allotted to others, the whole city would be ruined. In this perfect community, based upon eugenics (although the word did not then exist), and a kind of functional communism, there was however, to be a concession, if not to democracy then to social mobility, in the provision that auxiliaries of merit might be promoted to become Guardians; correspondingly, of course, an unsatisfactory Guardian might find himself relegated to the role of Auxiliary.

Plato's pupil, Aristotle, although possibly a still more important thinker, since he was the first true scientist as well as a philosopher, is less relevant to this chapter. His *Politics* was less concerned with the theory of the State than with the ethical aims of politics. The aim of the State—by which he meant no more than a self-governing community of villages—was to produce gentlemen of culture. A government that thinks only of itself is a bad government; one that cares for the whole community, a good one. In the rich, varied, but microcosmic world of the city-States, with it's rapid changes, seizures of power or usurpations, Aristotle discerned six main types of government—three good, three bad. The good ones were monarchy, aristocracy and polity (that is, constitutional government). The bad ones were the corruption of the good: tyranny (the corruption of monarchy); oligarchy (a debased aristocracy); and democracy (a worse form of polity). Why was aristocracy better than oligarchy? Because the aristocrats were presumed to be men of virtue who ruled for the good of all, whereas the oligarchs were men of wealth ruling primarily in their own interest. Democracy was bad, however, for it implied that the poor held power and exercised it without regard for the interests of the rich. (That the slaves should have rights never entered into these speculations; Aristotle did not disapprove of slavery, so long as it was confined to those who were slaves by nature.)

It is hard for us in the days of the mass-State and of galloping technology, to relate Aristotle's ancient ideas to our contemporary experience. Two of his passages, however, deserve special attention: his discussion of the causes of revolution, and his prescriptions for the tyrant who wishes to stay in power.

Aristotle thought a democracy (even in his rather pejorative sense of the term) less likely to be threatened by revolution than an oligarchy. Since oligarchs assumed themselves to be superior to the common herd, each oligarch was potentially under threat from a rival who might assume superiority over all others. Democracy, on the other hand, was based on an assumption of equal rights for citizens, and therefore less likely to foster the rise of a usurper. Revolutions, wrote Aristotle, arose from inequalities, numerical or qualitative: either from large numbers claiming an equality denied them, or from a minority claiming a superiority denied them. In all revolutions, the condition leading up to them was the desire of the many for equality, and the desire of the minority for effective superiority. In democracies, revolutions were due mainly to demagogic attacks on wealth, leading the wealthy to combine, and the outcome was the establishment of an oligarchy or of a tyranny. In oligarchies, they sprang from the oppressive conduct of the oligarchy or from dissensions among the oligarchical body. In aristocracies, they arose from the jealousy of those excluded from power, personal ambitions, great inequalities of wealth. Under monarchies, injustice and arrogance were the causes of insurrection, or fear, or contempt for incompetence, coupled with ambition. Tyrannies were overthrown by collision with external forces, or by private intrigues in the tyrant's entourage.

It will be seen that Aristotle was possibly the first to perceive the economic factors of rebellion; and that he made no distinction between insurrections and *coups d'état*. It is true that he was writing long before revolutionary war had been thought of.

When it comes to prescriptions for preventing revolution, Aristotle begged as many questions as he answered. There should, he wrote, be government propaganda through education, and the law should be respected, even in small things. Moreover, there should be justice in law and administration, that is 'equality in proportion, and for every man to enjoy his own'. Few modern politicians would publicly dispute this proposition.

The section on tyranny (Book V, 11) is more realistic; and indeed, as Bertrand Russell pointed out, there was an 'ironically Machiavellian' touch about it.[1] '. . . whereas the power of a king is preserved by his friends, the characteristic of a tyrant is to distrust his friends, because he knows that all men want to overthrow him, and they above all have the power.' He defined the three aims of the tyrant as sowing distrust among his subjects, taking away their power, and humbling them. Alternatively, the tyrant should imitate the king in that 'he should pretend a care of the public revenues, and not waste money making presents of a sort at which the common people get excited when they see their hard-won earnings snatched from them and lavished on courtesans and strangers and artists'. Old Nick advising Caesar Borgia could not do much better.

Alone among the ancient city-States, Rome became a great empire. Rome's contribution to the study of State institutions was, perhaps for that reason, through example not philosophy. The kings of ancient Rome in that twilight between prehistory and reliable chronicle were elective, not hereditary. Their power was limited, but not to excess, by an advisory Senate of 100 elders and a popular assembly of clans (*curaie*). It was the assembly that elected the king. The more prosperous farmers called themselves patricians and arrogated class privileges to themselves. The less fortunate, called *plebeians*, sought the patricians' protection.

In the early Republic (which tradition unreliably dates from 509 B.C.), the *imperium* or power that had been the king's was shared equally between two consuls, originally called *praetors* or generals. Either could prevent the other from acting, but neither could force the other to act. From these early times, the Romans, though in a cultural sense rustic and brutish, displayed their innate genius for social and political organisation. Over the armed forces, they held power of life and death; their rule over the city was enforced by the summary police power of the *coercitio*. They were elected by the *comitia centuriata*, but they owed their *imperium* to the *comitia curiata*, later represented by 30 lictors. There was an advanced judicial system, in which criminal cases were handled by the *quaestores parricidi* or investigators of murder. Treason, however, was referred to the *duouiri perduellionis*.

[1] Bertrand Russell, *A History of Western Philosophy* (London, 1946) p. 214. My quotations from Aristotle are from the standard Benjamin Jowett edition of *Politica* (Oxford, 1921).

Later the *quaestors*, whose responsibilities included the collection of fines, became the State's main financial officers and as such were attached to the consuls as comptrollers. Civil cases were handled by arbitration until, in 367 B.C., the consuls set up a special office of *praetor* for this purpose.

At times of crisis, the Senate could override the consuls by appointing a dictator, known as *magister populi*, to restore unity of command. But the dictator, although he had absolute power while in office, had to resign when his task was completed or at the expiry of six months —whichever came first.

In two centuries of wars, the Romans defeated the Etruscans and the Samnites to extend their hold over all Italy. During this period, the natural conflict between the patricians and the plebeians deepened in intensity. In this confrontation, the plebs were not without resources, not least their vastly superior numbers. They seem to have invented the strike as a political weapon, which they wielded five times with considerable effect. The most celebrated of these occasions happened in 494 when the plebeians, oppressed by debt, seceded to the Sacred Mount, forcing the patricians to tolerate the institution of *sacrosanct* officials known as tribunes, whose powers, though never legalised, derived from the unanimous support of the plebs and were consolidated by custom. In time, the tribunes gained admission to the Senate and a right of veto over any proposed law or decree. They presided over the *Concilium Plebis*, which defended the rights of the plebeians against the official Assembly of the People. Fines imposed by the tribunes on the *Concilium* were collected by the *aediles* who used the money to make free distributions of corn to the poor and to repair public buildings. Later, they came to exert a general police power.

Having subdued the tribes of Italy, the Romans defeated Carthage in the Punic wars. Syracuse was conquered, and the Macedonian monarchies were absorbed. In turn, Spain, Gaul and England fell under Roman rule. The conquering Julius Caesar, fresh from these victories, returned to Italy, routed the forces of his rival Pompey and entered Rome, where he set up a dictatorship. By contemporary, and even later, standards, it was a benevolent one. Land drainage and town planning relieved unemployment; colonisation abroad relieved the pressure of population in Rome; taxation was improved; citizenship was granted to non-Romans, diluting the power of the Senate; magistrates and senates after the Roman model were set up in the provinces.

It was not a popular rebellion, but a conspiracy of the disgruntled, that removed Julius Caesar by assassination in 44 B.C. Thirteen years later, Caesar Octavianus, styling himself Augustus, became the first Emperor, ushering in a 'Roman peace' that was to last almost uninterrupted for 200 years.

Christianity injected an entirely new, and in some respects a backward-looking, element into the concept of the State. The most important Christian writers, in this context, were St. Augustine, St. Thomas Aquinas and Martin Luther. The first two virtually span the medieval age; the third is the voice of the Reformation, after the rationalism of the Renaissance. Shortly after the sacking of Rome by the Goths in A.D. 410, St. Augustine (354–430) wrote *The City of God* to contest the denigration of the Church by the barbarians who had attributed the disaster to the desertion of the ancient gods. He distinguished between the earthly and heavenly kingdoms. Rome was earthly and sinful. The heavenly kingdom or City of God was the society of the elect whose knowledge of God was obtained in the only possible way, through Christ. The earthly city was represented by the State; and the City of God by the Church. The State could partake of the City of God only by submitting to the Church in all religious matters. Basing itself upon St. Augustine's teachings, the medieval Catholic Church considered itself above the State and claimed the right to enthrone or depose kings. The doctrines of St. Augustine underlay the nebulous concept of the Holy Roman Empire (the term was first used by Frederick of Swabia—Barbarossa—in the twelfth century), although strong emperors contested the superior authority of the Pope.

The classical Greeks had argued that the city-State was the natural fulfilment of the life of man; St. Augustine saw it as ordained by God to mitigate the consequences of Man's Fall—that is, as a remedy for sin. St. Thomas Aquinas (1225–74) rejected this view of Augustine's and revived the Aristotelian theory that man is a political and social animal by his nature. Since man was created by God, it followed that God intended man to live in societies, and this argument led Aquinas to reject another notion of Augustine's: that earthly cities are evil and that the good society can be achieved only in heaven. Aquinas argued, however, that States, though natural, could be good only if they rested on what he called the Natural Law, that is if they conformed to God's moral principles, including that of justice.

An advocate of an elective monarchy, with the consent of the governed, but with an aristocracy to provide leadership and administration, Aquinas nevertheless went some way to justifying revolt against tyranny in certain circumstances. Indeed this concession was implicit in his theory of the Natural Law. For if any edict should offend against the Natural Law, it had no moral validity in his eyes. He did not, however, advocate reckless civil disobedience or rebellion, but enjoined prudence. Unjust laws were 'acts of violence rather than laws'. It might, however, be necessary to abide by them, although they were not binding in conscience, 'to avoid public scandal or public disturbance'.

Luther (1483–1546) approached politics from a theological standpoint. Believing that men were saved by repentance and God's grace alone, he utterly rejected the Church's claim to a special place between man and God on the ground that men needed the sacraments to attain salvation. Temporal leaders, he taught, derived their power directly from God and therefore rebellion was in all cases wrong. He denied the right of subjects to resist a tyrannical ruler, and that of the Pope to depose him. 'Rebellion,' he wrote, 'is not just plain murder; but it is like a great fire which sets a land ablaze and lays it waste; therefore rebellion brings with it a land full of murder and bloodshed; it creates widows and orphans and destroys everything, like the greatest of all disasters.' Thus, through theology and his own revolt against the claims of the Papacy, Luther came to similar conclusions about the horrors of anarchy as the English philosopher Hobbes (see below).

Although a contemporary of Martin Luther's, Niccolò Machiavelli (1469–1527) seems to belong to an entirely different era. Luther was an essentially medieval figure, even though he was a rebel against Rome; Machiavelli, with his sceptical realism, was the first truly modern political thinker. All scholars are agreed that Machiavelli himself was not 'Machiavellian' in the pejorative sense in which the word is normally used—an evil reputation derived entirely from his short, shocking and brilliant work, *The Prince*. I am less concerned to defend Machiavelli against his detractors, however, than to point out that he was the first European thinker since ancient times to base his speculations entirely upon direct observation of politics, without the intrusion of theology, and the first ever to analyse the reality of politics without aspiring to define a political ideal. Politics, Machiavelli perceived, was about power; and just as a State needed power to stand up to other States that might challenge it, so a ruler needed to understand the laws of power to maintain his rule, without which he would be denied the chance to carry out his work.

Machiavelli wrote as a patriot, both for Italy as a whole and, more specifically, for the city-State of Florence, which he held to be superior to the other city-States in the intelligence and culture of its citizens.

From his study of history and of contemporary events, from his own experience as a travelling diplomat, he elaborated the doctrine that the State has reasons of its own that transcend the needs of individual citizens. In practice, *all* States, whatever the degree of public approval or disavowal of the Machiavellian doctrine, have exercised this *raison d'état*.

At some time in the late medieval age, the term State, derived from the Latin *status* (which referred to men's legal rights) first came into general European usage. National boundaries were less important then than they have since become, and the term 'State' transcended linguistic barriers, so that the German *der Staat* is immediately understandable to the English-speaker or to those whose tongue is French (*l'état*), Italian (*lo stato*) or Spanish (*el estado*). Machiavelli, however, took it for granted and never bothered to dissect its elements. The first philosopher to do so was Jean Bodin (1530–96), a Frenchman born three years or so after Machiavelli's death. Although a less important writer than Machiavelli, Bodin deserved his niche in history for his treatise *De la République*. Despite the title of his book, his own preference was for a monarchy whose power should be tempered by a States-General. In the fashion of the time, he used the term 'republic' in the sense of a commonwealth, which he defined as 'the rightly ordered government of a number of families and of those things which are their common concern by a sovereign power'. Sovereignty was the distinguishing mark of the State; and the sovereign alone had the right to make law, wage war, conclude alliances and sign peace treaties. All appointments to public office, moreover, devolved upon him as of sovereign right.

With Hobbes (1588–1679), the philosophy of the State takes a giant intellectual leap forward; although there will always be moral reservations about his view of the State's legitimate powers. There is some controversy about the extent to which the thought of Thomas Hobbes was conditioned by the turbulence of the period through which he lived (he was born in the year of the Spanish Armada, grew up during the religious upheaval of the Reformation, and took refuge in France when the English Civil War broke out; he wrote his great work—*Leviathan*—in Paris). It has been argued that he already subscribed to the principle of royal absolutism before writing *Leviathan*, and that his thinking could therefore not have been the outcome of the Civil War. Hobbes himself may perhaps be allowed a say in the matter, and he declared that his work had been 'occasioned by the disorders of the present time'. In this, he was no different from other philosophers:

from Aristotle and the city-States; from Augustine, haunted by the sack of Rome; from Luther, appalled by the moral degeneracy of Rome and the sale of Papal indulgences; from Machiavelli, trying to make a career in the anarchic turmoil of the warring Italian city-States. Of a sceptical and ironic turn of mind, wielding a witty and vigorous English prose, Hobbes saw in absolute authority the only logical solution to the intolerable problem of anarchy.

In a passage as famous as any in political literature, Hobbes defined the 'state of war'—which he implied, without precisely saying so, was the state of nature—in a manner half mythical, half historical. He saw it as a condition of chronic insecurity with men (and women) in un-restrained competition for scarce resources, each fearing death at the hands of others, and each ready, in the last resort, to inflict death in the interests of survival. Nothing, he reasoned, could be worse than this state in which there were

> ... no arts; no letters; no society; and which is worst of all, con-tinual fear, and danger of violent death; and the life of man, solitary, poor, nasty, brutish, and short.

In this state, all were equal (and women the equals of men), not in the sense of equal value or endowment, but in that of ultimately equal vulnerability to sudden violence and death. In this situation, men enjoyed one inalienable right, above all others: that of self-defence. Their only escape from perpetual fear and insecurity, however, lay in the surrender of most other rights to a sovereign power; indeed, specifically to a king, or to an assembly, to wield power through the Leviathan of the State. There being no natural law (except to kill or be killed), the sovereign, in return for guaranteeing peace and security, had the absolute power to legislate. Conversely, the citizen had the absolute duty to obey it. The sovereign's laws defined justice and in-justice, and it would be presumptuous of the citizen to question them since—to the extent that he did—society would move back towards the abhorrent state of war from which the sovereign protects him. The sovereign's power could not be diluted—for instance by Parliament—for competing authorities meant no authority and might (as happened in Hobbes's time) lead to civil war.

It will be seen that *Leviathan* is the ultimate case for authoritarian government. But it would be quite wrong to see it—as some com-mentators do—as the precursor of totalism. For Hobbes, while advocating undiluted power, limited the sovereign's rights in some interesting specific ways. Nothing, for example, could deprive the citizen of his inherent right of self-defence. If the sovereign takes actions that threaten men's lives, they are within their rights in resisting him. More important still was his explicit limitation of the sovereign's rights to the regulation of his subjects' *outward* behaviour. A man's thoughts were his own: '. . . the inward thought, and belief of men . . . human governors can take no notice of (for God only knoweth the heart).' Since the principal distinguishing characteristic of the modern totalist State is its presumptive right to control the thoughts of its subjects, forcing them all into a single ideological mould, Hobbes is in no sense the prophet of Fascism or Communism.

I know of no evidence that the evolution of the State itself, as distinct from the theory of the State, was in any discernible way influenced by the writings of Thomas Hobbes. In his own day, *Leviathan* pleased nobody. Oxford University burned it publicly as 'false, seditious and impious'; Parliament cited his atheism as one of the causes of the Great Fire of London; even the Tories, those supporters of royal absolutism, were disquieted by the reasons adduced by Hobbes to support his espousal of that cause. For they rested their case upon the divine right of kings and therefore saw the sovereign as the instrument of God's will; whereas he thought that the people, faced with the dreadful alternative of anarchy, were bound, in their own interest, to surrender all power to the sovereign. Thus absolutism, in Hobbes's eyes, could be said to rest upon the authorisation of the governed—a dangerously democratic notion in the seventeenth century.

   In fact, the State went on as though Hobbes had written nothing. By beheading the sovereign, Cromwell had dealt a death-blow not merely to Charles I but to the principle of the divine right. True, the monarchy was restored, but things could never be the same. Elsewhere —most notably in France—the divine right continued to be asserted. But there, too, not much more than a hundred years after the English Restoration of 1660, the monarch was deprived of his throne, his head and his divine right.

The influence of philosophers is a fascinating but inevitably inconclusive subject; as is the incidence of best-sellers, and quite possibly for similar reasons. The least influential are those who are too far in advance of their times, although time may catch up with their teachings and bring them posthumous glory. But every now and then, a thinker happens to be the right man at the right time. Attuned to the popular mood or appetite, which he divines before the public is quite aware of it, he expresses aspirations which reflect those of millions. Four such, in very different ways, are Rousseau, Locke, Mill and Marx.

Although Jean-Jacques Rousseau (1712–78) was not the first of these in chronology, I shall deal with him first, because Locke, who preceded him, and Mill who followed, should really be considered together. One of the difficulties with Rousseau is that he was in no sense a systematic thinker. This may help to account for the fact that he has been widely hailed as the inspirer of democracy, and denounced as the pathfinder of the totalitarian State. Writing during the second World War, Bertrand Russell saw Hitler as 'an outcome of Rousseau'.[2] But his emphasis on the 'general will' and on what would nowadays be called 'participation' seems to me much closer to the kind of State Mao Tse-tung has established in China, with its 'mass line' and enforced participation of the people in 'socialist construction'. It is true, on the other hand, that his other leading idea—the sovereignty of the people—can be used to justify democracy in the Western sense; but only if it is considered in isolation from the rest of his doctrine.

Since all philosophers are, to some extent, the captives of current knowledge and wisdom, it is not surprising that much of Rousseau now seems demonstrably nonsense. In Rousseau's case, however, it is perhaps harder than with most others to separate the nonsense from the rest. For me, to take a subjective view, the most nonsensical of Rousseau's doctrines is the notion of the natural nobility of man. In antithesis to Hobbes, Rousseau held that in his natural state, man was good without being moral; it was civilisation that made him a moral being; but having failed to improve, it had corrupted him. More specifically, the institution of property was the origin of social injustice. In *Emile*, Rousseau advocates a 'natural' form of education, by direct experience in preference to excessive book learning, although he himself was a self-taught man with a passion for books. This approach displeased established authorities, since it implied that the Church or the priest was not necessary to an appreciation of God. It influenced modern educationalists, such as Froebel and Montessori, and may have a bearing on the decline of reading ability at the hands of 'progressive' teachers in Britain, during the two decades after the mid-twentieth century.

It is, however, in *The Social Contract* (1762) that Rousseau's most coherent political philosophy is found. Starting from a standpoint radically different from that of Hobbes, Rousseau nevertheless reached conclusions in some respects rather similar. There comes a

[2] Russell, *op. cit.*, p. 711.

time in the state of nature where men need to unite to form a society in the interests of self-preservation, and to fulfil man's nature as a citizen. In so doing, each individual surrenders all rights to the community as a whole. This process is what Rousseau calls 'the social contract', and its outcome is the State. There was undoubtedly a mystical (that is, hazy) element in his own definition of the social contract: 'Each of us puts his person and all his power in common under the supreme direction of the general will, and, in our corporate capacity, we received each member as an indivisible part of the whole.'

Everything, then, depends on what is meant by 'the general will'. On this key point, Rousseau is obscure. He appears to say that it means what is common in all men's desires once each has discarded selfish interests. But who is to define the outcome? I am ready, with David Thomson, to give as an example the refusal of the British people as a whole to submit to Hitler after the evacuation of the British expeditionary force from Dunkirk in 1940.[3] But such occurrences are very rare. A 'general will' does not usually emerge spontaneously with any clarity in the more humdrum questions of everyday life. That is why delegation of some kind to an elected assembly has been deemed necessary by the theorists of Western democracy, but Rousseau will have none of it. For him, there can be no dilution of the will of the people. His ideal democracy was that of the city-State, and what we in the West call democracy, he termed 'elective aristocracy'. He regarded all subordinate associations within the State as against the general will, and advocated an imposed State religion. His ideas are therefore, in their sum, closer to the present-day communist-controlled regimes than to those of the pluralistic societies with representative government.

Having momentarily rejoined Hobbes in advocating the surrender of all personal rights to the 'sovereign', Rousseau parts company with him on the semantics of sovereignty. For Hobbes thought of the sovereign as an individual in whom the people vest all authority; whereas to Rousseau, the 'sovereign' was synonymous with the people as the expression of the general will. Although Rousseau is an obscure and at times a confused thinker, who can be made to mean different things to different men, it seems to me that the long-term implications of his philosophy are totalist; whereas those of Hobbes are authoritarian. The difference is a vital one.

John Locke (1632–1704) and John Stuart Mill (1806–73) were the greatest prophets of liberal democracy and their influence, like

[3] David Thomson, ed., *Political Ideas* (1966), pp. 97, 98.

Rousseau's but in a far more precise way, has been wide and profound. As a philosopher, Locke was a modern, and a man of common sense. As a political theorist, he was both a patriot and a revolutionary; and an advocate of selective tolerance. He originated the concept of enlightened self-interest (which does not translate easily into Latin tongues), and the doctrines of government by consent, and of checks and balances and the separation of powers. Since all these concepts are central to the representative democracies of Britain and the United States (and of countries that have borrowed from, or imitated, their examples), it is hard to exaggerate his influence.

Locke owed much to the protection of the first Earl of Shaftesbury, whose household he joined. That great Englishman, the founder of the Whig party and the pioneer of British commerce overseas and therefore of the special form British imperialism took, advocated religious tolerance at a time when the parliamentary supporters of Charles II wanted to force everybody to join the Church of England. But his advocacy of tolerance did not extend to Papists, whose loyalty to Rome, he thought, implied disloyalty to the Crown. When Charles II became a Catholic and accepted a pension from the Catholic Louis XIV, Shaftesbury turned against his king. In all this, Locke followed him. Their views made it perilous for them to live in London, and both men fled to tolerant Holland—that haven of dissidents, where Descartes spent twenty years.

The Catholic despotism of James II might almost have been designed to prove Locke right, and his *Two Treatises of Government*, written some ten years before the Glorious Revolution of 1688, but not published until after the event, was a philosophical justification for the rebellion that drove the king from his throne. Arguing that the sovereign derived his authority from the consent of the government and that James had forfeited the people's trust by arbitrary government, Locke drove the last nail into the coffin of the divine right of kings.

In a social sense, Locke was no revolutionary. His defence of rebellion in specific circumstances did not extend to advocacy of an entirely new system, but was intended to restore the 'natural rights' of the people, of which they had been deprived by illegal government. It is worth noting, in passing, that Locke was a staunch upholder of private property. His espousal of freedom, though passionate, was conditional. If one man's freedom is likely to endanger another's, it must be controlled. As a safeguard against abuse of power, he advocated the separation of the legislative power from the executive, and the judiciary stressed the need for independent judges. It is in the United States, rather than in Britain, that the adoption of Locke's ideas has gone furthest.

Mill, though not a true innovator, made his lasting mark by the passionate conviction with which he held his ideas, and the eloquence with which he expressed them. From Jeremy Bentham (1748–1832) he borrowed the Utilitarian notion of 'the greatest happiness of the greatest number', and from the great French observer of contemporary history, Alexis de Tocqueville (1805–59), the fear that unrestrained democracy might lead to 'the tyranny of the majority'. By far the most influential book Mill wrote was his essay *On Liberty*, in which two main ideas are expressed: the case for freedom of speech, and that of freedom for the individual. At the outset, he spelt out 'one very simple principle' which epitomises his philosophy: '. . . the only purpose for which power can be rightfully exercised over any member of a civilised community, against his will, is to prevent harm to others. His own good, either physical or moral, is not a sufficient warrant.'

In the name of his simple principle, John Stuart Mill called for complete liberty of conscience, speech and publication. It was only if all opinions could be freely expressed, he argued, that those hearing or reading them could decide where the truth lay; and he defended this view in one of his most eloquent passages:

'The peculiar evil of silencing the expression of an opinion is, that it is robbing the human race; posterity as well as the existing generation; those who dissent from the opinion, still more than those who hold it. If the opinion is right, they are deprived of the opportunity of exchanging error for truth: if wrong, they lose, what is almost as great a benefit, the clearer perception and liveliest impression of truth, produced by its collision with error. . . .

If all mankind minus one were of one opinion, and only one person were of the contrary opinion, mankind would be no more justified in silencing that one person, than he, if he had the power, would be justified in silencing mankind.'

His chapter on individuality advocated the tolerance of those who insisted on leading their own lives, so long as they did not harm others, and whatever the degree of their eccentricity.

It is not at all difficult to 'pick holes' in Mill's arguments, and many critics have claimed their right (which he would have defended) of doing so. I shall exert my own right to that end in a later chapter. For now, all that need be said is that Mill's plea for the individual has had less success than his advocacy of free speech. Its delayed fruit, which the author could hardly have foreseen, writing as he did in the hypocritical and constricting atmosphere of Victorian England, has been permissiveness and the enthronement of pornography in the name of freedom from censorship. (But I too am a captive of my time: the last sentence, though substantially true in 1973, when these words were written, may have ceased to be true when this book is published, and may be successively true and untrue at different stages of its lifetime.)

Although I have already mentioned Karl Marx, his philosophy marks so clear a break with the writers we have just considered that he needs a separate chapter.

MARX AND HIS FOLLOWERS

The ground covered in this chapter

Marx's evil influence—Praxis *and the attempt to change the world—ideology as a form of action—the class struggle—Marx's economic view of history—justification of revolution—dialectical materialism: Hegel upside down—Hegel precursor of totalitarian State—Marxism as Utopianism—Marx's theory of the State and its contradictions—Engels and withering away—durability of Marxism: substitute for religion—Lenin as living disproof of Marxism—seizure of power from Kerensky—Lenin on the State—the vanguard party—democratic centralism and totalitarian State—the Comintern—leftist adventurism—tyranny inherent in Marxism-Leninism—fundamentalist illusions—the Trotskyist fallacy*

THE MOST influential political thinker of the twentieth century has been Karl Marx, who lived all his life in the nineteenth (1818–83). His influence has been almost wholly evil, with few redeeming features. (Conceivably his only serious rival in these respects, and if influence is considered rather than the man's actual work, has been Sigmund Freud (1856–1939); but Freud is of peripheral interest, as distinct from Marx, who is central, to this study.)

Marx was a prolific writer: prolific in works, words and ideas. Though often obscure, turgid and prolix, he was capable of vivid and powerful writing, especially in the historical chapters of *Das Kapital*. I shall not attempt to summarise his entire philosophy; indeed, I am less concerned with his philosophy, as such, than with the influence it has had on men and events. I shall therefore concentrate upon the Marxian ideas that seem to me to have been the most influential: the theory of *Praxis*; the notion of class struggle and of the inevitability of revolution; and his contradictory views on the nature of the State.

With his *Praxis*, Marx broke entirely new ground. In the eleventh and last of his brief *Theses on Feuerbach* (1845) put it in this terse and striking form: 'The philosophers have only *interpreted* the world in various ways; the point however is to *change* it.'

Ludwig Feuerbach (1804–72) was a minor German idealistic philosopher, whose name might well have been totally forgotten today, had he not provoked Marx and his disciple Engels to write critical texts about him. The *Theses* hardly justified their ponderous title, being simply, in Engels's words, 'notes hurriedly scribbled down for later elaboration, absolutely not intended for publication, but . . . invaluable as the first document in which is deposited the brilliant germ of the new world outlook'. This verdict was true enough, for these notes, which the young Marx—he was 27—'scribbled' so hurriedly, contained the fundamentals of his thought.

Marx utterly rejected the contemplative role of the philosopher. The fundamental reality, as he saw it, was the material world; but knowledge of it was not to be explained merely as the impact of sensations upon the mind, for sensations were passive. Perception thus obtained was immediate, but needed to be transformed and completed by action (a theory now generally known as 'instrumentalism'). Arguing from these premises, the Marxists (that is, those influenced by Karl Marx) insist that theory and action are indissoluble. As R. N. Carew Hunt pointed out, theory and action (or *Praxis*) 'stand in much the same relation to one another as do faith and works in Christian theology'.[1]

The importance of ideology to Communists stems essentially from Marx's view of the *Praxis*. When Marxist writers produce ideological texts, their purpose is not, as it is with most non-Marxist writers, merely to produce ideas for discussion, for ideology is itself a form of 'action'. In practice (although this is not how Marxists would put it), ideology serves internally (that is, within the Communist party in opposition, or throughout the State if in power) to enforce obedience, conformity and cohesion. In other words, ideology has a *disciplinary* function. Externally (that is, beyond the State boundaries of Communist regimes), ideology fulfils parallel purposes: to subvert non-Communist regimes; to achieve, maintain or restore the unity of the international Communist movement; and to justify Soviet dominion over other Communist countries. In other words, externally, ideology has an *imperialist* function. The eleventh of the *Theses on Feuerbach* may thus be regarded as one of the theoretical roots of Communist totalism.

Of all Marx's theories, that of the class struggle seems to me to be

[1] In *The Theory and Practice of Communism* (1950; Pelican edn., 1963).

the most pernicious, for it trades upon envy and is a permanent incitement to violence and conflict. In its starkest form, it is expressed in key passages of *The Communist Manifesto*, which Marx and Engels jointly drafted in January of that year of revolutions—1848—as a programme for a political party of the working class. 'The history of all hitherto existing society,' they wrote in a dismissive phrase, 'is the history of class struggles.' It is best, I think, to quote rather than paraphrase the ensuing passage:

> 'Freeman and slave, patrician and plebeian, lord and serf, guildmaster and journeyman, in a word, oppressor and oppressed, stood in constant opposition to one another, carried on an uninterrupted fight, now hidden, now open, a fight that ended each time, either in a revolutionary reconstitution of society at large, or in the common ruin of the contending classes.
>
> In the earlier epochs of history, we find almost everywhere a complicated arrangement of society into various orders, a manifold gradation of social rank. In ancient Rome, we have patricians, knights, plebeians, slaves; in the Middle Ages, feudal lords, vassals, guild-masters, journeymen, apprentices, serfs; in almost all of these classes, again, subordinate gradations.
>
> The modern bourgeois society that has sprouted from the ruins of feudal society has not done away with class antagonisms. It has but established new classes, new conditions of oppression, new forms of struggle in place of the old ones.
>
> Our epoch, the epoch of the bourgeoisie, possesses, however, this distinctive feature: it has simplified the class antagonisms. Society as a whole is more and more splitting up into two great hostile camps, into two great classes directly facing each other—bourgeoisie and proletariat.'

If Marx had confined himself to noting the fact that throughout history some people, or groups of people (invariably in the minority) control the means of power and rule over others (invariably the great majority), he would have done no more than express in eloquent and impassioned language a truth which it was open to others to observe. The harm, if any, would have been limited. But Marx went further. Believing in *Praxis*, and therefore that theory must be completed by action, he set about to *change* the world. He did so by his economic view of history and his dialectical materialism. In the preface to his *Critique of Political Economy* (1859), he asserted that the principle governing all human relations was the pursuit of the production of the means to support life. In this situation, he argued, 'men enter into definite, necessary relations which are *independent of their will*' (my italics). At one stage of history, some people obtained control over the productive forces. This enabled the minority to exploit the labour of the majority. Marx developed these ideas in *Das Kapital*, an enormous work in three volumes (1867, 1885 and 1894), only the first of which was completed before the author's death. The other two were completed by Engels and published posthumously.

Marx intended *Capital* to be a text-book on economics, but as such it does not stand up to serious analysis in the light of later knowledge. Its force, however, lies in its justification of revolution. Marx argued that value is the product of labour alone, all profits being derived from unpaid labour time. Competition drives capitalists to accumulate capital, which becomes concentrated in monopolistic cartels and trusts. The lesser capitalists are thus driven back into the working class. Labour-saving devices and machines create unemployment by reducing the need for hired hands; but this also reduces capitalist profits and the capitalists are therefore forced to intensify their exploitation of the workers, whom unemployment forces to work on progressively more disadvantageous terms. The misery of the masses inevitably deepens, until they are forced to unite and overthrow the system.

It is worth noting that Marx, although he denounced the exploitation of the workers under capitalism, did not blame the capitalists as such (as his followers do), since he argued that they had no say in developments, being prisoners of economic forces acting independently of their will.

It was this element of predestination (shorn of divine determination) that gave Marxism its millenarian character: what happened was bound to happen, whatever men might do to prevent it, for all men were the prisoners of economic forces, the nature of which Marx claimed to have discovered for the first time.

Having established, to his own satisfaction, that capitalism was heading for a breakdown, and capitalist societies for revolution, it remained for Marx to decide what was to come *after* the inevitable revolution. The process of reasoning by which Marx reached his conclusion is known as 'dialectical materialism', and was not exactly original since it was borrowed from the thinking of an earlier German philosopher, Hegel (1770–1831). There was an original Marxian twist, however, in that Marx turned Hegel's teaching neatly upside down. This was Marx's own claim, and it was no more than the truth.

I am concerned here only with the barest elements of Hegel's philosophy that are relevant to this book, and in particular to Marxism. If Hobbes was the philosopher of absolutism, Hegel was, if only unwittingly, a precursor of the totalist State. He saw the State as 'the Divine Idea as it exists on earth', and advocated its worship. Moreover, he argued that war between States was necessary for their health. Against this, Hegel argued that the mature State would respect individual freedom. His conservative philosophy has perhaps been excessively maligned. At all events, he was held to have set the stamp of respectability upon the Fascist, and *a fortiori* the Nazi, regimes, providing war criminals with a philosophical justification for mass murders on the ground that they were merely obeying State orders. The Hegelian legacy is also visible, through its Marxist filter, in the Communist forms of totalism.

Plato had invented, or at least popularised, the *dialectical* method of discussion as a means of arriving at the truth. Each argument was to be opposed by another, which would then be opposed in its turn, so that errors would progressively be exposed. Hegel borrowed the dialectical concept and used it to explain the nature of the universe. He also borrowed from Plato the view that ideas are the only reality (and in this sense, is rightly classified as an exponent of 'idealist' philosophy). The highest, and only, reality was the Absolute, and all ideas were in process of change until the Absolute was reached, which was unchanging and permanent. Hegel's dialectical description of this process he called thesis, antithesis and synthesis. A proposition is affirmed: that is the thesis. Having been affirmed, it is negated; that is, a contradictory proposition is affirmed, which he called the antithesis. Then came the synthesis (which Marx called the 'negation of the negation'), incorporating what is true in both the thesis and the antithesis. The entire process is then repeated: that is, the synthesis becomes the new thesis, to which an antithesis is found, both yielding in turn to a new synthesis. And so on, *ad infinitum*, until the Absolute, which contains no imperfections and is therefore permanent, is attained.

As the Hegelian dialectic stood, it was a mystical and abstract concept. Marx sought to make it 'scientific' by substituting his materialism for Hegel's idealism. In his hands, thesis, antithesis and synthesis became stages of social development. Feudalism, for instance, was the thesis, changing gradually until the cumulative changes produced contradictions that could only be resolved by a 'negation'—that is, by a qualitative or dialectical change. At that point, feudalism was replaced by capitalism, its antithesis. But capitalism in its turn was destined to develop increasing contradictions, until in the end it yielded to the synthesis of socialism. Once socialism has been reached, contradictions are eliminated, for this is the Marxian version of Hegel's Absolute.

Although Marx claimed to have brought scientific method to the study of history and economics, he never adduced proofs of his assertions that would be accepted as such by any but his uncritical followers. The dialectical method 'works' only if arbitrary choices of categories are made. Feudalism did not break down because of its economic contradictions but because in most feudal societies, the king—the strongest of the feudal warlords—eliminated or subjugated the barons or other feudal rivals of his power. 'Capitalism' did not spring whole into the world as the 'antithesis' or 'negation' of feudalism, but as the result of a complex process that included the violent disproof of the divine right of kings, the decadence of Rome and the emergence of the Puritan ethic, new inventions, the spirit of inquiry of the Renaissance, and so forth. Nor is socialism the necessary synthesis, still less the materialistic Absolute freed of contradictions. In real life, as distinct from the fantasy-world of Marxism, the workers have not been driven progressively deeper into misery, but have become increasingly affluent consumers. Indeed in the United States, where trade unionism has been almost entirely free of the Marxist element, and even of non-Marxist socialism, the organised workers, concentrating upon the admittedly materialistic aim of getting the best possible deal for themselves by making capitalism work, have achieved unparalleled working class living standards.

True, the 'capitalist' world underwent a period of mass unemployment and crisis, in the depression of the 1930s, but partial answers, at least, were found to the 'contradictions' of capitalism, which showed an extraordinary capacity for self-correction that would have astonished Karl Marx. Nor has capitalism conformed to the Marxian prophecy by making a violent 'dialectical' change to socialism. The *successful* 'spontaneous' Communist revolutions on record—in Russia, China and North Vietnam, especially—occurred in countries in which only a small sector (though in Russia in 1917 a fast-growing one) could be termed capitalist. In his innocence, Marx had supposed that the revolution would occur first in the most highly industrialised countries, such as England or Germany. Fantastic though it seems to non-Marxists, the Bolshevik decision to embark on a break-neck

programme of forced industrialisation was made, at least in part, to
meet the requirements of the Marxian dialectic *after the event*.[2] In
China and North Vietnam, the Communists seized power, as the
outcome not of a Marxist–Leninist revolution, but of a peasant
insurrection in which the driving force was the old-fashioned virtue of
patriotism in the face of a foreign enemy; much the same was true of
Yugoslavia.

Elsewhere (e.g. in eastern Europe or in North Korea) Communism
was imposed by the Soviet army, or (in Cuba) was the fortuitous outcome of circumstances unforeseen by Marx. What Marx utterly failed
to allow for was the possibility that 'capitalist' States could adapt to
changed circumstances and (more or less successfully) tackle their
problems, such as unemployment or inflation, curbing the power of
monopolies, introducing social welfare programmes and combining
within their structures both private and public ownership of the means
of production.

But the literal fulfilment of prophecies appears to be of little interest
to the millenarian mind. The Marxist who calls himself such is obliged
to swallow the contradictions of Marx's philosophy, the most pernicious of which is that between the inevitability of socialism and the
identity of theory and *Praxis*. For if socialism is inevitable, because
determined by scientific laws independent of men's will, then there is
no need for the expectant to do anything but await its coming. But
Marx was a revolutionary as well as a thinker. He is not content to
wait for his 'laws' to prove themselves, but calls upon his followers to
'change the world'. Marx's followers are therefore in duty bound to do
everything to make the prophecies come true, to hasten the breakdown
of capitalism and the advent of the revolution. Non-Marxists who have
not studied Marxism often fall into the error of supposing that
Marxists are basically reformers with the courage of their convictions,
mere militants determined to remove the ills of the society in which
they live, if necessary by force. But to think on these lines is funda-
mentally to misunderstand Marxism: the Marxist is basically *opposed*
to reform, except for tactical reasons, because reforms, if successful,
retard the processes of history and the advent of socialism. This does
not prevent Communists, however, from advocating reforms if in
opposition, or from initiating them if they share power in a coalition,
since it may be of advantage to a Communist party to cultivate a false
image of reformism or to appear to be working loyally with, say,

[2] See Robert Conquest's Introduction to Milovan Djilas, *The New Class* (London, 1957; Allen & Unwin edn., 1966, pp. 7–8).

Socialist ministerial partners. But the end in view is invariable: the abolition of all non-Marxist societies and their replacement by 'socialism'.

For all its scientific pretensions, Marxism is as Utopian as the rival varieties of socialist philosophy Marx roundly condemned (St. Simon, Fourier, Owen, etc.), but his advocacy of revolutionary action makes it impossible to regard him with the amused or detached tolerance that can be accorded to other Utopians. As dreamers, they are mostly harmless. The Marxists, in contrast, being in duty bound to 'change the world', will stop at nothing to hasten the historical process. And since the Utopia they pursue is unattainable, they impose no time-limit on the infliction of suffering to reach their professed end.

It is at least possible that Marx himself would not have approved of the excesses and abuses of his followers, but who is to say? Convinced that the fulfilment of his prophecies was historically imminent, he certainly did not shrink from revolutionary violence in his own lifetime. But Marx's theory, despite the complexity of his outpourings, was essentially simple, and he did not see, or apprehended too late, the implications of his own contradictions. Of these, none was greater than his theory of the State. Seeing all States, without exception, as instruments for the protection of economic class interests, he found them all uniformly oppressive of the unpropertied. As Maurice Cranston points out, Marx passionately believed in freedom, by which he meant the condition that is denied by despotism.[3] Since the oppressiveness of the State (even of the relatively liberal, 'bourgeois' State of England, where he sought refuge from the despotism of his native Germany) was due to class antagonisms, did it not follow that when classes were abolished under socialism, the State would cease to be necessary? At this point, however, Marx is caught in his own contradiction, for he specifically advocates the need for the State to bring about socialism once the revolution has taken place. But if all States are oppressive, will the socialist State not be as oppressive as the rest? Marx never fully faced up to this dilemma, still less did he resolve it.

The programme of nationalisation outlined in the Communist Manifesto—involving State-ownership of the land, banks, industries and transport, the direction of labour, and the centralised control of education—clearly could not be implemented without a massive *expansion* of the organs of the State. Many years later, in the *Critique of the Gotha Programme* (1875), Karl Marx suggested that in time the

[3] See 'Marxism and Freedom', in Brian Crozier, ed., '*We Will Bury You*' (London, 1970).

period of State-communism that would follow the proletarian seizure of power from the bourgeoisie would yield to the Stateless communism of economic abundance—'from each according to his ability: to each according to his needs'.

At the time of his death, Marx had been planning to write a book dealing with the development of the State from the family and private property, using as his point of departure a book that had greatly impressed him when it was published in 1877: Lewis H. Morgan's *Ancient Society*. To this end, he made extensive notes, which Friedrich Engels (1820–95) later expanded into his book *The Origin of the Family: Private Property and the State* (1884). In this, the most complete expression of Marx's ideas on the State, Engels dismisses the problem of the State under communism in a much-quoted but paralysingly opaque passage:

> 'Government over persons is replaced by the administration of things and the direction of the processes of production. The State is not "abolished", *it withers away*.' (Itals. in original)

It is surely fair to point out that at this point, the Marxian dialectic simply broke down. For socialism (communism) is supposed to be the final synthesis that rounds off the dialectical progression from feudalism (thesis) and through capitalism (antithesis). The socialist 'synthesis' was supposed to bring the millennium, but for a phase (of indefinite duration), the State would be needed, both to build the economic base for abundance and to liquidate the bourgeois class, thus abolishing class antagonisms (the foundation of the State in Marxian theory). Yet the difference between the phase of State-communism, when the State would have greatly enhanced functions, and the classless communism of abundance, when the State would wither away, would clearly be enormous, implying no less a dialectical change than that from feudalism to capitalism, or from capitalism to socialism. Is the dialectic, then, to start all over again? Marx does not say; neither does Engels. Thus in the end, the Marxian Utopia is no less vague than the Heaven or Paradise of the early Christians, whose legacy Marx had condemned as the opium of the people.

Marx thought socialism/communism would come, inevitably, as the result of a revolution. At all events, this is what he preached, or claimed to have discovered. He saw the revolution as essentially the outcome of an alliance between the industrial workers and left-wing bourgeois elements, who would be discarded once their usefulness had ceased.

He saw no political role for the submerged working class (*Lumpenproletariat*) or for the lower middle class; or for that matter, for the peasants (it never occurred to him, of course, that the revolution would come in Russia). In later years, he occasionally wavered on the necessity or inevitability of revolution (though not on the overthrow of capitalism). He seems to have been puzzled by the apparent reluctance of English governments to behave in accordance with his theories. Instead of the masses sinking deeper into misery, their lot was actually being improved by successive reforms. Since 1848, Engels complained in a letter to a friend in June 1885, the English Parliament had been 'the most revolutionary body in the world'. He would have been deeply disillusioned at the spectacle of proletarian affluence in the mid-twentieth century.

Despite its monumental fallacies (to which we shall return) Marxism has proved extraordinarily durable, and the answer, I think, lies in its unique combination of millenarian promises with a claim to scientific method. Despite the decline in faith in Western countries (especially in Protestant ones), and in the attractive power of the Churches, there is no evidence at all that the inherent need for religion of Man as a species has in anyway weakened. Science, however, has largely destroyed the comforting certainties of the Bible stories and of miracles. Mysticism is out of fashion. In this situation, Marxism offers a refuge, for it provides not only a dogma and a prophet, but a reassurance that it is all scientific and modern. Moreover, since the October Revolution of 1917, it has also provided a church in the universal Communist Party; and since the events of 1948, 1956 and 1960, a set of heresies and rival centres of dogma, much as happened to the universal Church of Rome with the Reformation.

Lenin (1870–1924) was a living refutation of Marx's materialistic interpretation of history; as was Stalin. Seeing all history as resulting from the interplay of economic forces, Marx allowed no special importance to great men, on the ground that if, say, Napoleon had never been born, the historical 'necessity' of somebody like him would have thrown up somebody else. This contention is hard to disprove, although (as Carew Hunt pointed out), history could have done with a great man when Greco-Roman civilisation was collapsing, but none came forward. It is true that Marx had not yet told history what was expected of it.

At all events, Lenin's *personal* contribution to the history of his time was decisively important. Nor is it easy to argue that he was enabled to play his overwhelming role by the pull of economic forces; for it was only by the kind of fortuity that has no place in historical materialism that he happened to be the right man at the right place at the right time ('right', that is, in Marxist–Leninist eyes, for his real contribution to history was massively retrograde). As everyone knows, the Germans sent Lenin back to Russia from exile in April 1917, in a sealed train, in the hope that he would use his influence to stop the Russians fighting. But they almost decided *not* to send him back, and if they had not it is arguable that there would not have been a Bolshevik revolution and that the entire history of the world would thereafter have been different.

For Lenin played virtually no part in the overthrow of the regime of the Tsars in March 1917. The first post-Tsarist government, under Prince George Lvov, was not a Marxist one but a liberal democratic one. The Germans, however, had not miscalculated. After an abortive first attempt at a coup in July, Lenin seized power on 6 November (24 October in the Old Calendar: hence the 'October' Revolution) and promptly made peace on disadvantageous terms with the Central Powers, the better to consolidate his Marxist revolution.

Lenin was not, as Marx had been, a great innovative thinker. He was primarily a professional technician of revolution. However, he wrote voluminously, both as a pamphleteer and polemicist, and as a theorist of revolution and an interpreter of the Marxian texts. In consequence, Marxism–Leninism is by no means identical with Marxism *tout court*.

It is not my purpose to deal exhaustively with Lenin's political thinking. I wish only to draw attention to his ideas on the State and revolution, and on imperialism, all of which continue to influence revolutionaries.

As a good Marxist, Lenin identified theory and action, and at the height of his agitation to overthrow the Kerensky government—in August–September 1917—he wrote perhaps the best-known of his pamphlets, *The State and Revolution*. The first half of it is devoted to explaining the Marxian doctrine of the State as laid down by Marx and Engels. As we have seen, both men were vague about the role of the State after the revolution, and the meaning of its 'withering away' was left unclear. What Engels really meant, said Lenin (and Engels was not there to protest), was that the revolution would destroy the *bourgeois* State, not the State as such. As for the withering away, that would not take place until a much later stage. In the meantime, the proletariat would establish and maintain its dictatorship. The exploitation of man by man would cease and the coercive functions of the old order would now be exercised by the majority, not the minority. Differences of wealth would continue until abundance (still at a much later stage) made it possible to pay each 'according to his needs'. However, there would be no need for a bureaucracy, as any literate person was capable of 'accounting and control'.

When the German Social Democratic leader, Kautsky, attacked *The State and Revolution* at the end of 1918, Lenin replied with a vitriolic denunciation, *Proletarian Revolution and the Renegade Kautsky*, in which he asserted the new doctrine of 'proletarian democracy'. The 'labouring and exploited masses' would organise and administer the State in their own way, and this would be 'a million times more democratic than the most democratic bourgeois republic'. As Carew Hunt pointed out, the 'one-party system' follows from 'proletarian democracy' as a corollary: 'It is no more necessary that there should be two political parties than that a man should have two heads.'[4]

As regards revolution, Lenin was the arch-exponent of the small, tightly disciplined revolutionary party, which he saw as a vanguard. In *What is to be done?* (1902), he stipulated that there could be no revolutionary movement without a revolutionary theory (this was good Marxist *Praxis*). Armed with its advanced theory, the party would indoctrinate the masses. He rejected the notion, at that time prevalent, that the workers would spontaneously become revolutionary: it was the party's duty to lead the masses and make them revolutionary. Two years later, in *One Step Forward, Two Steps Back*, he advocated the principle of the ideological purge: the party should have a central directing organ and a central committee, from which unreliable elements were to be expelled.

These monolithic and totalist principles were further consolidated, after the revolution, in the *Theses of the Communist International* (1920), and the *Twenty-One Conditions of Admission to the Comintern* concluded with the principle of 'democratic centralism' as the basis of party organisation: that is, the lower party organs should be subordinate to the higher. At the Tenth Congress of the Communist Party (Bolsheviks), it was laid down that individuals and even groups should have the right of criticism until a decision was taken, but thereafter any attempt to create an opposition would be banned as 'fractionalism'. Armed with this principle, Stalin later crushed all opposition.

Lenin was convinced that the Russian revolution would not survive unless complemented by revolutions in other places, especially in

[4] *Op. cit.*, p. 182.

Western Europe. It was with the aim of fomenting world revolution that he set up the Communist Third International, or Comintern, in March 1919. Some fourteen months later, he published perhaps the most important of his pamphlets, *Left Wing Communism: an Infantile Disorder*. The irony in the title was directed at the newly formed Communist parties, which had been interpreting Lenin's teaching as implying total hostility towards all non-Communists. There were grounds for this interpretation as Lenin did indeed regard mere Socialists as the real enemies of the revolution in that they stood in the way of its ever happening by offering a gradualist alternative; whereas the bourgeois or right-wing parties could be eliminated at leisure once the revolution had happened. But the revolution was not happening of its own accord, as Lenin had hoped; and where it did, as with Rosa Luxemburg's Spartacist revolt of January 1919, it was rapidly crushed. It was essential, therefore, for Communists to work within governments, trade unions, parliaments, beating bourgeois politicians at their own game. Hence, *Left Wing Communism*.

The new guiding lines were these: Communists were to penetrate democratic organisations and exploit the freedoms of the 'capitalist' countries; and there would have to be a lengthy period of preparation to bring about the general breakdown of authority which Lenin described as a revolutionary situation. Here is a typical passage:

> '. . . Every sacrifice must be made, the greatest obstacles must be overcome, in order to carry on agitation and propaganda systematically, stubbornly, insistently, and patiently, precisely in all those institutions, societies, and associations to which proletarian or semi-proletarian masses belong, however ultra-reactionary they may be. And the trade unions and workers' co-operatives (the latter, at least sometimes), are precisely the organisations in which the masses are to be found.'

The importance of *Left Wing Communism* is hard to exaggerate, for the advanced countries of the West have obstinately declined to fulfil Marxist-Leninist predictions, yet the Leninist orders to infiltrate and agitate are still in force today, more than half a century after they were issued. It is tempting to laugh this situation off, but it would be foolish to do so. The Communists themselves take their 'agitprop' mission very seriously, indeed entirely without humour. Their strength lies in their continued will to work towards the revolutionary situation, seizing whatever crumbs of opportunity come their way, disregarding all setbacks. And in some Western countries, especially France and Italy, their numbers make them a formidable force which the 'bourgeois' parties cannot ignore.

Was the rapid decline of the Soviet system into a self-perpetuating tyranny inevitable? Was it inherent in the creed of Marxism, or peculiar to Leninism, or due to extraneous factors? These are important questions, for among Marxists who recognise at least that portion of the truth which was revealed by Khrushchev's famous 'secret' speech in February 1956 (when he denounced a selection of Stalin's crimes), a variety of excuses and explanations are on offer. The orthodox (Moscow-line) Communists blame it all on Stalin, and regard the phase of terror as a temporary aberration, even though they were absolutely uncritical of Stalin at the time. The Peking-line Communists, however, still revere the memory of Stalin, along with that of Marx–Engels and Lenin, even though Mao Tse-tung in his own quest for power, defied Stalin's advice; for them, the decline of the Soviet Union dates from the 'revisionism' of Khrushchev.

Neither of these attitudes adds noticeably to the world's dangers. Far more dangerous is the attitude of certain fundamentalists of the New Left, who argue that there was nothing wrong with Marxism, or even Marxism–Leninism, but the revolution 'went wrong' under Stalin and his successors because it degenerated into a bureaucratic tyranny. Thus, if it is common ground that the Soviet State is not what Marx or Lenin had in mind, two alternative deductions are possible. One is to shed one's ideological illusions and concentrate on making 'capitalism' work. This is the view of those who have recovered from the fanatic infection. But the incurable fanatics and revolutionary romantics, even when they dismiss the Soviet experiment as a failure, simply want to try again in countries more suitable than was Russia in 1917. After all, Marx never expected the revolution to begin in that backward country of peasants, and Lenin, in consequence, had serious misgivings about it, although these did not deter him from seizing power when authority was collapsing.

For the Trotskyists, Stalin alone was to blame. If Lenin's mantle had fallen on Trotsky, the revolution would have fulfilled its promise. For some extremist groups (notably the International Socialists in Britain, who hanker back to the 'pure' communism of Rosa Luxemburg and the German Spartacists), only Marx and Engels are inviolable; even Lenin is held partly to blame for the failure of the Soviet experiment through excessive 'bureaucratism' and centralism. They too want to start all over again.

All these arguments, it seems to me, are equally specious. The totalist State is inherent in the all-embracing claims of Marx himself. Until the Reformation, and in Spain until well on in the nineteenth century, the Church of Rome was an exclusive tyranny, whose claim to spiritual absolutism rested upon its position as God's own Church and upon God's guidance. Marx denied divine guidance, but proposed a substitute: dialectical materialism and scientific socialism. Science replaces God as the basis of infallibility. He claimed to have discovered a scientific guide to history and iron laws pointing to revolution and beyond that, at a time unspecified, to the earthly paradise of communism. Most of his claims and prophecies were demonstrably false, and to sustain the faith of the believers, and prevent non-believers from taking over, implied the existence of a coercive apparatus of State and party. But for all his wavering in his later years, he refused to face the implications of his own teaching.

Nor was Lenin markedly different from Stalin in his attitudes towards the State, the role of the party, the subservience of the organs of government to the party, and the need for a secret police. Stalin merely carried his usage of the Soviet institutions which Lenin had created to the extreme logic of the permanent terror. But it was Lenin himself who, within a few weeks of the October Revolution, set up the Cheka (ancestor of the KGB), and was soon using it with utter ruthlessness to eliminate all who stood in his way. Nor can much weight be given to the argument that things would have been different if Trotsky, not Stalin, had come out on top in the power struggle that followed Lenin's death; for there is no evidence that Trotsky was anything other than a ruthless fanatic.

The evidence, therefore, is overwhelming: any system based upon Marxism, and *a fortiori* on Marxism–Leninism, inevitably becomes a totalist autocracy. If further proof were needed, it may be found in a study of all existing communist regimes (with the possible exception of Yugoslavia, which has moved away from Marxism, although there was no guarantee that Marshal Tito's successors would not return to it). It is sometimes asserted, as though it were surprising, that such regimes differ markedly from one another. How else could it be, given the diversity of histories of the countries involved, and their enormous geographical spread? But the remarkable thing is not that they differ, but that they are so closely similar in the fundamentals of the State. Whether in North Vietnam or in Cuba, in North Korea or in Czechoslovakia, in China or the Soviet Union, there is an all-powerful ruling party; democratic centralism (the subordination of lower organs to higher) is practised; and the system has characteristically yielded a dictator (Mao, Ho Chi Minh, Fidel Castro, etc.). In all, the secret police has arbitrary powers. Moreover, there is, as yet, no record of a communist government yielding to a non-communist one. There is no philosophical reason for supposing that these autocracies are going to be perpetual; but it is clear that they are self-perpetuating.

THREE

THEORISTS AND OBSERVERS

The ground covered in this chapter

THE DIVERGENCE between theory and fact is not confined to Marx–Lenin and the Soviet State. Only the misguided, and the professional politicians, would claim to find harmony between the theory and the practice of representative government, even in countries such as Britain and the United States where the contrast is less glaring than elsewhere. It could indeed be argued that the divergence is no bad thing in that it protects ordinary people from the excesses implicit in fanatical or well-meaning attempts to make reality fit the dream.

Hitler and Stalin are among the fanatics who tried to make the world they controlled fit preconceived theories, and in so doing caused immeasurable suffering. Similarly, but on a mercifully smaller scale, attempts to make the practice of democracy conform to theoretical expectations are likely, to the extent that they are successful, to make systems unworkable. Proportional representation, for instance, is theoretically closer to the ideal of representative assembly than Britain's highly undemocratic tradition of 'first past the post', whereby approximately half the population is unrepresented for having given its votes to losing candidates. But in places, such as Holland, where proportional representation is practised, the outcome is a multiplicity of parties that virtually guarantees prolonged ministerial crises and unsatisfactory coalitions.

It is wise, then, to distinguish between political theorists and observers, the former advocating courses of action, the latter recording, as far as they are able, things as they really are. Since the deaths of Marx, Engels and Lenin, there have been many theorists and considerably fewer observers. Among the former, however, there has not been a single writer whose influence compares with those of men like Locke, Mill, Marx or Lenin. It may be logical, therefore (since this is not a treatise), to consider the theorists and observers in groups.

The other totalists

We have already considered some of the precursors of the totalist State: Hegel, Marx, Engels and Lenin. Among those who should be added to this list are Mazzini and Mussolini, Gobineau, H. S. Chamberlain, and Hitler. It would be wrong, I think, to include Nietsche, for all his love of war and worship of power, because his romantic exaltation of the Hero was incompatible with a comparable worship of the State, which he did not profess.

The writers and political adventurers I have just named are prophets or creators of totalist regimes conventionally labelled 'right-wing', especially those of Fascist Italy and Nazi Germany. Count Joseph-Arthur de Gobineau (1816–82) was a Frenchman, whose four-volume *Essay on the Inequality of Human Races* inspired the later Nazi doctrines of racial purity. That it did so, however, was almost accidental. He was a friend of Richard Wagner's, who became a leading member of a Gobineau Club in Germany and used it to spread anti-Semitic ideas.

Houston Stewart Chamberlain (1855–1926) went further still in his involvement with Wagner, by marrying the composer's daughter. Born British, he was naturalised German, and his book, *The Foundations of the Nineteenth Century* (1899) became a kind of semi-official bible of pan-German expansionism. In *Mein Kampf* (two volumes, 1925–8), Hitler praised Chamberlain, but far surpassed him in the brutal vehemence with which he stated his views. His vision of a 'folkish State', devoted to the procreation of an Aryan master-race to the expulsion or liquidation of Jews, and the enslavement of the Slavs, were nebulous. His turgid prose was incapable of precise formulations, and he did not spell out his plans for the structure and administration of the National Socialist State. The totalist end-result, however, was implicit in the utter fanaticism of his racist and expansionist views.

Initially, at any rate, Mussolini was less nihilistic than his German imitator who later became the senior partner in the Rome–Berlin Axis. His ideas of revolutionary nationalism were partly derived from Giuseppe Mazzini (1805–72), who preached the unification and greatness of Italy. But too much should not be made of this debt. Mazzini envisaged an international community of nation-States, none employing force, all sovereign and equal. Mussolini, with his exaltation of war and conquest, had a different view of nationalism. Beginning his political career as a Socialist, he specifically abandoned socialism in his essay, *The Political and Social Doctrines of Fascism* (based on a draft by Giovanni Gentile, and published in 1933), on the ground that it was divisive. He exalted the nation-State and sought to bind the whole nation together. Since individuals have opinions and private groups have separate interests, neither individualism nor private groups could be allowed. The outcome could only be the 'totalitarian State'—a term used by Mussolini in a speech in 1930. But Gentile was probably the first to use the word 'totalitarian', in a speech on 8 March 1925; not longer after (22 June) Mussolini himself used it in a public attack on the cowed remnants of the opposition in the Italian Chamber.[1]

So discredited has Fascism become that it is only fair to add that the idea of the Corporative State, which Mussolini launched (and which Franco, Salazar and others adopted with varying degrees of success) was not, in itself, an altogether bad one. The idea that different professions, trades and industries should be represented in an advisory assembly need not be automatically condemned just because Fascism was a Bad Thing. Nor is the concept of trade unions representing employers, workers and the State an unintelligent one, although it attracts the anathema of trade unionists in Western countries who value above all else the unfettered right to strike.

The democrats

The democratic State is by its nature pluralistic. That is at once its strength and its weakness. Its strength, because the right to express dissident views, or to oppose within an assembly, absorbs and mitigates frustrations; its weakness too, because a pluralistic society cannot remain pluralistic if it tries also to be a police State, and is therefore

[1] See Leonard Schapiro, *Totalitarianism* (London, 1972), p. 13.

vulnerable to the extremist groups which it tolerates and which desire its destruction.

Representative democracy, as it exists today, is essentially the product of events in the United States and France in the eighteenth century, and of the thinking that preceded and followed these events in both countries and in England, where revolutionary change had occurred a century earlier. The interaction of thought and deed was in fact crucial. There are really three strands in democracy of the Western types: the radical, the conservative and the egalitarian. All are liberal (with a small l and in the British acceptance of the term) in that all, to a greater or lesser degree, tolerate the expression of ideas that differ from, or contradict, their own. It follows (although not all are willing to accept this self-evident fact) that all three strands (and their inevitable sub-strands) have more in common with each other than any has with the totalism of the so-called Right or the so-called Left; a proposition to which I shall return. It is important to add that no democracy is conceivable except within a framework of law and order, the absence of law implying either anarchy or the perversion of the legal process, and of order the breakdown of a society; while the absence of both law and order connotes gang rule.

Leaving aside the ambiguous figure of Rousseau, we have dealt with two of the major precursors of modern democracy in Locke and Mill. The former, especially, was the great advocate of the rule of law. His message was transmitted, and transmuted, by the Baron de Montesquieu (1689–1755); adopted and adapted by two great Americans, Benjamin Franklin (1709–90) and Thomas Jefferson (1743–1826); broadened and placed in a central tradition by Edmund Burke (1729–97).

That attractive, wise and witty man, Montesquieu, enormously erudite by the standards of his day, but physically too lazy to see for himself whether the things he read in books were true or not, anticipated so many things that it is hard to make a concise selection. The Welfare State and full employment; a critique of the arms race; the fear of universal destruction by war; enlightenment in judicial punishment; the abolition of slavery—the list is almost endless. But two aspects of Montesquieu's thought are particularly relevant to this book: his advocacy of checks and balances, and his belief, which permeates his great *L'Esprit des Lois* (1748), that the spirit behind the drafting and application of constitutions and individuals is more important by far than the texts themselves. Today, this belief commands fairly wide acceptance, at least in democratic countries; but in his day, it had a revolutionary impact. It has often taken a genius to think of the cliché of a later age. As for checks and balances, Montesqueiu essentially borrowed the idea from Locke and assumed, quite wrongly, that it was already in force in England at the time. In his admiration for the English, or rather of what he thought the English had already achieved, he advocated a constitutional and responsible monarchy, with a division of legislative, executive and judicial powers. Looked at now, from our later perspective. Montesquieu appears as an enlightened conservative; if his ideas seemed revolutionary in his day, that was because the society in which he lived was heading for the self-destruction of blind despotisms.

Imported into America, Montesquieu's ideas (reflecting, I repeat, Locke's) had a great influence upon the leaders of American independence; although, since their object was to rebel against the English King, they applied the principles of checks and balances not in a monarchy but in a Republic. Historically, the American revolution predated the French by a few years and brought modern democracy into being about a century earlier than either France or England (counting the advent of French democracy from the proclamation of the Third Republic in 1870, and of British from the introduction of the secret ballot in 1872; but admittedly, this dating, especially the second, is arbitrary: England's democracy, in particular, evolved so gradually, and in fits and starts, that any number of dates could be named to fit its 'beginning'). At all events, the Americans were first. They enjoyed the unique advantage of being able to make a fresh start in a new country, and the signal luck of being able to draw upon the wisdom of a number of exceptional men. Outstanding among these were Jefferson and Franklin. Men of thought as well as of action, they were associated with two of the most remarkable documents of modern times: the Declaration of Independence (1776), which Jefferson wrote, and the American Constitution (1787), in the drafting of which Franklin played a leading part as one of the Founding Fathers who met that year at Philadelphia to represent the original thirteen States.

From the first, both the Declaration and the Constitution illustrated, in both a good sense and a bad, the relative unimportance of documents, as compared with the spirit behind them and the intentions of the men behind institutions. 'All men,' announced Jefferson with touching optimism, 'are created equal', and 'are endowed by their Creator with certain unalienable rights, . . . among these . . . Life, Liberty and the pursuit of Happiness.' It was noticed later that the supposed equality of all men did not, at the time, extend to the Negro slaves in the southern plantations. But it took nearly another century, and a bloody civil war, to extend at least a theoretical equality to those initially less equal than the rest.

Still, the intentions of the Founding Fathers were of the highest. Both Franklin and Jefferson had observed the political ferment in France on the spot, Jefferson succeeding the older man as Minister in Paris. Typically, Jefferson proposed to the leaders of the Third Estate, on 3 June 1789, a compromise between the king and the nation. It would be wrong, however, to suppose that the ideas of the French revolutionaries deeply influenced Jefferson, except in a heightened awareness of excesses to avoid; after all, he had gone to Paris as the seasoned revolutionary whose faith in the equality of men was enshrined in the Declaration of Independence.

That faith, in turn, permeated the Constitution itself, which conferred upon the President something of the majesty of an elected monarch and far more power than any constitutional one; yet separated the legislative power (exercised through Congress) almost completely from the executive; creating not only an independent judiciary, but one which (through the Supreme Court) has the final say on the legality of the government's actions and the laws passed by Congress. Edmund Burke provides a natural link between the ideas of the American and French revolutions. Paradoxically—at least at first sight—he supported the first and violently condemned the second. Yet the paradox was possibly more apparent than real. (It has been claimed on Burke's behalf that it is impossible to find any contradiction between the speeches he made in defence of the independence of England's American colonies, and his later writings attacking the excesses of the French Revolution.) Essentially a pragmatist, he did not assert the right of the colonists to independence so much as deny that any good could come of crushing their rebellion. 'The question with me,' he declared, 'is not whether you have a right to render your people miserable, but whether it is not your interest to make them happy.'

It was on similarly humanitarian and pragmatic grounds that he condemned the French extremists in his explosively successful pamphlet, *Reflections on the Revolution in France, and on the proceedings in certain societies in London relative to that event* (1790). Writing during the events he was describing and at a time of headlong, uncontrollable change, Burke at first underestimated the importance of the Revolution in European history, and took no account of the grave social ills and the blindness of those in power, which together made the event inevitable. But although the Revolution was the occasion of his

Reflections, its significance far transcends the occasion. From it emerged a system of evolutionary change that has profoundly influenced British political thinking; and not only among Conservatives.

A Whig turned Tory, Burke was a Godly man and saw the social contract as essentially divinely ordained. What he feared and resented among the revolutionaries was the presumption of their Utopianism and the brutality with which, in the name of abstract principles, they claimed the right to sweep everything away—the good with the bad, the accumulated beauties and wisdoms of the past along with the abuses and the privileges of the great and noble. In the lawlessness and incipient terror of the Revolution, he saw the denial of justice to all, and the foundations for a future arbitrary and absolute rule. (In this, he was right, for Napoleon was soon to come.) Emphatically, Burke was no reactionary, no partisan of the static polity or stagnant society. For the virtue of tradition, of the multiplicity of customs and sentiments that constitute a community's heritage, could only live if it changed as the years passed. In life, and especially the life of politics, there was no instant, no final, solution; no document could abolish the past, with its evil and its good. Progress had to be by reform, not violence; by experiment, not doctrine. Despite the Fabians' attachment to doctrine, there was much of Burke in Webbs' concept of the 'inevitability of gradualness'.

There is room in democracy, however, for the radical strand, so long as those who espouse it renounce violence. Nor is all value to be denied to documents and declarations (although in writing this, I am conscious of sitting outside myself in arguing against a deeply ingrained scepticism). The value of such texts, except when they constitute Law, lies in the statement of ideals to which a majority of the community may subscribe, even if the performance of the community falls short, as it inevitably will, of those same ideals. The danger begins when the radicals attempt to enforce the unenforceable, trying in the process to coerce the recalcitrant, negligent or apathetic. That way lies despotism. The advantage of the plural society is that, at least to a degree, it is self-correcting. When the radicals go too far (and if they have not already damaged the democratic process beyond repair), the conservatives, the empiricists, those in possession of common sense, will reassert themselves and stop the damage. With time, experience and the habits of alternation, each side may learn to live with the other and not to exceed the boundaries beyond which the other side can no longer live with changes contemplated or enacted.

There is room then, for Tom Paine (1737–1809) as well as for Edmund

Burke in the democratic polity; on condition that enough people resist the temptation to try to apply his principles literally, completely and instantly. Burke opposed the French Revolution; Paine, it is well known, was its apologist. Having failed as a staymaker, as a low-grade Excise Officer and as a tobacconist, he went to New England in 1774 and became a political journalist. With only a few years of grammar school education behind him, he developed a vigorous and forthright literary style that was to make him, in the face of much persecution, one of the most successful authors of his age. In his first book, *Common Sense* (1776), he defended the right of the American colonies to independence. Back in England in 1787, he went on to Paris to live through the days—glorious in his eyes—of the French Revolution. From General the Marquis de La Fayette, two years later, he received the keys of the Bastille after it had been stormed by the revolutionary mob, so that he should present them to George Washington.

Burke's *Reflections on the Revolution* drove Paine to a fury of polemical creativity. His answer to it was *The Rights of Man*, published in two parts in 1790 and 1792. Castigating Burke's 'pathless wilderness of rhapsodies', he asked what the author of the *Reflections* meant when he denounced the French Constituent Assembly's *Declaration of the Rights of Man and the Citizen*. Did he mean to deny that *man* had any rights? If he did, then he must mean that there were no such things as rights anywhere, for who was there in the world but man? If this was not what Burke meant, then one had to inquire what those rights were and how man came by them originally.

In the course of his first pamphlet, Paine translated the French *Declaration of Rights* and defended each article in turn. It is a measure of Paine's persuasiveness, as well as of the powerful appeal of the original French document, that merely to summarise the stipulated rights is to list things which today we (in certain countries) take for granted (at least in principle):

—The political equality of all citizens.
—Respect of private property.
—Sovereignty of the nation.
—Eligibility of all citizens for public service.
—The obligation imposed upon all men to obey the law, expression of the general will.
—Respect for opinions and beliefs.
—Freedom of expression and of the press.
—Equitable distribution of the taxes freely agreed by the representatives of the country.

If Paine had confined himself to translating the French *Declaration*, interpreting its provisions and advocating their validity, he might well have escaped official censure. But he used it to berate the monarchy as a 'silly, contemptible thing', to denounce the Bill of Rights as a bill of wrongs and insults, and to make fun of England's unwritten—and therefore, in his eyes, non-existent—Constitution. For these and other irreverences, he was convicted of seditious libel and fled to France, where he joined the Convention.

There, however, he was soon to learn that revolutions tend to devour their children. Robespierre turned against him and flung him into a cell in the Luxembourg Palace. He died in New York, however.

In Part Two of *The Rights of Man*, Tom Paine vigorously expounded the principles of what would now be called the Welfare State, advocating a kind of reverse income tax with which to double relief for the poor, educate their children and look after the aged. For these passages, as well as for the work as a whole, his pamphlet became a working man's bible. Tom Paine therefore constitutes a natural link between the radical and egalitarian strands in modern democracy.

The egalitarians

At a time when only property-owners (and not many of them) had the vote in England, and there was no secret ballot, Tom Paine was bold enough to advocate universal suffrage and invite the common man to assert his right to play a part in the political process. The logic of this stand, by his own premises, was unimpeachable; its wisdom, now that the principle is so widely accepted, remains questionable. If all men are regarded as born with equal rights, then one cannot, in logic, disfranchise those who lack money, property or education. (It is worth remembering that despite the English Reform Acts of 1832, 1867 and 1884, it was not until 1928 that women came to be regarded, for the purpose of voting, as the equals of men.)

Although Paine did not invent the principle of equality, he was one of its most impassioned disseminators. It does not seem to have occurred to him, however, that property might have something to do with existing inequalities; or he would not have subscribed as uncritically as he did to the French revolutionaries' defence of property as one of man's natural rights. He was a radical, but not a socialist.

The credit, if credit is due, for first using the word 'socialism' is usually ascribed to Robert Owen (1771–1858), whose *Co-operative Magazine* first carried it in 1827. A capitalist turned social reformer,

Owen founded the consumers' co-operative movement, promoted the Factory Acts, paved the way for the modern trade unions, founded the model village of New Lanark (successful); then lost his money, prestige and the public goodwill with his disastrous communal colony at New Harmony in Indiana. His reputation is therefore mixed, for he is remembered both as an advanced social pioneer and as an unpractical Utopian.

Owen's French counterpart, and almost exact contemporary, was Charles Fourier (1772–1837), who saw the solution to the new problems of the first industrial age in a free and voluntary association of capital and labour. His ideal communities—called 'phalanxes'—each consisted of exactly 1,620 people, the male and female of the 810 types of temperament Fourier believed constituted the entire range of character possibilities. They all failed.

More realistic, and more important, than Fourier was another contemporary, the Comte de Saint-Simon (1760–1825). His extraordinary life was a strange mixture of romantic involvement and ambitious unpracticality. He fought in the War of American Independence, was gaoled in the Luxembourg during the French Terror, speculated in land to some personal profit and launched schemes to build a waterway connecting Madrid to the sea and to join the Atlantic and Pacific oceans by a canal. His writings were prolific but attracted little attention during his lifetime, and no fortune for their author. He died poor two years after a suicide attempt.

After his death, the followers of Saint-Simon formed a school, soon rent by factionalism, and Saint-Simonism—enshrining the master's doctrine as interpreted by his followers—had a lasting influence on socialist thought in France and elsewhere. The distinguishing features of Saint-Simonian socialism are: the advocacy of an industrialised State directed by modern science; a hierarchical élitism in which power would be wielded by industrialists and scientists; a form of Christianity in which society is given the goal of abolishing poverty; complete equality of the sexes; promotion and monetary incentives for merit. Saint-Simon anticipated modern notions of technocracy and productivity, and even the managerial revolution. Despite the Christian element, his ideas had a great influence on Lenin, doubtless because, unlike other socialists, he was not an egalitarian but an élitist and an authoritarian.

Because of the failures of Owen and Fourier, and those of other social theorists of the period (among whom Etienne Cabet and Louis Blanc), Karl Marx dismissed the lot of them as 'Utopians'. But, as

Milovan Djilas pointed out, Marx too was a Utopian and the only difference between his followers and theirs was that his gained power. Having done so, they did not attain their goals, for 'Utopianism, once it achieves power, becomes dogmatic, and it quite readily can create human suffering in the name and in the cause of its own scientism and idealism'.[2]

It would be easier to write about socialism if it were possible to produce a generally accepted definition of it. But this aspiration has proved infinitely elusive. There are almost as many definitions of socialism as there are socialists. To some it connotes the public ownership of the means of production, distribution and exchange (a paraphrase of the controversial Clause 4 of the British Labour Party's Constitution); to others, it is, more vaguely, 'about equality'; to most, it implies national and local welfare schemes. In Sweden, it is considered not incompatible with the private ownership of capital resources. In Burma, it has much to do with the sharing (and possibly—though this is not spelt out—with the creation) of scarcity. 'Arab' socialism, the late President Nasser's vehicle for his brand of pan-Arab nationalism, had (or has) more in common with Salazar's Portugal than with Khrushchev's Russia. India, which manages to preserve a democratic framework, calls itself 'socialist'; and so do the totalist societies of Eastern Europe, the communist Far East and Cuba. One could go on.

However well-known these facts are, taken individually, it is as well to recall them, given the pervasiveness of semantic pitfalls. In the context of this chapter, the point I am making is simply that the socialists and egalitarians have a place in the democratic social contract—along with the conservatives and radicals—only to the extent that they believe in and practise pluralism. If the point is reached where they seek to impose irreversible social changes upon a majority or a substantial minority to whom such changes are intolerable, they thereby cross the thin dividing line between pluralism and totalism. Likewise, the conservatives who reject or unreasonably resist the introduction of necessary reforms are opting out of the consensus. The trouble, as in all politics, is that we are dealing with variables. What is a 'necessary reform'? To whom is it necessary? What is an 'intolerable change'? To whom is it intolerable? The give-and-take implicit in the discussion needed to resolve such questions is what constitutes democracy.

Marx's sweeping rejection of any form of give-and-take made his

[2] Milovan Djilas, *The Unperfect Society: Beyond the new class* (New York, 1969), pp. 4 and 5.

followers of later generations natural and irreconcilable enemies of democratic societies, which paradoxically offered them the facilities —such as freedom of speech—which they deny others once in power, and which they enjoy and exploit for their own purposes. No group of thinkers was treated with greater contempt by Marx and Engels than the 'Utopian' socialists; and among these, it is interesting to note, he included the Frenchman Pierre-Joseph Proudhon (1809–1865) who, in some respects at least, ought to have been a thinker after his own heart (but whom, in fact, he despised as a typical lower middle-class, self-educated vulgarian). Indeed, when Proudhon proclaimed that 'property is theft', he was adopting a starting point remarkably similar to Marx's call for 'the expropriation of the expropriators'. Yet there was a fundamental cleavage between the two. Marx wanted to professionalise revolution and pretended to have found a scientific method for the changing of society on preordained lines. Proudhon was essentially an anarchist. He advocated a libertarian revolution, which would preserve freedom and equality for all in a non-State, avoiding the ghastly danger, as he saw it, of the emergence of a new governing élite no less tyrannous than the old. Proudhon is thus a natural bridge between the egalitarians and the men of violence.

The destroyers

Mikhail Bakunin (1814–76) acknowledged Proudhon as his master. But he was not content, as Proudhon mostly was, to philosophise about anarchism; instead, like Marx, he wished to change the world. Having served in the Russian imperial guard in Poland, he quit, wandered in Western Europe and, along with Richard Wagner, took part in the doomed defence of the Dresden revolutionary government in 1849. Arrested and handed over to the Tsarist authorities, he was sent to Siberia, but escaped and returned to Western Europe. Later in his adventurous career, he brought Anarchist revolution to Spain, briefly basking in the short-lived triumph of the independent 'cantons' in southern Spain and Barcelona during the First Republic of 1873. His simple and intoxicating message, as outlined in his letters and *God and the State* (1882) consisted of three principles: atheism, insurrection and the destruction of the State. God must go, since religion assumed man to be evil, whereas his natural goodness would spontaneously create libertarian communism once the twin evils of the Church and the State were removed (by force, since violence was the only way to destroy the instruments of oppression).

Let us be fair to the Anarchists. Not all were Bakuninists; not all practised assassination or deposited bombs in vulnerable places. There was a gentler brand of Anarchism. One of its earliest advocates, the Englishman William Godwin, wanted the overthrow of all State institutions and even of social ones, such as marriage. He argued his case in his book *Political Justice* (1793), but relied upon the good sense of citizens, not on their violence, to achieve what he preached. Similarly gentle was Bakunin's saintly rival, Prince Peter Kropotkin (1842–1921), whose dream society was one 'in which all the mutual relations of its members are regulated not by laws, not by authorities . . . but by mutual agreement between the members of that society and by a sum of social customs and habits . . . .'

But gentleness was a minority practice among Anarchists: the bomb-throwers predominated. In Georges Sorel (1847–1922), the apostles of violence found their greatest prophet. An ex-Marxist and a retired engineer, Sorel was much influenced by the irrationalist theories of the philosopher Henri Bergson. In his *Réflexions sur la violence* (1908), he preached the need for violence by the working class and the myth of the general strike—a total stoppage of production leading to the collapse of society—as a spur to revolutionary action. He is usually regarded as the first philosopher of 'syndicalism'—the doctrine that considers trade unions (*syndicats* in French) as the natural heirs to power after the general strike has overthrown bourgeois capitalism. For all his espousal of the working class, Sorel seems to have had only a minor impact upon the organised workers, although the basic ideas of syndicalism are by no means dead. His disillusion may account for the fact that he turned to royalism in his last years.

There are two basic absurdities in Anarchism and its syndicalist offshoot, one moral, the other logical. The moral one is the supposition that men are naturally good and that, if left to themselves, they will spontaneously set up good organisations that will obviate the need for a State. In fact, the few anarchist social experiments in historical experience—such as those of the Anabaptists of the 16th century, and the Spanish anarchists during the Civil War—rapidly degenerated into blood-stained tyrannies. The logical absurdity is linked to the moral one. Bakunin created secret revolutionary conspiracies whose members were totally obedient to his will. An earlier anarchist (before the term was in general use), François-Noël Babeuf (1760–97), also envisaged violent revolution led by a conspiratorial élite which would impose an egalitarian society from above. What neither Babeuf nor Bakunin seems to have grasped is that the conspiratorial organisation, once in power, would itself form the nucleus of a new State, unless overthrown by a rival élite. For that is the nature of power and of the human political animal. In Babeuf's case, the dilemma resolved itself when the Directoire got wind of his plotting and sent him to the guillotine; which he cheated by stabbing himself to death at the last moment.

The trouble with these political fantasies is that the total failures of their advocates does not deter their disciples, either at the time or later. The Babeufs and Bakunins do not achieve revolutions, but they do create revolutionaries, as the contemporary cases of the Angry Brigade in Britain and the Red Army Group in Germany illustrate. The harm done by the prophets of violence thus long outlasts their passing.

The observers

The Utopians (including Marx) wanted to change the world; others were content to observe it and analyse the political process. As James Burnham rightly observed, these writers were in the tradition of Machiavelli in that they tried to see things as they really were, neither obfuscating the truth in a maze of misleading words, nor mistaking wishes for reality, nor advocating the impossible.[3] By explaining the nature of power, they are the natural defenders of the freedom of those whom the powerful would deprive of it.

In a commentary on James Burnham's book, *The New Machiavellians*, I have already presented a slightly revised interpretation of the four writers whose work he analysed:[4] Gaetano Mosca (1859–1941), Robert Michels (1876–1936), Vilfredo Pareto (1848–1923), and Georges Sorel, whose inclusion in the group rests on dubious grounds and whose work is considered earlier in this chapter. I shall not, therefore, repeat myself in detail, but confine myself to reproducing my summary of the principal findings of the Machiavellians (including Burnham himself) about the nature of politics in any organised society:

—The fundamental subject-matter of political science is the struggle for power.
—All societies are ruled by an élite, the main objective of which is to maintain its own power and privilege. This does not, of course, rule out the conferment of benefits upon society as a whole; but that is not the primary objective of the ruling élite.
—Self-government, or democracy as the term is generally understood in the West, is a technical impossibility. All groups except

---

[3] James Burnham, *The Machiavellians* (London, 1943).
[4] See Brian Crozier, *The Masters of Power* (London, 1969), pp. 333–42.

those whose membership is very small throw up ruling oligarchies.

—The published programmes or stated objectives of all political élites, both before and after they are in power, are political myths designed to perpetuate their power. (This does not, of course, rule out the possibility that parts of a political programme may be practical and realisable. Any parts of a programme that are not clearly attainable within a generation clearly partake, however, of the nature of myths.)

—No social structure is permanent. Each ruling élite must renew itself or perish. If its resistance to renewal is too rigid, it will be overthrown and a new élite will take the place of the old. (Contrary to Marxian analysis, and to Anarchist and New Left expectations, the revolution of the proletariat does not lead to the classless society, or abolish the class struggle. A new élite—that of the strongest of the revolutionary groups which could be the Communist Party—takes the place of the old, constituting what Milovan Djilas called the 'new class'.)

To these, it would be fair to add the essential kernel of truth in Burnham's earlier (and still his most famous) book, *The Managerial Revolution* (1941), summarised as follows:

—The control of the world is passing into the hands of the managers. Capitalism has virtually lost its power and will be replaced by the rule of the administrators in business and government.

—The capitalist system will soon disappear. Continuous mass unemployment, colossal unpayable national debts, wholesale destruction of food while thousands starve, show that it no longer works. The future governing class will not be the possessors of wealth, but the possessors of technical or administrative skill. Already they alone are satisfied, keen and confident.

As Burnham wrote his famous work in 1940, it must be owned, in retrospect, that he showed remarkable percipience. Behind the pervasive slogans about capitalism, communism and fascism, he had perceived that the real control of government and society had already passed (especially in Russia) or was fast passing (as in America) into the hands of the managerial élite, and out of the hands of the owners of the means of production. His analysis, however, has always seemed to me to be open to criticism, less for its findings than for its author's assumptions. Dr. Burnham wrote as a very recent ex-Marxist; indeed, to be accurate, as an ex-Trotskyist who, not long before, had still been convinced of the essential truth of Marxism–Leninism, though quickly disillusioned with the fruits of the Bolshevik Revolution.

So pervasive is Marxist teaching, and so persistent are its teachers, that even non-Marxists need to be on their guard against uncritical acceptance of its basic assumptions. How many non-Marxists, for instance, unthinkingly use the term 'capitalist system'? How many assume with the Marxists, that the capitalists wield (or at any rate wielded) political power because of their ownership of the means of production? Yet neither assumption (especially the first) stands up to critical scrutiny.

There is not, and never has been, a capitalist *system*. The term 'capitalism', in proper usage, is merely descriptive of an evolutive condition. Capitalism just happened, as the result of a myriad circumstances, by far the most important of which were the ingenious industrial inventions of the 18th century. Moreover, it has never ceased to evolve, so that today's capitalism of multinational companies and mass shareholding already bears only a distant resemblance to the capitalism Burnham was writing about in 1940; and a progressively fainter one to the unbridled builders of the great capitalist fortunes—the Fords, the Rockefellers, the Mellons—at the turn of the century and in the 1920s, and to the remoter days of Marx and Dickens.

In contrast, the 'Communist system' really is a system, imposed from above by the deliberate political decisions of a ruling élite.

Nor do economic and political power necessarily or invariably coincide. A striking example of this is found in Malaysia and other South-East Asian countries where the economic power was overwhelmingly concentrated in the hands of the Overseas Chinese, while the political power was wielded, first by the British or other imperial powers, and later by the Malay or other indigenous authorities. There was a time, of course, in England and other countries, when the wealthy, by virtue of the aristocratic principles and the laws of inheritance, did constitute the ruling few. But this power did not, and probably cannot, survive the introduction of universal suffrage. Nor can it be said, even in 'capitalist' countries where conservative governments are in power, that the great companies necessarily get their way: the trade unions have become too strong for that. In Germany under Hitler, the capitalists became an instrument at the service of the gangsters in power. In Sweden, where the means of production remain largely in private hands, it would be hard to argue, after decades of socialist rule, that government is in the interests of the capitalists, let alone that it is they who give the political orders.

It is on this point, indeed, that the 'theory of convergence' (beloved by John Kenneth Galbraith) breaks down. The argument is that the Communist and capitalist Powers, facing similar problems because these are inherent in advanced industrial societies, will inevitably find similar solutions and will gradually come to resemble each other more and more. The fallacy in this reasoning arises from the assumption, whether or not acknowledged, that Marx was right in identifying economic with political power. The fundamental difference between the totalist Soviet bloc and the pluralist societies is political, not economic. On one side, all decisions are in the hands of the tiny ruling élite, which is self-perpetuating, and no opinions or practices of which they disapprove are allowed. On the other, the élite is much wider, more readily changeable, and the government is liable to be overthrown every few years at the polls. 'Convergence' is therefore an absurdity unless the political system is changed on one side or the other.

Varieties of the State

Looking at the world in 1974, and allowing for very wide national variations, one discerned that existing States fell broadly into one or another of the following categories:

1. *Representative democracies:* the United States and Canada, Britain, France and other countries of continental Western Europe; India and Ceylon; Australia and New Zealand; some Latin American countries.
2. *Authoritarian governments:* Spain, Portugal,[5] Greece.
3. *Totalist regimes:* the USSR and all other Communist countries, including China and Cuba; certain near-Communist regimes (Algeria, Guinea, etc.).
4. *Despotisms:* Haiti, Uganda (under Amin), Libya (under Gaddafi); Saudi Arabia, etc.
5. *Discriminatory but representative regimes:* South Africa, Rhodesia.

In the above list, 'authoritarian' comprises dictatorships, such as Franco's or that of the Greek colonels. Inevitably, there is some blurring or overlapping. To most visitors, for instance, Yugoslavia

---

[5] I.e., before the military *coup d'état* of 25 April 1974 which brought pledges of a wholesale restoration of political liberties interdicted since 1926.

appeared (and usually was) a much freer country than any other under a Communist government. As with Spain, Yugoslavia allowed its nationals to work abroad in large numbers, and welcomed tourists, also in large numbers and with minimal formalities. In practice, the workers managed their factories, and in theory they owned them (but only in theory: a matter that was easily disposed of by inquiring whether the Yugoslav workers could *sell* the factories they 'owned' to the highest bidder). Ultimate power, however, was held by the League of Yugoslav Communists and (while he lived) by President Tito, as was shown periodically whenever a purge of party functionaries was thought necessary, for instance in Croatia in 1971-2. This left Yugoslavia awkwardly poised between categories 1 and 2.

Anomalies abound. In Chile, a minority coalition of the Left under President Allende initially kept precariously within the Constitution, but by relentless pressure and harassment of private enterprise and the ruthless use of formerly dormant legislation, was laying the bases for a Marxist economy—until its overthrow in September 1973. Was it still, before the military coup, a category 1 government? In Sweden, the outward forms of democracy were respected, but the determined isolation of dissenters and the growing encroachments of the State, together with the official encouragement of sexual permissiveness, produced a society which a well-informed observer has characterised as that of *The New Totalitarians*.[6] Did Sweden continue to occupy its traditional place in category 1?

Categories 2 and 3 need explanation. It is widely assumed that there is little to choose between authoritarian and totalist governments; yet in one important sense, they are mutually antithetical. Authoritarian governments seek to abolish politics; totalist governments seek to involve the entire population in politics. In Franco's Spain, since the decline of the Falange in the 1950s, and even earlier, it was possible to live a full life so long as one did not indulge in politics outside the recommended forms. Citizens could travel freely, and (since the structural reforms of the late 1950s) the economy was overwhelmingly in private hands. In China—the ultimate totalist regime—it was impossible to opt out of politics, since the entire people was kept permanently involved under the vigilant eyes of the Communist Party cadres. It is fair to add, however, that if ordinary people were far freer in authoritarian Spain than in totalist Russia, the lot of politically active dissidents was only marginally better for Spaniards than for

[6] The title of Roland Huntford's book (see p. 4).

Russians. The distinguished journalist and writer, Calvo Serer, although a member of the supposedly 'ruling' Opus Dei, was deprived of his newspaper *Madrid* (closed down in November 1971), of many of his assets and very nearly of his personal liberty, and driven into exile. Ostensibly, the reason for these misfortunes was an alleged technical breach of the law involving an ownership arrangement between his newspaper and a bank; the real reason doubtless lay in the fact that his paper had carried a series of articles mildly critical of Franco's constitutional provisions, while Sr. Calvo Serer himself had written an article in *Le Monde* which attracted the regime's disapproval. Despite this unfortunate case (and others like it), the differences between categories 2 and 3 remain important.

As for category 4, I use the term 'despotism' to characterise the dictatorial regimes of relatively primitive countries, such as those named.

Category 5 needs more explanation. South Africa and Rhodesia were both, though in unequal degrees, racist regimes, and both have been called 'fascist' and 'police States'. Neither epithet was quite true, however, although elements of the police State were present in both, especially South Africa. Yet in both countries the independence of the judiciary was remarkable, and the press had not been absolutely muzzled, although it was under pressure. It was therefore accurate to call them 'discriminatory but representative regimes'. True, it was the white minority, not the black majority, that was properly represented; but taking the population as a whole, the degree of representation was greater than in the countries in categories 2, 3 and 4; and greater than, say, in England before the introduction of universal suffrage.

* * *

This long and occasionally digressive exploration of the development of the State in theory and practice must end here. Its purpose was not to exhaust the subject (or possibly the reader) but to further understanding of the target of revolutionaries, since the State, in all its infinite variety, is what they want to bring down.

We now turn to recent and contemporary history. The next chapter analyses the consequences of the two World Wars, leading in the end to the bi-polarised world of the two super-powers. The revolutionary challenges dissected in the ensuing chapter need to be seen against this background of power relationships, and especially against the growing power and expansive foreign policy of the Soviet Union, which interprets 'peaceful co-existence' and '*détente*' as a licence for the unlimited subversion of other countries.

I suggest, with reference to the summary classification of the 'varieties of the State' attempted in the present chapter, that in the light of the current revolutionary challenges and existing power relationships, the alternatives that face pluralist societies in the event of an inimpeded descent into anarchy are either the authoritarian reaction or 'the long night of totalism'.

How, then, should pluralist societies deal with the revolutionary challenge? Are there ways of containing political extremism within the law? To answer these questions, we need to consider both the techniques of revolution and those of counter-insurgency and counter-subversion. These are the themes of Part III.

PART III

The Contemporary Scene

ONE

THE STAKES

The ground covered in this chapter

Consequences of First World War—Lenin's seizure of power—Fascism, Nazism and Japanese militarism—technological yields of Second World War—the altered balance of power—economic sequels: Germany and Japan—loss of colonial empires—irrelevance of United Nations—recovery of Western Europe—Soviet hostility—NATO and EEC—problems of poverty—fallacies exposed—problems of affluence—acceleration of scientific discovery—the world in 1974—the super-Powers and the deterrent—regional power centres: Far East, Middle East, Africa, Latin America—America retreats, Russia advances—aid to clandestine movements—consequences of Vietnam war—détente and Ostpolitik—Cold War and 'peaceful co-existence'—alternatives to pluralism: authoritarian and totalist 'solutions'

THE WORLD of the 1970s, in which we lived when this book was written, was the product of two cataclysmic wars, and of an exploding technology to which each of them made dramatic contributions. The First World War (1914–18) left France exhausted, Britain weakened though still powerful, and Germany smarting under a sense of injustice and humiliation. In the exhaustion of France and the punitive provisions of the peace settlement of 1919 lay the seeds of further conflict; and it is true, though paradoxical, that a major but delayed consequence of the war that was to have ended war was the Second World War of 1939–45. By far the most significant consequence of the Great War, however, was the collapse of the Tsarist State, which gave Lenin and his little gang of revolutionaries the chance to overthrow the short-lived democratic government of Alexander Kerensky and create the most enduring of the century's totalist experiments.

Between the wars, Fascism flared into strenuous life in Italy which, though it had fought on the victorious side, had entered the Great War late and had been routed by the Central Powers; and Nazism was created by the fanatical will of an inspired madman swept to power on the mass vote of a demoralised and humiliated people after an unsatisfactory experience of parliamentary rule. A mere twelve years after Hitler's rise to power, the Third Reich, which was to have destroyed Bolshevism and lasted 'a thousand years', collapsed in the fire and blood of a new *Götterdämmerung* in the Berlin bunker where the dictator took his own life. In Italy, the Fascist regime had already collapsed and the Italian partisans had hung Mussolini and his mistress by the heels in a public square. In Japan, where a militarist regime had overrun South-East Asia and parts of China but, in its hubris, made the error of attacking a quiescent America, two large cities were destroyed by the first (and so far the only) atomic bombs dropped in anger; Tokyo was destroyed by fire; and the Emperor accepted unconditional surrender, giving General Douglas MacArthur his historic opportunity to introduce the Japanese to parliamentary democracy.

The technological yields of the Second World War were prodigious. The A-bomb—an American–British–Canadian development—ushered in the nuclear age; the jet engine—a British invention—heralded the new age of fast air travel; the V-2s—a German achievement—were Man's first incursion into space; and penicillin and antibiotics—discovered in Britain—revolutionised medicine.

The Second World War altered the balance of power more profoundly than the first. In Western Europe, there was, in relative terms, a collapse of power, with Germany prostrate, France demoralised by defeat and debilitated by occupation, and a Britain still strong but no longer prepared to shoulder the imperial burden. The age of the superpowers began. For some years the United States was incontestably the greater of the two, with a monopoly first of the atomic, later of the hydrogen bomb. But Stalin's seizures of territory or acquisitions of ideological satellites greatly extended the boundaries of the Russian empire while, in east Asia, Mao Tse-tung's victory in the Chinese civil war created, for some years, an apparently monolithic Eurasian land mass under communist rule. Acquiring in turn the atomic and hydrogen bombs, the USSR was the first to put a man in orbit around the earth and by the 1970s had reached strategic parity with, and indeed a slight edge of superiority over, the United States.

The economic sequels to the Second World War were totally unforeseen. The defeated powers, Germany and Japan, after a few difficult years, made recoveries that were generally regarded as 'miraculous'. Both were relieved, for a time, of the necessity to provide for their own defence, and having lost the taste for adventurous foreign entanglements, concentrated upon the fulfilment of material ambitions —to such effect that Germany, although divided, emerged as the economic giant of western Europe, and Japan as the third economic power in the world and—at least until doubts were raised by the oil crisis of 1973—apparently destined to overtake the Soviet Union before too long as the second after the United States.

The loss or surrender of the great European colonial empires was a further consequence of the war. The Dutch in the East Indies, and the French in Indochina and Algeria, fought to retain their possessions (although General de Gaulle placed no real obstacles in the path of the French-speaking African territories that wished to gain sovereignty). The British surrender, though on the whole more graceful, was no less final. The Belgians panicked and pulled out of the Congo with undue precipitation. The Americans had been the first to concede independence to any former colony (in this case, the Philippines). Only the Portuguese—a special case because of the length of their tenure, their absence of racial discrimination and an awareness that the territories they ruled in Africa were not nations but tribal conglomerates—saw no reason to withdraw.

The emergence of dozens of States, some entirely new, others a revival of ancient sovereignties, finally relegated the ill-conceived United Nations to total irrelevance: its inception rested, in any case, upon the mistaken assumptions that the war-time alliance between the pluralist West and the totalitarian East would endure, and that the disturbers of the peace would continue to be Germany and Japan, which had lost both the means and the will to be a threat.

Generous beyond all historical experience, the Americans set stricken non-communist Europe on its feet (and would have done the same for eastern Europe if Stalin had not vetoed the Marshall Plan); and distributed largesse, not always to wise effect, to the countries of the Third World. At the same time, they tried, under President Truman and President Eisenhower's Secretary of State, John Foster Dulles, to contain an elusive menace described as 'communism'. The assumption that the Communist empire would permanently remain a monolith was, however, shattered in 1956 and ensuing years when the Soviet leader, Nikita Khrushchev, denounced some of Stalin's crimes and China went its own way, as Yugoslavia had done when Stalin was still alive.

In the face of the power and hostility of Stalin's expanded empire, the Western countries, including the US, united for their own collective defence under the North Atlantic Treaty of 1949. In this and in certain other respects this external threat was beneficial to those threatened. It caused the French and the Germans, for instance, to bury the national rivalries that had brought them to grips three times in seventy years, forming the nucleus of the European Economic Community and in time, it was hoped, of a united Europe.

The EEC rapidly proved its capacity to force the economic growth of its member-countries. It regenerated France and Italy; while Britain, which had initially stayed outside, condemned itself to relative stagnation. In general, the rich countries were growing richer, while the poor countries, in relative and sometimes even in absolute terms were growing poorer. This growing gap was widely regarded as tragic and, on flimsy evidence, as a source of future world conflict, and many well-meaning people who ought to have known better expended much time and eloquence in calling for its reduction, although it was not difficult to demonstrate mathematically that this aim was impossible of fulfilment. Logically, indeed, the increasing wealth of the rich nations in no way added to the misery of the poorer ones: the important thing, whether on humanitarian grounds or for the prevention of conflicts, was clearly to reduce the poverty of the poor even if, while this was happening, the gap between them and the rich did not cease to expand.

It had been widely supposed, on the argument that the 'imperialist' countries had exploited their colonies, that independence would bring prosperity—an absurd notion that was encouraged both by Marxists, who may have believed it to be true, and by liberal opinion in the Western countries, which may not have believed it but fostered it in the apparent belief that those who expressed such views would thereby be relieved of the burden of collective guilt. For some years, the richer countries of the pluralist and totalist worlds competed fiercely with each other for the privilege of aiding the poorer countries although it was in time perceived that such aid, while instrumental in keeping ruling groups in power, had little bearing on the economic fortunes of the receiving countries. (India, though a major recipient of both Western and Soviet aid, made despairingly slow progress in *per capita* income; Japan, generously aided by the Americans, rapidly reached take-off point). Aid, in other words, was a help to those who made the best use of it, not to others. (The key factors in reaching take-off appear to be hard work and native ingenuity; luck; the absence of stifling religious or social traditions or the readiness to discard them; education and vocational training of the right kinds; birth control and abortion; and, not least, minimal government interference except, as in Japan and Brazil, in protecting local industry from foreign competition in the early stages of development.)

Leaving aside the nonsense frequently talked about aid and economic development, poverty does remain a problem, of course, in the context of this book; not *per se* but to the extent that it provides fertile ground for the political agitator and the propagandist. In this sense, even the false problem of the widening economic gap acquires a reality of its own. Directly linked with poverty are the related problems of disease and exploding population. One of the major factors in Japan's astonishing economic expansion was its success in stabilising population growth (through legalised abortion, voluntary sterilisation and contraception). If India's population were 200 million instead of about 450 million, its ability to feed, clothe and house its citizens would be dramatically improved. The control of disease, however, is a mixed blessing in that it increases the survival rate at both unproductive ends of the age scale. If the delicate young survive, and the old live longer, the burdens on productive adults increase. Against that, disease debilitates a working population. The problem is therefore complex. Advanced medicine without economic growth is a recipe for social disaster. To state this problem is easier than to solve it.

If the poor have problems and collectively constitute one, so have and do the rich. The strains and stresses of urban life in advanced industrial societies increase dramatically. The incidence of mental and heart disease rises sharply, as does the consumption of drugs, whether legally or illegally. Modern man (and woman) smokes, drinks or drugs himself out of pain or merely out of the surrounding world. Tranquillity and oblivion are available, at a price; a situation of rising benefit to the pharmaceutical industry, to the brewers, distillers and wineries, and to the tax authorities. As modern man (and woman) consumes more, so he pollutes the air he breathes, the water he drinks, the shores, seas and rivers he might be sunbathing upon or swimming in; so too does he fill the air with the abomination of noise (none more intolerable than piped music, that ultimate infringement of individual privacy and right of choice).

He builds high, to the greater benefit of property developers and the climate of investment, and proportionately diminishes the visual and aesthetic amenities and the cultural heritage; for good measure, he creates new social problems inherent in the anonymity of apartment life and its destruction of community example and restraint, thus adding to the rising crime wave. In recent years, these problems, instead of being taken for granted, have been given the honour of wider recognition; and words like 'ecology' (the study of man in his environment) have come into general use. It is fashionable, nowadays, to have a Ministry or Department of the Environment. Solutions are still remote; but at least the problem is acknowledged: it would be difficult to solve it if it were not.

Nor is the picture unrelievedly black. Technology may create problems; but it solves them too, and adds to, as well as subtracts from, the amenities of civilised life. It can shorten hours of work and eliminate drudgery. Modern woman, with her dishwasher and washing machine, is spared the worst horrors of the kitchen sink that afflicted her mother and grandmother. (True, she is less likely than they, if affluent, to enjoy domestic help: the supply of under-privileged labour having drastically diminished.)

Even that sourly hostile enemy of technology, Herbert Marcuse, gives full credit to the blessing of stereophonic music (an attitude which parents of teenage children will not necessarily share). Science and technology are indeed neutral: you can programme a computer to memorise and calculate; or to kill and destroy. It is no good arguing, as Marcuse does, that: 'In the face of the totalitarian features of . . . society, the traditional notion of the "neutrality" of technology can no longer be maintained. Technology as such cannot be isolated from the use to which it is put; the technological society is a system of domination which operates already in the concept and construction of techniques.' The fallacy in this determinist argument is not difficult to spot, for it is not technology but its makers and consumers as a whole who determine the use to which it is put.

What is certain is that the possibilities created by technology are almost infinite, while the problems it raises have hardly begun to be thought about. Technology has placed men on the moon and enormously improved the capacity to kill at a distance (a capacity to which Robert Ardrey attributes man's escape from barbarism, since it was only when the bow and arrow made it possible for individual men, as distinct from men hunting in packs, to kill their prey that individual achievement and inventiveness enabled man to escape from cave life). Electronic devices enhance the killing power of the East German regime against those of their citizens seeking to cross from East to West Berlin. Devices similar in scientific principle enable machines instead of men to make car parts and assemble them. The first industrial revolution produced machines that replaced human muscle power; the second yields machines that simulate certain thought processes while still ultimately dependent upon human programming.

Nor does technology alone exhaust the resources of science for the discoveries of the new biology, of experimental psychology (the study of the human brain), ethology and evolutionary zoology are perhaps no less momentous. We know not merely a little more but dramatically more about the origins and components of life, about the birth of the universe, about the age of man and evolutionary changes in the human brain. It must be assumed that we stand on the threshold of still more momentous discoveries and inventions.

All this—the consequences of the two world wars, the acceleration of scientific discovery, the persistence of poverty and its multiplication through galloping population growth, and the unsolved problems of the technological age—all of it, is relevant to the study of conflict. The point, I submit, is that for the first time in history, man has the technical power either to destroy his universe or to provide health and abundance for all. It is not in science that he is backward or recessive; but in morality, political wisdom and social organisation. It is against this background that the revolutionary challenges of our day have to be seen.

The stakes

I deliberately refrained, in the preceding passage, from concluding with some facile phrase, such as 'the choice is ours' or 'it is up to us to choose between abundance and annihilation'. For we are all individuals and unlikely in fact to make any choice at all, or indeed, given the complexity of modern government, to be given the chance to make one. It is nevertheless worth analysing some of the main political options that are available in the contemporary world and pointing to the probable consequences of selecting some in preference to others.

To do this intelligently, let us first look at the world, as it stood politically and in terms of power in 1974. The two main centres of military power were still Russia and America, roughly equal but possibly with a slight strategic advantage to Russia, achieved through a vast expansion in the construction of Intercontinental Ballistic Missiles and nuclear submarines after the removal of Khrushchev in 1964. On this world scale of capacity to inflict major damage from afar, all else was largely hypothetical. Although the accession of Britain to the EEC in 1973 greatly strengthened the chances of creating a 'United States of Europe' with common foreign and defence policies, this prospect still seemed far off. Certainly there was no *European* deterrent, although two major members of EEC, France and Britain, possessed deterrents of a kind. The British one, dependent upon supplies of Polaris missiles from America, was obsolescent as American technology moved on to new generations of submarines and missiles. The French one, though increasingly impressive, lacked credibility, in the sense that it seemed unlikely the French would ever use it and expose their country to total destruction. Tentative Franco-British talks had begun, with the aim of producing a joint deterrent for European use, but great problems remained, still unsolved. Could the West Germans be excluded for ever from access to nuclear weapons or at least a say in their possible use, as members of the Western Alliance? Would the Americans consent to make their nuclear technology available to the French, from which they had been debarred until then by the American Atomic Energy Act?

In the Far East, the Chinese had acquired a deterrent of their own, but with limited means of delivery. They had the power to destroy Siberian towns (or Tokyo, or Delhi), but not Moscow or New York. The Japanese had acquired gigantic economic power, but still seemed seared by the remembered loss of two cities under atomic bombardment, and reluctant to build a nuclear force of their own.

Apart from these actual or potential centres of nuclear power, all other power centres were regional. In the Far East, the most formidable of these regional powers was North Vietnam, still bent upon the conquest and absorption of other components of the former French Indochina empire. But some other countries in South and East Asia had big armies: South Vietnam still undefeated after 16 years of war; Indonesia (largely untested); India (which had defeated Pakistan).

Between the Arab–Israeli wars of 1967 and 1973, the military scene in the Middle East was dominated by two impressive regional powers: Israel, whose efficiency and supremacy in combat had been proved repeatedly; and Iran, rapidly developing and openly preparing to dominate the Gulf area in the vacuum left by the departure of the British.

South of the Sahara, Nigeria and Sudan, each emerging from a civil war, had armies to be reckoned with; otherwise, the armed forces that counted were white-commanded—those of Portugal in that country's African territories; and of South Africa.

In Latin America, where armies, traditionally, had played a more important part in domestic politics than in war, a potential great power was emerging in that huge and fascinating country, Brazil; but Brazilian interests seemed likely for many years to be concentrated upon economic development and the satisfaction of material needs, rather than upon any regional adventures. The only local State that had consistently interfered in neighbouring affairs was communist Cuba which, however, had by 1973 been satellised by the Soviet Union and thereby lost much, though not all, of its power to act alone.

Inevitably, the outlook for the world in 1973 was deeply coloured by the changing foreign policies of the super-Powers, and by the curious partnership evolving between them. The shortest way of expressing the change is that Russia was driving forward, and America pulling back. During the two years that followed Khrushchev's unsuccessful nuclear confrontation with President Kennedy in 1962, the external policies of the Soviet Union were relatively quiescent. They were marked, for instance, by a reluctance to get drawn into the Indochina war and by comparative inactivity in Africa. This apparent timidity may have been one of the reasons why Khrushchev was removed in October 1964. At all events, the changes made after his departure were swift and dramatic. The most momentous was undoubtedly the decision, taken early in 1965, to launch a programme to achieve strategic superiority over the United States. By late 1971, the Russians had in fact achieved superiority in ICBMs, increased their lead in conventional forces and made a start with an Anti-Ballistic Missile (ABM).

Concurrently, the Soviet government had launched a vast programme of naval expansion, which was soon marked by a great build-up in the Mediterranean, the establishment of a naval presence in the Indian Ocean, greatly increased activity in the Atlantic and Caribbean areas, and so forth.

Nor was the new forward policy confined to the armed forces: in overt State policies as well as in clandestine subversion, there was a renewed emphasis on expanded activities. The National Front for the Liberation of South Vietnam (or NFLSV, the political front of the Vietcong terrorists and guerrillas) was allowed to open an office in Moscow in November 1964—a remarkable development after seven years of war and at a time when the Vietcong already had offices in Peking, Havana, Cairo, Djakarta and East Berlin. In February 1965, the Soviet Premier, Kosygin, visited Hanoi and his visit marked a decision—again, after seven years of war—to provide North Vietnam (and through it, the Vietcong) with large quantities of modern weapons.

The drive to find client States was pressed with renewed vigour. Egypt was virtually satellised, until President Sadat in July 1972 expelled most Soviet personnel; treaties were signed with Egypt (May 1971), India (August 1971) and Iraq (April 1972); and in 1969–71, the Russians brought much of the Cuban administrative machine indirectly under their control, while a secret Soviet-Cuban pact led to the construction of a base for Soviet nuclear submarines at Cienfuegos.

In contrast, American policy, especially during the latter part of the same period, was marked by a declining interest in playing a world role. This is not to say that America was returning to the isolationism of the 1930s, or that it had suddenly ceased to be a super-Power. But certainly the contrast with the recent past was striking. President Truman had committed his country to the 'containment' of communism; had provided the bulk of the United Nations force that prevented communist North Korea from conquering the south of that divided country; and had pledged his country to defend Europe against Soviet encroachments. President Eisenhower and his Secretary of State, Mr. Dulles, had initiated the Manila Treaty of 1954 to contain communism in East Asia, had inspired the Baghdad Pact (CENTO) to do the same for the Middle East, and greatly extended America's network of bilateral alliances throughout what was popularly known as 'the free world'. President Kennedy took the fateful decision to intervene with ground forces in the Vietnam War, and stood up to Khrushchev when offensive Soviet missiles were installed on Cuban soil.

Presidents Johnson and Nixon, however, reversed the trend. Vietnam eroded America's will and exacerbated such domestic problems as drugs and urban violence. Political dissent fed upon it and the impact of the protest movement was a major factor in President Johnson's decision not to seek re-election in 1968. By 1970, President Nixon seems to have decided that the Vietnam war was unwinnable and started to seek ways out of it. Imaginatively, he sought to do so in the wider framework of a general attempt to reduce the tensions of the world and the dangers of general war. The attempt was marked by the President's visits to Peking (February 1972) and Moscow (May 1972), and by the attempt to end the nuclear arms race in the Strategic Arms Limitation Talks (SALT) between the US and the USSR. The successful policy of 'Vietnamisation' enabled the Americans to withdraw their ground forces from Vietnam, although the war itself continued, despite 'cease-fire' agreements negotiated for Vietnam, Laos and Cambodia in the early months of 1973.

The American withdrawal was widely considered a defeat, not least in America itself. Yet it is best described as marking a costly stalemate. The criterion of 'victory' or 'defeat' in a revolutionary war, such as that in Vietnam, revolved around the occupancy of power in Saigon, the southern capital. The Americans had intervened to prevent the

take-over of the whole of Vietnam and of the two neighbouring States
—Laos and Cambodia—which had appeared imminent early in 1962,
when the American command was set up in Vietnam. When they
withdrew eleven years later, the Communists had still not achieved
power in Saigon, and the government and army of South Vietnam were
vastly stronger than their predecessors had been. Against this, the
strategic position favoured the Communists, who controlled large
areas of Laos and Cambodia.

The point, however, is that the Vietnam War had proved a bitterly
frustrating experience for the American government, and especially
for the armed forces, whom it seriously demoralised. America's allies,
especially in the Far East but in Europe, too, drew the lesson that they
could not, in a protracted struggle, count on the continued support of
their major ally. America's will was in question, and as always the will
was no less important than the material means of policy. The American
executive's *capacity* to conduct a foreign policy at all, moreover, was
further weakened by a series of leaks and scandals, especially the so-
called Watergate affair involving the bugging of Democratic Party
headquarters during the Presidential election campaign of 1972,
allegedly on orders from the White House.

The Russians, on their side, were quick to profit from so favourable
a turn of circumstances. In 1966, they had launched a fresh campaign
(there had been an earlier one in the 1950s) in favour of *détente* and a
European Security Conference. The campaign, initially unsuccessful,
was given considerable impetus when the West German government
of Herr Willy Brandt, which came to power in September 1969,
launched its *Ostpolitik*, reversing the rigid policies of its predecessors
and seeking an accommodation and better relations with East Germany and the Soviet Bloc. The outcome was an important series of
arrangements: treaties between Bonn and Moscow; a four-Power
agreement on Berlin; and an All-German Treaty signed on 21 December 1972.

In the improved atmosphere fostered by the West German *Ostpolitik*
and the Nixon Doctrine, agreement was reached on the convening of a
Conference on European Security and Co-operation (which opened at
Helsinki in July 1973 and was resumed later at Geneva), and on talks
in Vienna between the Warsaw Pact and NATO Powers on Mutual
and Balanced Force Reductions. SALT, meanwhile, had yielded an
American decision to accept a slight strategic inferiority relatively to
the Soviet Union. The new strategic understanding between the US
and the USSR was enshrined in various treaties or agreements

concluded during President Nixon's visit to Moscow (May 1972) and Mr. Brezhnev's return visit to Washington (June 1973).

The situation was paradoxical, in that the United States remained immensely powerful but opted for strategic retreat; while the Soviet Union negotiated from a position of great military power but deep economic weakness, the most striking sign of which was the inability of the regime, 56 years after the Bolshevik Revolution, to feed its own people. The strategic deal, however, coincided with a phase of incipient energy shortage in the US, and was complemented by arrangements for vastly increased Soviet–American trade, giving Russia access to American technology in return for the provision of natural gas and other Soviet resources. On both sides, and indeed in the press of many European countries, it was proclaimed that the Cold War was at last being buried—a proposition that could be accepted only if the Soviet definition of the Cold War prevailed; that is, if it were conceded that the Cold War covered only the hostile deeds and words of the 'capitalist' countries against the Soviet Union, and not those of the Soviet Union against the industrial countries of the West. Moreover, on the Soviet side, there had been no renunciation, even for public consumption, of the doctrine of 'peaceful co-existence' which, as frequently defined in Moscow, implied the 'intensification of the international class struggle', that is of Russia's systematic attempts to subvert and undermine the 'capitalist' and 'imperialist' countries and indeed all countries not subservient to the Soviet Union; in other words of what we in the West normally understand by the Cold War. The importance of such definitions far transcends the temporary joys of semantic skill. For neither in Moscow, nor in Washington nor at Helsinki did the Soviet Union renounce the aim—asserted as a right—of aiding, training and supplying revolutionaries all over the world; of spying on and subverting Western countries; and of attempting to gain or reassert control over all Communist parties.

These were the realities behind the existence in many countries of revolutionary groups dedicated to the overthrow of existing institutions.

In Part II, 3, I presented a short list of categories of States (representative; authoritarian; totalitarian; despotic; and discriminatory but representative). Here, I am concerned only with the first three. Let us rename two of them, and present the following alternatives: pluralist, authoritarian and totalist. This book is, of course, largely though not entirely addressed to people who live in pluralist societies. There is no need of reminders that existing pluralist societies are imperfect; but the evidence (freely available, since these *are* pluralist countries) is overwhelming that the great majority of their citizens would rather live in such societies than in any others. A substantial minority would like a greater degree of authority; and in most places a very small minority would opt for the totalist 'solution'. (In France and Italy, however, the minorities apparently willing to entrust their fate to totalist parties were disturbingly large.)

Now the point of shortening the previous list and renaming two of the possibilities is that in realistic terms, there are only two feasible alternatives to pluralism: the authoritarian and the totalist. Should France, for the sake of argument, drastically change its system of government, it was hardly likely that it would find itself under a primitive despotism such as the Libyan or the Ugandan. The last major change (under de Gaulle in 1958–9) had been in the direction of greater central authority. The next might be still further in the same direction; or in the collectivist and totalist direction. Similar alternatives faced all the other representative democracies, in greater or lesser degree according to their histories and circumstances. In the case of countries, such as Britain and the United States, with large coloured minorities, an authoritarian change could well include features akin to those characteristic of Rhodesia and South Africa.

I should make one thing clear: I am not making any precise forecasts, since political predictions are vulnerable to the exposure of actual events. What I am doing is to point out that representative democracies, by virtue of their natural tolerance, are themselves highly vulnerable. Although their faults are to some extent self-correcting, they have no prescriptive right to permanency, and in historical terms their advent is too recent to encourage faith in their indefinite survival. All pluralist societies include groups of extremists impatient of gradual reform and bent upon rapid change, if necessary by violent means.

The stakes in 1974 were therefore high. Indeed, they could be no higher: for what was at stake was no less than the survival of a way of life. In most Western countries at that time, the main threat came from what was conventionally but unsatisfactorily known as the Left, but the outcome of the confrontation was not necessarily a 'left-wing' totalist regime: it was just as likely to be an authoritarian regime of 'the Right'. In the longer term, however, events might be determined by the gigantic power and messianic ambitions of the Soviet Union at a time of American reluctance to continue with its post-war role of world power and defender of the West.

TWO

THE REVOLUTIONARY CHALLENGE

The ground covered in this chapter

Public fear of violence—revolutionary challenges of our time; nationalists; left extremists; Communist parties; unimportance of extreme Right—no fascist power bases—expansion of Soviet power—subversive centres—target countries—competitive subversion—transnational terrorism—danger of irreversible changes—Soviet 'right' of intervention—popular front techniques: Chile, France—new Soviet sophistication—clandestine aid for terrorists—importance of New Left to Moscow—weakening the State: importance of power bases—revolutionary aims compared (Communists, Maoists, Trotskyists, Anarchists)—'right-wing backlash' and totalist prospect

ALL CHALLENGES to law and order, whether from the Right or the Left or merely criminal, are to be feared by the mass of ordinary citizens who merely wish to live their lives at peace and go about their business unhindered. This fear is generally felt in the initial stages of a rebellion against the State. If, however, the State is weak, inefficient or timid and fails to restore order, or makes itself unpopular by harsh measures—such as internment without trial—that are nevertheless ineffectual, then the time may come when a majority of those expressing opinions will opt for the rebels—whether through fear, through weariness or because, having lost faith in the State, they are willing on balance to take their chances with the counter-State. What is certain is that the vast majority of people have only a short-lived tolerance of violent anarchy.

I am not directly concerned with criminal violence, except to the extent that it overlaps, as it often does, with revolutionary terrorism. Especially in the initial stages, for example, terrorists often rob banks or kidnap people for ransom for fund-raising purposes. Such activities constitute common law crimes. Equally, it is of little concern to the passengers of a highjacked airliner whether the motivation of the highjackers is political or not: the threat to their own lives is the same either way. In Northern Ireland, many of the activities attributed to one or other of the contending terrorist factions were often thought to be the work of ordinary criminals taking advantage of the general violence and hoping to deflect attention and escape attention by adopting a political label.

The revolutionary challenges of our time, however, are not confined to groups practising violence. Indeed some Communist parties committed, at least for the time being, to the 'constitutional path to power' must be granted a better chance of achieving power than smaller groups dedicated to violent methods. This was still true, in 1974, of the French and Italian parties. Where Communist parties achieve power, however, the changes they introduce are, if experience is the guide, irreversible.

In the 1970s, extremist challenges of all kinds, including those properly to be regarded as revolutionary, fell into the following broad categories:

1. *Ethnic, religious* or *nationalist*. Most of these groups, though not all, could be labelled, without straining accuracy too far, 'right-wing'. They included, for instance, the Provisional wing of the Irish Republican Army (IRA) and the Palestinian group *Al Fatah*, with its extreme terrorist wing, Black September. But there were a few ethnic or nationalist groups of the extreme Left, the most notorious in recent times being the *Front de Libération Nationale du Québec* (FLQ). The Regular wing of the IRA, which was Marxist-dominated, also fell into this category.
2. *The revolutionary Left.* This in turn could be subdivided into four main groups: the Trotskyists (by far the most important because of their discipline and international organisation); the Anarchists (of which the Red Army Group in Germany, better known as the Baader–Meinhof gang, and the much smaller Angry Brigade in Britain, were examples); the Maoists (whose label, usually self-conferred, was often misleading since it might imply simply a devotion to revolutionary violence and a hatred of Soviet 'bureaucratism', and not necessarily any understanding let alone espousal, of the creed and revolutionary techniques of Mao Tse-tung); and the 'Guevarists' who owed their inspiration to the late Che Guevara. To these should be added a profusion of groups or movements whose ideology was confused and whose tactics were incoherent but whose general character was of the revolutionary Left.

3. *The orthodox Communist parties,* more or less loyal to Moscow and more or less responsive to the current Soviet line, which advocated a 'constitutional path to power' for Communists in general, while not excluding more or less clandestine assistance to non-Communist extremists. Among the true (but not necessarily Moscow-line) Communist parties, however, were a number—the most important being the North Vietnamese, the North Korean and the Cuban—that were actively engaged in revolutionary violence or assistance to terrorists.

4. *The ideological extreme Right.* At the time of writing, groups that could be labelled 'fascist' or 'neo-fascist', except with pejorative intent only, were few and relatively unimportant.

This relative unimportance of the ideological extreme Right needs to be spelt out, because recent historical memories of fascism and war have made many people naturally receptive to a sustained and highly successful communist campaign pointing to the supposed revival of fascism as the only real political danger in the world today. That two at any rate of the fascist regimes of the 1930s were a major threat to international peace and security is a matter of historical record. I am alluding to Germany and Italy; the Japan of that period, although it became an ally of the Rome–Berlin Axis, is more properly described as an ultra-nationalist and militarist regime than as a fascist one. But it is arguable that the war-like tendencies of Fascist Italy and Nazi Germany were due in far greater degree to the character and ambitions of Mussolini and Hitler than to the theories of the corporative State which Mussolini introduced. At all events, the regimes of Franquist Spain (which initially had fascist aspects) and of Salazar's Portugal, whatever may be thought of them, have never constituted a threat to world peace. (Portugal's African wars, whether or not they are regarded as colonial, are essentially *defensive* campaigns against left-wing tribal and rascist insurgents using the methods of revolutionary war; they are not a threat to neighbouring countries, except to the extent that these harbour or shelter the insurgents.)

The era of the fascist wars is over, however. Germany and Italy were utterly defeated, and so was Japan. In 1974, fascism (even if the meaning of this much-abused term is stretched to include a military dictatorship, such as that in Greece between 1967 and 1973) entirely lacked a power base. Although 'neo-fascist' parties have emerged in Germany and Italy, their share of the vote remained very small. Nor could the various murder squads of the extreme Right in Latin American countries, for instance in Guatemala and Brazil, be regarded as 'fascist': they were essentially the militant arms of supporters of regimes threatened by urban or peasant guerrilla groups of the extreme Left—in other words, they represented a defensive reaction to an existing challenge.

The lack of a power base, and the absence in contemporary 'fascist' groups of the mystique of war that distinguished Italian fascism and German National Socialism, are very important. Although I would not rule out the emergence of authoritarian regimes in any of the contemporary representative democracies, should it prove beyond their capacity to deal with existing revolutionary challenges, there were in 1974 no grounds for supposing that 'fascism' would again become the threat to international security that it was in the 1930s.

None of this was true of communism in its various forms, or of the proliferating Marxist or anarchist groups throughout the non-communist world. In contrast to the Axis Powers, the Soviet Union emerged from the Second World War with its territory greatly enlarged, and later turned into a super-Power. Although the monolithic communist land mass of Stalin's day no longer cohered, the competing centres of communism—China, North Korea, North Vietnam and Cuba—had this in common that all were opposed to 'capitalism' and 'imperialism', that is, to the pluralist societies in which we lived. Fascism had no significant power base; communism had many, including two of the biggest and most powerful countries in the world. If for no other reason than this, the revolutionary groups and parties of the extreme Left were infinitely more dangerous than those of the extreme Right to the survival of the pluralist societies.

There were, however, additional grounds for this assertion. I have referred to *power bases*. By this I mean simply sovereign States with greater or lesser power at their disposal. Wherever they may be, Communist parties do not stand alone: although liable at times to be sacrificed if the expedient tactical interests of, say the Soviet Union so demand, they can in normal times count upon the backing and often the material support of Moscow (or Peking, or Pyongyaung, or Hanoi, or Havana, as the case may be). Moreover, communism (of whatever variety) is an active, proselytising, messianic creed: not content with waiting for history to do what they say is historically inevitable, Communists everywhere are duty-bound to work constantly for the overthrow of 'capitalism'; and indeed for the overthrow or subversion of all non-communist States.

To the extent that Communist States provided aid to revolutionary groups beyond their borders, or worked to subvert non-communist States, they constituted *subversive centres*. All the Communist States named in the preceding paragraphs were subversive centres; and so were most of the East European States, especially those most closely under Moscow's control: Czechoslovakia, East Germany and Bulgaria.

But this does not exhaust the list of subversive centres. In the Arab Middle East and Africa in 1974, a number of countries could be described as subversive centres, in the sense that they provided money, training, equipment, accommodation and other facilities, for terrorists or guerrillas operating in other countries, which it is convenient and accurate to describe as *target countries*. In Africa, the subversive centres were: Algeria; Libya; Egypt; Guinea; Republic of the Congo (Brazzaville); Zambia; and Tanzania. In the Near East, they were: Iraq; Lebanon (largely against its will); and Syria. In Latin America, Cuba was for some years the only significant subversive centre; and it remained one when these lines were written. Chile under the left-wing Allende coalition, however, emerged as a subversive centre, partly on behalf of the Russians, Cubans and North Koreans, but possibly also on its own account.

The target countries included: (in Latin America) Mexico, Guatemala, Colombia, Venezuela, Peru, Bolivia, Brazil, Argentina and Uruguay; (in Africa) all the Portuguese territories, Ethiopia, Chad, Cameroun, Rhodesia and South Africa; (in the Near and Middle East) Jordan, Israel, Oman, Turkey and Iran; (in South and East Asia) India, Bangladesh, Burma, Thailand, Malaysia, Singapore, Indonesia, South Vietnam, Laos, Cambodia, and the Philippines; (and in Europe) Britain, Spain, Portugal, France, West Germany, Italy, Holland, Greece, Yugoslavia, and Cyprus. Inevitably, the list is incomplete, and there is some overlapping as some countries were the targets of more than one subversive centre, while others—e.g. Spain— were the targets of indigenous terrorist groups operating from within the country.

Without going into excessive detail, I have said enough, I hope, to indicate the international nature of the revolutionary challenge. But two further concepts need to be explained if the full complexity of the revolutionary picture is to be grasped. These are: *competitive subversion* and *transnational terrorism*. I originally coined the first of these terms in 1964 to describe the competing activities of the Russians and Chinese in South-East Asia, Africa and Latin America, where they supported rival factions that might expend at least a part of their energies in squabbling with, or shooting at, each other instead of at the putative enemy. In some areas, notably in 'white' southern Africa, Chinese competition against Soviet efforts had the effect of largely nullifying the latter.

This was, of course, beneficial to the target country, but it would be naïve to suppose that the benefit was unalloyed. In the days of mono-lithic communism, the job of the local security services was relatively simple in that it could fairly be presumed that Moscow was behind most subversive efforts. In the 1960s and 1970s the Chinese, the Rus-sians, the Cubans, the North Koreans and others might all be involved in a given situation, and the job of intelligence-gathering and of counter-measures was thereby greatly complicated. Moreover, com-petitive subversion may operate at the local and domestic level as well as internationally. If, for instance, Communist, Trotskyist and Anarchist groups are competing for the attention of trade unionists in a given industry with the object of bringing them out in a strike for political ends, the job of the management (and of the local security services, whether in France, Italy, Britain or elsewhere) is to that extent more difficult or complicated.

Transnational terrorism is of more recent origin, both as a phenome-non and as a concept. In the widespread student riots of 1968, it first came to public notice that a small and international nucleus of ring-leaders was involved in organising demonstrations in Paris, London, New York and other cities. It later became apparent that different terrorist groups were involved in a new form of co-operation. Some of these groups operated in countries that tolerated or encouraged their presence, and others in places where their activities were illegal and liable to suppression if discovered.

It is this trend which I term 'transnational terrorism', in preference to 'international terrorism' and such expressions, freely used in the press, as 'terrorist international'. In fact, there was *no* terrorist inter-national in that, as far as is known, there was no organisation that really qualified for such a designation, although a number of individual terrorist groups were affiliated to the Trotskyist *Fourth International*, with headquarters in Brussels.

There were indeed earlier instances of the phenomenon: what was new was its rapid development since 1968. A good example, among many that could be quoted, was that of the Lydda airport massacre on 30 May 1972. It was later established that the three young Japanese who massacred 25 people that day, and wounded 78 more, were mem-bers of an extreme left-wing terrorist organisation named the United

Red Army; that the brother of one of them was one of a United Red Army group that had hijacked a Japanese airliner to North Korea in May 1970; that the whole operation was planned by the Popular Front for the Liberation of Palestine; that the Japanese had been trained in camps in Lebanon; and that the gunmen had collected passports in Frankfurt and weapons in Rome, in each case by arrangement with local terrorist groups.

Such links between terrorist groups across the frontiers were in no sense surprising in view of the ideological similarities between them. Contacts were facilitated by the speed and frequency of jet travel; while the enormous expansion of airport traffic stimulated the new terrorist activity of highjacking, not all of which, of course, was politically motivated, while adding intolerably to the strain on, and cost of, security controls.

Propinquity, television and self-dialling international telephonic communications also contributed, in a way not possible in earlier days, to the elaboration and imitation of new terrorist techniques. Apart from highjacking one of these, characteristic of recent years, has been the kidnapping and occasional murder of diplomats and other public figures. Letter-bombs, made possible by the miniaturisation of detonating devices, were a further contribution to revolutionary technology.

Because of the spectacular nature of some of their deeds, the terrorists, transnational or local, attracted far more attention, as a rule, than the Communist parties which, in the past few years, had tended almost to merge with the surrounding scenery and increasingly to gain acceptance as political parties like the rest, or if not the same, as having lost the revolutionary drive and propensity for violence that once made them so feared. In the long run, however, the Communists were probably still more dangerous than the disparate groups that had turned to terrorism, which mostly lacked a solid support base, and which were often shortlived.

All experience shows that the changes the Communists would introduce into society would be irreversible and in the true sense revolutionary since the features that distinguish pluralist societies would be systematically removed. That rule by Communists (or indeed by Marxists of any label or none if sincere in their beliefs) would involve the total expropriation of private enterprise has never been disguised but is only one of the revolutionary changes which communist rule would entail. More fundamental still would be the disappearance of the fundamental liberties: of freedom of speech and expression, of the press and other media, of freedom from arbitrary arrest and the right to a fair trial if arrested; the freedom to form political parties and independent trade unions; the right to dissent and opposition. The list could be considerably lengthened and is in no sense fanciful, since all such rights and liberties have been abolished in practice (even if guaranteed by the constitution) not only in the Union of Soviet Socialist Republics but in all other countries practising a form of communism, with the possible exception of Yugoslavia—and even there, the exercise of liberties is intermittent. It is fair to assume, therefore, that the conditions that result from a communist take-over of power are inherent in the doctrine of Marxism or Marxism–Leninism. Nor can it be argued that these conditions obtained only in countries in which communism was imposed under Soviet pressure and which remained under Soviet control; for similar conditions obtained in China, North Vietnam and Cuba, where the local Communists achieved power unaided, or virtually unaided, by the Russians.

Moreover, whenever the people or government of a satellite country has rebelled against the prevailing uniformity, as in East Germany in 1953, in Hungary in 1956 and in Czechoslovakia in 1968, the Soviet army has marched in to restore the threatened orthodoxy. Mr. Dubcek's mortal sin in 1968 was to open the door to pluralism by calling in question the right of the ruling Communist Party to a permanent monopoly of power. It was for this that he had to be removed; and it was because Mr. Ceauşescu of Rumania had *not* breached this principle that his remarkable freedom of manoeuvre in foreign policy was tolerated, though not approved; doubtless it was this also that saved Marshal Tito's Yugoslavia, despite all the other concessions he had felt able to make towards a freer life for his people (and which his successors might well withdraw).

As I have said, some Communist parties were still using force in 1974; nor had the others formally renounced it in all possible circumstances: all they did was to admit that in certain circumstances, a constitutional road was more likely to lead them to power than a violent one. It was this proposition, first adumbrated by Khrushchev at the Twentieth Congress of the Soviet Communist Party in Moscow in 1956, that caused the major rift in the international communist movement, including the ideological split between Peking and Moscow. What, then, is meant by 'the constitutional road (or path) to power'? There are a number of variants, but the basic principle is the formation of what in the 1930s was first called a 'popular front'—that is, a coalition with the social democrats and/or other parties left of Centre, or a temporary electoral alliance, to be rewarded in the event of victory at the polls, by the allocation of suitable portfolios to the participating parties, including the Communists.

This method won a notable success in the 1970 Presidential elections in Chile, when Senator Allende, a Marxist–Socialist, led a coalition of left-wing groups, including the Communist Party, to power on a minority vote in a triangular contest. Once in power, and having acquired the economic ministries—economics, labour and finance—the Communists, working to the letter though not the spirit of the Constitution, started laying the economic foundations for a fully Marxist State. Within the first three years, the new coalition had brought most of Chilean business under State control, and in so doing produced the highest rate of inflation in the world at that time and general stagnation of the economy, marked by shortages of all kinds, including food.

In France, the Communists, in alliance with the Socialists (led by M. François Mitterrand, who had publicly praised the Chilean experiment as a possible model for France), came remarkably close to victory in the parliamentary elections of 1973; and in Italy, the powerful Communist Party stood permanently in readiness to take advantage of any electoral arrangement which the other parties might offer, should circumstances force them to weaken in their resolve to keep the party out. In at least two key West European countries, then, the prospect of communist governments was not one that could be dismissed out of hand.

Where did Moscow stand in this complex situation? There can be no doubt that the Russians disliked and distrusted the wilder varieties of revolutionaries now so prevalent in the world. They have often said so, especially in party documents, and in publications such as *Kommunist*, the theoretical organ of the Communist Party, or in the *World Marxist Review*, which serves as an ideological link between the Soviet party and other Communist parties throughout the world. But disapproval does not necessarily preclude occasional praise, or even selective material aid. In this respect, the Soviet Communists were a good deal more supple and sophisticated than they used to be. In Stalin's day, any Communist Party that stepped out of line would be sharply brought back into line; and anathema for 'adventurism' would be directed at the wilder left-wing groups or factions.

But this was before the denunciation of (some of) Stalin's crimes by Khrushchev, and the great ideological splits in the world communist movement. Moreover, in the more advanced industrial countries, at least between 1956 and 1968, violent revolution was seen to stand no chance whatsoever of success. The Russians, however, could not disinterest themselves entirely from the accusations of bourgeois softness, revisionism, loss of revolutionary intent and zeal, that were made from Peking, and indeed from Havana until the Russians, by relentless pressure, brought Fidel Castro to heel. Nor could they ignore the fact that many potential young recruits to the Communist Parties turned against Moscow after Hungary in 1956, and again after Czechoslovakia in 1968. In disgust, many of these young people turned to other and more obviously revolutionary groups: the Trotskyists, the Maoists, the Anarchists. Was Moscow to lose all such recruits for apparent lack of revolutionary zeal? The solution found was twofold. On the one hand, in carefully selected situations, lip service could be paid to causes even if the Russians disapproved of the groups involved and of their leaders. Continuing support of this kind has been given to the IRA in Ulster and to the Palestinian guerrillas; and even to the occasional rebels in the Andean countries of Latin America, who were given a programme all their own, in the Quechua language, on Moscow's Radio Peace and Progress.

Beyond that, however, the Russians, could and did provide clandestine aid in the form of money, arms, training, supplies to selected groups of terrorists or guerrillas, even where Moscow specifically disapproved of them on ideological grounds or held their methods in contempt. A particularly striking example was the Soviet-sanctioned shipment of arms from a Czechoslovak trading agency to the Provisional (that is, the non-Marxist) wing of the IRA, which was seized at Schiphol airport in Holland in October 1971. But other examples have come to light, and since this kind of activity is clandestine, it must be assumed that what is seen is only the tip of a much larger iceberg.

While this was going on, the leading 'orthodox' Communist parties —not only in France and Italy, but also in Venezuela, Uruguay, Brazil and Chile—disclaimed violent intent and indeed denounced the violence of the groups that practised it. It must be assumed from external evidence that this generally more sophisticated approach to the problems of revolution was the outcome of deep reflection in Moscow upon the extraordinary events of 1968. Within the first half of that year, President Johnson of the United States announced that he would not be standing for re-election; President de Gaulle was very nearly overthrown after violent rioting in the streets of Paris and of provincial towns; and Mr. Dubcek admitted the principle of pluralism in Prague.

In all three cases, the so-called New Left was deeply involved: in America through the protest movement; in Paris in the persons of the rioting students; and in Prague because Mr. Dubcek, to the general approval of the unorthodox Left everywhere, virtually established a New Left government within the 'Socialist commonwealth'.

If, the Russians may have reasoned, the New Left can bring down an American President, almost force a French President out of power, and displace the Moscow-line Communists in a satellite country, then it has clearly become a force to be reckoned with. The first sign of the Soviet change of course was the appearance of articles in the press attacking, instead of merely deriding, the New Left. But the policy of selected aid to revolutionaries, which was already in force in a number of countries of the Third World, was greatly widened as the activities of the revolutionaries themselves grew in scope.

It would, however, be a bad error to suppose that the Russians necessarily hoped for the ultimate victory of groups they aided. What is far more likely is that they hoped to make such groups dependent on Soviet help, so that in time, they would gain control over the leadership, regardless of ideological differences, regardless indeed whether the recipients initially denounced the 'bureaucratism' of Soviet socialism. Since their power was overwhelming, their resources vast and their patience infinite, such aims were in no sense vain or excessive.

There was further ground for hope in Moscow in all that happened in the late 1960s and early 1970s. The Russians, and the Communists who more or less echo the Soviet line, may dislike left-wing 'adventurism', but they cannot help noticing that protests, demonstrations, terrorism and political strikes weaken the States that suffer them, forcing their governments either to take unpopular measures or to stand exposed for their impotence in the face of violence, and, especially in the latter event, damaging the economy. In this situation, the Communists really cannot lose. Posing as the party of order, as the alternative government, or at all events as a desirable partner in a coalition of the Left, they are, as the saying goes, 'sitting pretty'. If the wilder revolutionaries 'win', provoking the total breakdown of the State, the disciplined Communists, enjoying (in Europe) the proximate support of the powerful Soviet Union, know that they are the most likely to take over power, restoring the State indeed, but in their own image. But should the revolutionaries lose, the Communists, having dissociated themselves from the excesses of the extremists, may see their 'moderate' status further enhanced and their eligibility as ruling partners improved.

It is in this context that the proximity or distance of the power base or subversive centre is of the greatest importance. If the State were to break down in the face of revolutionary and criminal violence in the USA, the Communist Party would be in no position to take over because of its feebleness in numbers and the lack of a proximate power base. (Cuba, though under Soviet control, would be inadequate in this sense.) The more likely change would be a military take-over.

In West Germany, the situation was dramatically different. Should the young revolutionaries succeed in the aim enshrined in Rudi Dutschke's slogan, 'The Long March through the Institutions', and so weaken the institutions and the armed forces from within that the Federal government decided to quit NATO, the beneficiaries would not be the Trotskyist Fourth International in Brussels, but the Soviet Union. In such a situation, the Federal German Republic, for all its relative size and wealth, would be ripe for a take-over by the relatively poor and underpopulated German Democratic Republic to the east.

These are, of course, mere hypotheses. But they were not beyond imagining in a world in which the United States had opted for strategic retreat while the Soviet Union was at the height of its expansive policy; and especially in a Europe in which the EEC had yet to unite its foreign and defence policies and lacked credible means of retaliation against the overwhelmingly powerful monolith to the east.

Such, then, was the revolutionary challenge in all its complexity.

Aims and probabilities

The aims of revolutionaries do not necessarily bear more than a slender resemblance to the shape of future events. But it is worth spelling out the aims, because only thus can the nature of the present threat be understood. In 1974, the aims of the Marxists among the revolutionaries were similar but not identical. Thus:

—*The Communists*, if in power, would set up a 'people's republic', initially on the model of the regimes of Russia's European satellites. The democratic parliamentary parties would gradually, or suddenly, be squeezed out of existence. All businesses in private hands—including farms as well as industries, banks, insurance, commerce and the rest—would be nationalised. All power would be concentrated in the hands of the Politburo of the ruling party. A secret police with sweeping and arbitrary powers would be established, and the judiciary would become an 'instrument of the revolution', that is, would be subordinated to the ruling party. The usual liberties would be abolished. Foreign policies would probably be aligned on Moscow's.

—*The Trotskyists*. Although Trotskyist ministers are not unknown in coalition governments and their behaviour is comparatively mild, it is clear from the extensive press and literature of the many violent Trotskyist groups that in the unlikely event of their finding themselves exclusively in power they would do all the things the Communists would do, possibly with greater speed and brutality. They would, however, remain independent of Moscow.

—*The Maoists*. Alignment with Peking would be probable. Otherwise, the various Maoist parties, usually styling themselves 'Communist Party of . . . (Marxist–Leninist)', would do most of the things the Communists would do, but with a far greater emphasis on 'participation' (that is, the forced involvement of the entire population in the political process, with endless indoctrination classes and self-criticism sessions, ubiquitous street committees and other features of the Maoist State).

—*The Anarchists*. Although the prospect of an Anarchist seizure of power is extremely remote, the capacity of Anarchists (such as the Baader–Meinhof gang in Germany) to weaken the State and strain the security services should not be underrated. Most, though not all, active Anarchist groups stemmed from the violent Bakunin stream of Anarchism. They continued to preach the need for self-governing local organisations, such as workers' councils, without a central State authority.

It is as certain as anything in politics can be that the Trotskyists, Maoists and Anarchists, and the many variants upon these basic themes, stand no chance whatever of achieving power in any advanced industrial country. Their capacity, singly or collectively, to weaken the State by damaging the economy and provoking a breakdown of law and order is, however, far from negligible.

I shall be turning in later chapters to the problem of containing this kind of situation in a democratic and pluralist State. What needs to be said at this point is that if it got out of hand—that is, if the government reacted weakly and too late, and a collapse of the State appeared imminent, one of two outcomes was likely. If the local Communist Party was strong, and especially if the country was close to Soviet-controlled territory, it could well take over, perhaps after a brief enjoyment of power by the wilder revolutionaries. More likely, especially if the local Communist Party was weak and if the Soviet power was remote, was a military seizure of power, with the advent of an authoritarian State.

One of the most striking examples of the entire cycle of democracy–violence–breakdown–authoritarian rule is Uruguay, where on 27 June 1973, the President dissolved Congress and the Army took over: the press was muzzled, schools and colleges were closed down, and political meetings were banned.

In the end, then, a revolutionary movement that had appeared to be heading for success had brought, not the revolution but an authoritarian regime; had brought, in fact, what it has become fashionable to call a 'right-wing backlash'.

The French experience in 1968 is illuminating on several counts, not least because it happened in a major European country, a member of the Western Alliance. Groups of student revolutionaries, mostly Maoists and Trotskyists, by rioting of unsurpassed violence, almost forced the resignation of General de Gaulle, in a country that had appeared prosperous and reasonably content with his mildly authoritarian presidential democracy. He was saved by his own will-power, by the readiness of the army to defend the Fifth Republic, and not least, by the refusal of the powerful Communist Party to make common cause with the extreme Left. Supposing, however, that de Gaulle's will or physical strength (at 77) had failed, and he had chosen the easy way out of resigning. The Socialist leader, M. Mitterrand, had already declared his readiness to form a government. But in the circumstances then prevailing, no government of the Left could function without the participation of the Communist Party. The Communists indeed, would have been the senior partners in any ruling coalition. If the riots had continued (as they might, since communist rule was not what the students had in mind), the Communists would have insisted on strong measures. Within months, France would have had a fully communist government and would have denounced the Atlantic Alliance.

Before this had happened, however, the Army, or a part of it, might well have decided to challenge the new government. There would have been no de Gaulle to avert civil war, as in 1958. Would a communist government, thus challenged, appeal to the Soviet Union in the name of the French people? Such questions, though hypothetical, are not wild. It was only by the narrowest of margins that they did not arise in real life.

The possible consequences of revolutionary violence must not, therefore, be ignored, once it has begun, and even if its initial manifestations appear feeble and controllable. If unchecked, its consequences may be either an authoritarian State or a totalist State of the Left, allied with Moscow. Neither would be to the taste of the great majority of citizens, though the former is clearly the more tolerable. For one thing, it is not necessarily permanent. For another, it may leave the majority with the opportunity to lead a tolerably full life, so long as they opt out of politics. The totalist outcome is worse: it is probably irreversible; and it seeks to involve everybody in politics, whether or not that is their wish.

It remains for us, in this section, to consider some of the techniques of revolution used today; and the problems of prevention and repression in the contemporary State.

THREE

TECHNIQUES OF REVOLUTION

The ground covered in this chapter

*Lenin's revolutionary party—Debray and 'spontaneous' revolution—
Mao's doctrine of revolutionary war—special circumstances of China
—Truong Chinh and Vo Nguyen Giap—differences between China and
Vietnam—Guevara, Debray and Marighella—'urban guerrillas'—the
practice of revolutionary war—early signs of insurgency—creation of
subversive apparatus—terrorism, guerrilla war and 'final offensive'—
aspects of terrorism—coercive and disruptive terrorism—a barometer
of support—terrorist failures—successful revolutionary wars: China,
Vietnam, Algeria—psychological causes of defeat—the constitutional
path: the Chilean example*

THERE ARE techniques for demolishing a building, and there are
techniques for demolishing a State. Revolution has become a science,
though it can never be an exact one, just as it is beyond the capacity of
even the most experienced demolition team to calculate exactly and in
advance just where every bit of rubble and speck of dust will land
when bricks and mortar crumble under the bulldozer.

The interaction of theory and technique is a fascinating study in
itself. There are revolutionary textbooks, some of them extremely
influential. Most of the latter were written by successful revolutionaries, and the question that arises is whether they acted out their
theories, or theorised about their actions. The answer can hardly be
straightforward, but it is generally true that the most influential textbooks of revolution were written *after* the event.

The exceptions, however, are of some interest. In his famous
polemic, *What is to be Done?* (published some fifteen years before the
Russian Revolution of 1917), Lenin called for the creation of a
centralised revolutionary party to lead the struggle, and defined the
content of the revolutionary agitation which he saw as essential to
the general breakdown of authority, which he described as the
revolutionary situation. But even Lenin could not foresee the exact

circumstances that would enable him and his small band of fanatics to seize power—not from the Tsarist State, which had already collapsed independently of the Bolsheviks, but from the democratic government of Kerensky. The fact that the communist revolution in Russia actually happened in two stages, however, deeply influenced two generations of more obscure communist theoreticians of revolution. And it was not difficult to see a parallel in the Cuban experience, where an initially non-Marxist revolution turned later in a Marxist direction, though without (as in Russia) a further *coup d'état*.

Another exception (to which I shall return later) was that of the French revolutionary theorist Régis Debray who, inspired by the Cuban experience, sought to provide a theoretical basis for 'spontaneous' revolutions elsewhere. It is relevant to note that his theorising was singularly unsuccessful in terms of practical results.

Among the most successful and influential revolutionaries of our time were the Chinese and Vietnamese Communists, and in both countries, experience preceded theory. By the time Mao Tse-tung published his doctrine in two essays—*Guerrilla Warfare* (1937) and *Strategic Problems of China's Revolutionary War* (1938)—he had already been at war, either with the Nationalist central government or with the Japanese, for about ten years. The China of the 1920s and 1930s, in which he fought, was overwhelmingly a country of peasants, and plagued by warlords and landlords. Moreover, it was, as it remains a land of continental dimensions, over which the central government of Chiang Kai-shek had failed to establish a generally accepted authority. Finally, this vast but, at the time, chaotic country, was the victim, in 1931, and again in 1937, of an unprovoked aggression by Japan's militaristic regime.

Mao, having decided to break with the Marxist–Leninist theory of proletarian revolution, which he rightly judged to be ill-suited to the conditions of a peasant nation, set about organising a peasant revolt. In so doing, he was able to appeal to the peasants' land hunger and need for protection against both the central government and the warlords. Although Chiang Kai-shek had inherited the mantle of the revolutionary Nationalist, Sun Yat-sen, who had overthrown the Chinese monarchy, Mao had no difficulty in representing his administration as feudal and reactionary and later as incurably corrupt. Moreover, Mao could, and did, represent his struggle as a *patriotic* one against the Japanese invaders, while by harassing Chiang's forces, he could divert them from the task of repulsing the Japanese and deny the Nationalists' claims to equally patriotic motives.

In combination, if not singly, all these circumstances made China a very special, indeed a unique, case. But Mao was sufficiently hubristic, or ethnocentric, to suppose that the theories he distilled from this very unusual situation would be universally valid and applicable. He envisaged a protracted war in three stages. During the first, the revolutionary forces would be weak and must preserve their strength, if necessary by retreating. Retreat, indeed, especially in a country as vast as China, led naturally to the second phase: the enemy's lines of communication, by this time, had been stretched to the limit and he had to pause to consolidate his gains. While he was doing this, the revolutionaries would do two things: harass the enemy with guerrilla action, and begin equipping a regular army for the third and final stage—that of the revolutionary final offensive. In this, the enemy is surrounded by a hostile population thoroughly infiltrated by revolutionary guerrillas; his forces are exhausted and demoralised; and the revolutionary army has grown strong enough to move in for the kill.

Mao stipulated a thoroughly politicised army—that is, an army that knew what it was fighting for and was subject to constant ideological discipline through a Soviet-style system of political commissars: the exact opposite of the usual Western army. Although Mao had little to say about communism (the overt appeal, being, as I have mentioned, to patriotism and land hunger), the Communist Party remained firmly in control of the armed forces throughout the struggle despite expedient political alliances with other parties destined for later emasculation (the so-called 'United Front' tactic).

Although the most famous of the Vietnamese revolutionary leaders was Ho Chi Minh, he was not himself a theorist of revolutionary war. The two main theorists (who were also practitioners of the art, or science) were Truong Chinh and Vo Nguyen Giap. Both men adopted Mao's theory, but adapted it with slight modifications to Vietnamese conditions. Truong Chinh (an assumed name meaning 'Long March' in tribute to the legendary trek of the Chinese Communists to the caves of Yenan), in *The Resistance Will Win* (1947), went along with Mao in distinguishing three phases of revolutionary war which, however, he restyled the stages of 'contention', 'equilibrium' and 'general counter-offensive'.

Giap's most important theoretical work is *The War of Liberation and the People's Army*, which appeared in 1950 at the height of the first Indochina war and should not be confused with *People's War, People's Army* (1961), a collection of essays of largely propagandist character. Accepting Mao's three stages of revolutionary war, he elaborated the last. As Giap saw it, four conditions would have to be fulfilled before the final offensive could be launched. The people's army must have established absolute psychological (he called it 'moral') superiority in its own eyes and in those of the people; it must have improved its supplies and, in general, its material resources; the international situation would have to be favourable; and finally, the people's army must have confidence in victory in the face of declining confidence on the enemy side. It will be seen that the first and fourth conditions are virtually the same. The most interesting is the third— the need for an increasingly favourable international situation. Giap did not elaborate the point sufficiently for clarity. He was probably referring to the help which the communist Viet Minh organisation was getting from China and Russia, as well as to international opinion about the French 'colonial war', and indeed to adverse views of the war in France itself. In that sense, this point overlaps with the first condition—absolute 'moral' superiority over the enemy.

There is an important difference here between the Chinese civil war and the first Indochina war. In the latter stages of the Chinese war, the 'international situation' was certainly important to Mao: Japan was being defeated, and Russia intervened at the last moment, making vast quantities of war material available to the Communists in Manchuria. But there is no exact parallel between the Chinese and Vietnamese situations. Mao was fighting both the Japanese and Chiang Kai-shek, who in turn were fighting each other; when Japan was defeated, he went on fighting Chiang. The morale of the Japanese invaders was never an important factor, since morale remained high until the sudden collapse came shortly after the dropping of the atomic bombs on Hiroshima and Nagasaki. In Vietnam, however, the Viet Minh were fighting the French and the French-sponsored Vietnamese government forces. As time went on, declining French morale was a major factor. Criticism of the 'dirty war', of its mounting cost, its 'colonial' character and the methods used—together with the corruption the war had brought in its train, both in Indochina and in France—grew rapidly, especially after the death of General de Lattre, the Commander-in-Chief, early in 1952.

Apart from the Vietnamese adaptations of Mao's theory, the most original contributions to this date have come from Latin America: specifically, from the late Ernesto 'Che' Guevara and his French admirer, Régis Debray; and from the late Carlos Marighella, a Brazilian ex-Communist who left the party and led an 'urban guerrilla' movement.

Generalising from the particular case—as singular in its way as China's—of Fidel Castro's successful challenge to the Batista regime in Cuba, Guevara argued that the orthodox Communists—in Moscow and Peking—were wrong in stipulating that a revolution could succeed only when 'objective' conditions were ripe. The mere fact of fighting, he argued, would create the right conditions for a successful revolution. This was one of the key arguments in Guevara's manual on *Guerrilla War*. Debray, in *Revolution in the Revolution?*, went further still, by rejecting the concept of a united front, and even that of a special leading role for the Communist Party. Until victory had been achieved, he wrote, both the political and military leadership must be vested in one man, and throughout the struggle military priorities must take precedence over politics.

With Marighella and his *Minimanual of the Urban Guerrilla* (1970), we have an arresting attempt to make the strategy of peasant warfare successful by a tactically intermediate phase of urban terrorism. Marighella's originality, however, probably lay in the fact that he put his theories down on paper, for an almost identical combination of tactics and strategy was observable in other places long before the *Minimanual*: in Vietnam during both Indochina wars, in Cyprus during the EOKA troubles of the 1950s, and in Algiers and other towns during the Algerian war, to give only three examples. The catchphrase 'urban guerrillas', which serves the media well, has caught the public imagination, but there is nothing particularly new about the phenomenon, except to the extent that in some countries of the Third World, especially in Latin America, the increasing relative affluence of the cities has drawn to their outskirts a vast population of landless peasants and workless labourers, who live in shanty towns of their own making, creating explosive social problems that lend themselves to revolutionary exploitation.

Nor was Marighella's strategy all that different from Mao's or Giap's, in that he envisaged a war in three phases: the formation of cadres and the collection of supplies (what, on the side of authority, would be called the creation of a 'subversive apparatus'); guerrilla operations; and at last a war of movement with the countryside encircling the towns. In common with other Latin American revolutionaries, however, Marighella was soon disabused of his initial assumption that the peasants wanted the intellectuals to liberate them. In the face of their apathy, he sought to create the conditions for a civil war by launching a campaign of urban terrorism that would, he reasoned, provoke an excessive reaction on the part of the authorities, thus alienating moderate opinion, which would rally to his support. That his campaign did provoke a reaction which many would consider excessive is true enough; that many moderate intellectuals were revolted by official security measures and supported his urban guerrillas is also true; but in the end, the military regime (which had seized power in 1964) was strengthened, the guerrillas were smashed, and Marighella himself was killed in a street ambush in November 1969.

I do not propose to pay much further attention to theories of revolution and of revolutionary war, *per se*. Although such theories are important as symbols and rallying points of youthful protest, they differ markedly from the actual practice of their exponents, and the practice is undoubtedly more important than the theory. Although time and history outlive men, so that what is true today is not necessarily true at some future point in time, it is fair to say now, in the mid-1970s, that as theorists Guevara, Debray and Marighella failed utterly, Guevara and Marighella, however (though not Debray), had some highly practical things to say to aspirant revolutionaries about methods and techniques. Marighella in particular wrote with chilling precision about the choice and use of firearms and there was evidence that his advice had been heeded as far away as Northern Ireland.

Let us look, then, at what actually happens in a revolutionary war, as distinct from what the theoreticians claim or advocate. In this respect, Marighella, minor figure though he is, shares with the far greater figure of Lenin a quality of cynical candour which Mao, Giap and Chinh totally lack. Lenin took no trouble at all to conceal from the 'bourgeois', 'capitalists' and 'imperialists' of the world the lurid fate that he reserved for them. This openness was the expression of the boundless contempt he felt for their stupidity (and who, in the euphoria of *détente* and East–West trade in the mid-1970s, can sensibly hold him to be wrong?). He made no secret of his advocacy of a tightly-controlled revolutionary party; nor did Marighella hide his view that the first thing revolutionaries should do was to train an élite and make sure it had arms.

The nearest Mao Tse-tung came to utter candour was in his dictum that 'power grows out of the barrel of the gun'. But neither he nor his Vietnamese disciples said much about organisation, or about the need that might arise to terrorise people into conformity and obedience. (It is true, however, that because of the uniquely favourable circumstances I have mentioned, there was relatively little *need* for terrorism of ordinary people during China's long civil war than in any other comparable situation in contemporary history. This was signally untrue of Vietnam, but the Vietnamese theorists conceal their cruelty. Here again, Marighella was candid, at least to the extent of calling for 'death for spies', just as Grivas, the right-wing Greek Cypriot terrorist, ran a 'death for traitors' campaign.)

I have already (in Part I, 2) defined revolutionary war at some length, and I shall not repeat the definition here, except to say that it aims at the total destruction of the environment in which the 'enemy' —the State—operates. It may be more useful, at this point, to switch the perspective, and look at the phenomenon from the standpoint of those who suffer under revolutionary war—the public, that is, the people in the true (as distinct from the revolutionary) sense, or those who are required to cope with it: the authorities and the security forces.

From this antithetical standpoint, everything looks curiously different. At first, indeed, there may be nothing at all to see. If the rebels are expert conspirators, even the security service—assuming the threatened country has one—may be unaware of what is happening. The first thing the police and the public may hear about could be the theft of pharmaceutical stores, or of supplies of gelignite from some warehouse. A bank or two may be held up and the fact that the motive may have been ultimately political could remain unknown, perhaps for months. At some later stage, a police station or two might be raided for any firearms kept there. A high school teacher or a university lecturer may notice that one or two students, very likely reading for a degree in Politics or Sociology, have absented themselves without a convincing explanation. Later on, one of them may be seen, or caught, distributing anti-government pamphlets.

In the language of counter-insurgency experts—a new breed of men, made necessary by the prevalence of situations that call for their skills—any one of these incidents may (or may not) be an 'indicator' of an impending insurgency. The raid on a police station and the distributing of 'subversive' leaflets probably indicate that the organisation is fairly far advanced.

This first, or invisible, phase of an insurgency is in fact extraordinarily difficult to detect. Many countries are simply not geared to face this kind of situation. A police force trained, as is proper, to cope with crime, including violent crime, is not necessarily equipped to sense an impending political explosion; still less to suppress it when it has broken out and its revolutionary character has become clear to all. More sophisticated countries may have a first-class security service —an MI-5, a *Direction de la Surveillance du Territoire*, a Federal

Bureau of Investigation—but the prevailing spirit of tolerance may inhibit action until it is dangerously late.

Authoritarian States are better equipped than pluralist ones to deal with this kind of internal threat but by no means immune to it. Only totalist States, by virtue of their all-pervasive police surveillance, may be considered to have total immunity.

But what, in fact, are the revolutionaries doing during the invisible preparatory phase of their insurgency? If they are serious revolutionaries and mentally steeled for the long haul, they are creating a *subversive apparatus*—essentially, a clandestine network of activists and sympathisers. The activists may be grouped into secret cells, only the leader of which knowing the identities of the other members. Sympathisers there must be, to provide space and facilities for training in terrorism, sabotage and guerrilla war, to carry messages, to guarantee food supplies and shelter, to organise rudimentary hospitals. Journalists of the written or spoken word, or of the fleeting image, must be enlisted, and well-placed informants who will keep the revolutionaries in the picture about the plans and movements of the security forces. If opposition parties are legal, the rebel movement, even if it is itself outlawed, will try to recruit covert supporters among them, to make speeches tending to present the revolutionaries in a good light, or to ventilate the real or supposed grievances of the oppressed, and to discredit the government's attempts to deal with them.

The invisible phase may take months or even years. When the preparatory work is well advanced, and if it has escaped destruction, if not detection, by the security forces, Phase 2 will begin. In practice, of course, things are less systematic than this passage may make them sound. The leadership does not decide that Phase 1 is over and declare Phase 2 open. Rather, when the leaders feel their movement has adequate supplies of arms, ammunition and medicaments, access to food and information, and a well-knit organisation, it will begin, at first on a small scale and later, if successful, at an accelerated pace, to stage incidents of terrorism. Phase 2 may be lengthy; if it is also successful, it may be followed by Phase 3—guerrilla war—and if that too is successful, the insurgency may graduate to the final phase of outright war, with or without international complications, culminating in a final offensive and the collapse of the central administration.

In practice, extraordinarily few insurgencies ever reach this final phase, beloved of the theorists and advocates of revolutionary war. Of all the hundreds since China's 'patriotic war', only three may be said to have been at least partially successful, apart from China's.

Two of these were the first and second Indochina wars, and the third was the Algerian war. In each, the 'enemy' was an alien colonial power, and in each (despite the defeat of the French at Dien Bien Phu in 1954, which was not in itself militarily decisive), the victory of the rebel side (a partial one in Indochina) was due to the collapse of the authorities' will to fight on. (Cuba is sometimes cited as a further example of success for a revolutionary insurgency, but that is misleading: the corrupt Batista dictatorship collapsed in Cuba, giving Fidel Castro and his rather underworked guerrillas a walkover into Havana.) In most insurgencies, the rebels remain 'stuck' in Phase 2, and even if they successfully launch guerrilla warfare, they may be driven back from time to time to terrorist tactics.

Terrorism, then, is a constant of revolutionary wars, or wars of 'national liberation', and is so even if the revolutionaries style themselves 'freedom fighters' or use other similarly euphemistic designations. A child who has a leg blown off by a bomb is no less injured if the man who threw or deposited it claims to be fighting for 'the people'. By its nature, terrorism is an emotive subject, and whenever a terrorist campaign is in progress, such expressions as 'senseless terrorism' or 'apparently motiveless violence' are invariably heard or seen. This is understandable, since the minds of ordinary people are profoundly shocked and disturbed by terrorism and recoil from attempts to understand it.

Yet terrorism, except when it is the work of the demented, is never 'senseless' or without motive. The most satisfactory way of explaining terrorism is by considering the purposes for which it is used; for the purposes in turn determine the techniques selected. The most important distinction to be made is between *disruptive* and *coercive* terrorism (although in practice there is inevitably some overlapping between the two, as terrorists do not necessarily ask themselves such semantic questions before they toss a bomb or kidnap a diplomat).

The aims of *disruptive terrorism* include the following:

—To gain publicity for the movement, and arouse admiration and emulation.
—To secure funds and build up the movement's morale and prestige.
—To discredit and demoralise the authorities.
—To provoke the authorities into taking excessively harsh repressive measures, likely to alienate the population and force a rising spiral of official expenditure in arms, lives and money, resulting in public clamour for the abandonment of counter-action.

Coercive terrorism complements the disruptive kind, by:

—Demoralising the civil population, weakening its confidence in the central authority, and instilling fear of the revolutionary movement.

—Making an example of selected victims, by torture and/or death, to enforce obedience to the leadership of the movement.

I have not listed these purposes in any special order of either chronology or importance. When terrorism starts, the movement may be seeking both to disrupt normal life, to harass, stretch and discredit the authorities, and to bring waverers to heel. The FLN terrorists of Algeria tortured the unwilling or the 'traitors' with red-hot pokers or boiling water poured from a kettle. Mutilation, too, was much favoured, nose or tongue, lips, ears or sexual parts being cut off by knife. The Vietnamese Communists frequently disembowelled their selected victims. The IRA, relatively gentle, chose to beat those selected for punishment, or tar and feather them; in worse cases, they shot their victims through the knee-caps.

When Arab terrorists of the so-called Black September group murdered eleven Israeli athletes during the Twentieth Olympic Games at Munich in September 1972, they gained world-wide publicity. True, their deed provoked widespread horror and revulsion, but among other Arabs, especially the young they sought to influence, the Munich massacre aroused admiration for the daring and self-sacrificial courage of the terrorists. The wave of kidnappings of diplomats or businessmen, especially in Latin America, during the early 1970s, not only served publicity ends, but also swelled the coffers of the revolutionary movements, while discrediting governments shown to be incapable of protecting the people in their care.

It is worth pointing out that although terrorism is normally a central feature of revolutionary war, it has also been used by many groups or movements that do not practise anything recognisable as revolutionary war. For example, the explosions perpetrated by such contemporary anarchist groups as the Baader–Meinhof gang in Germany or the Angry Brigade in England did not, as far as can be discerned, constitute the preliminary phase of a carefully planned campaign likely to lead to the destruction of the State, although this Utopian aim may have been in the backs of the minds of the terrorists. Violence, in a sense, became an end in itself, and even a way of life.

Similarly, although revolutionary war normally (and certainly in theory) comprises a guerrilla phase, the terms 'revolutionary war' and 'guerrilla war' are not, as is often thought, synonymous. The scope of the former is infinitely wider than of the latter. Guerrilla or partisan war is defensive and tactical. It involves the harassment of regulars. It may be nationalistic or patriotic, but it is not necessarily political. Revolutionary war, on the other hand is essentially political and social. It may, during certain phases, involve guerrilla action but its aims are vastly more ambitious than those of partisan war. It may, as in China, Vietnam and Algeria, comprise an appeal to patriotism against a foreign aggressor or occupier, but the aims transcend 'liberation' in the conventional sense.

It is also worth noting that although revolutionary war is essentially a Communist doctrine (and more precisely a Sino-Vietnamese one, with the Latin American deviations as the inevitable heresies), it has been practised by non-communists, such as the Algerian FLN, who learned it from the Viet Minh in Indochina, and by the IRA Provisionals who picked up tips wherever they could.

Since so much has been written on guerrilla war and its tactics and techniques, I do not propose to enter into this aspect of the subject here. Instead, I return to terrorism with a few further observations.

One is that terrorism is *a barometer of revolutionary success*. Being, by common consent, a weapon of the weak, it is extensively used in the initial stages, when the movement is at its weakest; its abandonment or relaxation may denote increasing strength and confidence; and reversion to it probably indicates declining strength, and is likely to follow military defeats.

Similarly—and this second observation is the converse of the first—terrorism is also a fairly precise indicator of public support or its absence. In situations where the revolutionaries find it necessary to kill more people on their own side than on the enemy side, it must be presumed either that their cause is widely opposed or that, at least, it leaves the population indifferent. When writing my first book on this general subject, my researches yielded the interesting ratio of 3:2, or three-fifths: that is, of every five victims of terrorism, three belonged to the side of the terrorists, and only two to the enemy side. The arresting point is that this ratio was valid in such widely different situations as Cochinchina, Malaya, Kenya and Cyprus, during specific periods under review. I should add that when and if such situations graduate from terrorism to guerrilla war or beyond (that is, from Phase 2 to Phases 3 and 4), the statistics no longer hold good, although the coercive principle is likely to reassert itself in the event of a reversion to terrorism.

How effective is terrorism? A general conclusion from the facts of the post-war period was that terrorism is a useful auxiliary weapon rather than a decisive one. It may even be counter-productive, if it goes on too long, by sickening and alienating the population, who may turn to the authorities for protection. This was true of Algiers in 1957. It is clear, however, that where the population has been cowed—that is, in the strict sense, 'terrorised'—by the revolutionaries, it will turn to the authorities only if the security forces begin to register successes. And as such successes are heavily dependent on information from the population, a measure of luck may be necessary—in the form, for instance, of tactical errors or indiscretions on the terrorist side—before the tide begins to turn. On the other hand, in situations where support for the insurgents is virtually total (as among the Jewish population of Palestine before the creation of Israel, and among the Egyptians in the Suez Canal Zone in the 1950s), and a 'Death to Traitors' campaign is therefore unnecessary, terrorism directed solely against an occupying power can be devastatingly effective.

The general truth of these propositions is confirmed by recent experience. Of contemporary outbreaks of terrorism in places as widespread as India, Indonesia, Ceylon, Ulster, West Germany, Italy, Turkey, Uruguay, Brazil, Peru and many more, none has brought decisive results for the terrorists. Most have been defeated, though some lingered on inconclusively. In some cases, (Brazil, Uruguay, Turkey) the outcome was authoritarian rule. Nor did success in any measurable sense other than strictly local and temporary, mark the efforts of the new breed of 'transnational terrorists'—that is, of the groups operating in countries not their own with the help of similar groups in scattered places. In such conditions, and with the aid of jet travel and transistorised technology, spectacular deeds can be accomplished. But they could not, in the nature of things, be decisive, since the targets (world Jewry, capitalism, imperialism) were too vague, diffuse and scattered to allow of a conclusive concentration of effort on key points. It is possible by terrorism to accomplish the destruction of a State; it is possible to weaken the pluralist way of life, but not to bring about the simultaneous downfall of the centres of non-communist industrial society as a whole.

In the light of the general rule of terrorist failure, it is worth looking more closely at the reasons for the few successes of revolutionary war. The special conditions of the Chinese civil war make it so atypical an example that there are no useful lessons to be derived from it in this context. The first and second Indochina wars and Algeria, however, do provide lessons that are valid in other cases and places. It is an arresting point that the terrorist side in both Indochina wars fulfilled some, but only some, of their war aims. Throughout the period spanning the two Indochina wars (1946–73), and indeed ever since the creation in 1930 of the Communist Party of Indochina, the ultimate war aim of the Vietnamese Communists was to gain sovereign control not only over Vietnam, but also over the other components of the French empire in Indochina: Cambodia and Laos. The more limited and specific aims of the first Indochina war were: to evict the French; and to gain power in the whole of Vietnam. The first of these aims was fully achieved in 1954; the second, only partially, in the sense that the southern half of Vietnam remained out of communist hands.

The second Indochina war was inherent in this partial failure, and this time the specific and limited war aims were: to get rid of the Americans; and to bring the south under Communist control. Again, the first aim was achieved, but the second remained elusive. The cease-fire agreement of 27 January 1973 provided for the withdrawal of the United States forces; but the Communists, although they had proclaimed a 'Provisional Revolutionary Government' in South Vietnam, controlled only sparsely populated territory and were not in power in Saigon. The war went on.

It is arguable, therefore, that the Algerian war was the only *completely* successful application of the theory of revolutionary war, yielding in the end a regime of the extreme Left that was nevertheless not, in the orthodox sense, Communist, and transferring sovereignty from France to the revolutionaries.

The relevant point, however, is that in all three cases, the alien power (termed 'colonialist' or 'imperialist') was forced to withdraw, and *in none was the withdrawal the consequence of military defeat*. In all three cases, in fact, the withdrawal was due to psychological factors: the war weariness, the failure of will, the unwillingness to fight apparently interminable wars. And in each instance, this weariness, this failure, this unwillingness, were due to what I have called the rising spiral of expenditure ('raising the cost of the war'), and the mobilisation of public opinion against the war through the protest movement (not necessarily initiated, but generously supported, by the international communist movement and the communist powers) and international diplomatic pressures, channelled *inter alia* through that egregious body, the UN. In all three cases, the revolutionaries were helped in that they could claim to be fighting against an alien power (an advantage denied to them in Indochina after the withdrawal of both the French and the Americans). The Chinese Communists had a similar advantage in the presence of the transgressing Japanese. In all the purely indigenous cases on record, the revolutionaries have been either contained or defeated.

The constitutional path

By its nature, political violence commands attention and attracts the headlines. But in a well-organised modern State, with vast power at its command, violence is not automatically the best way of achieving a revolution. The Russians—or more precisely, the group of leading Communists who supported the then boss of the ruling party in the Soviet Union, Khrushchev—decided in 1956 to abandon the thitherto sacrosanct Leninist principle of the inevitability of violence in the revolutionary process. He did not, as is sometimes mistakenly assumed, renounce revolutionary violence altogether; he merely decreed that in certain circumstances, the transition to socialism might be achieved by parliamentary means. This widening of revolutionary options was to remain one of the enduring points at issue between Moscow and Peking.

There is some evidence that when Khrushchev announced this change of doctrine—which came as a traumatic shock to many Communists in different countries—he was much under the influence of the late Palmiro Togliatti, the Italian Communist leader, who could see that in his country at least, the mass party he led stood a good chance, in the long run, of achieving power by constitutional means, but risked losing all if it provoked repression by going for power through violence. Togliatti was right, and Khrushchev was right to listen to him.

The 'constitutional path' or road to power means, then, keeping within the law and constitution of the country. It may also mean taking advantage of every possible loophole within the law. And politically, it implies an alliance of convenience between the local Communist Party and other parties left of centre in the imaginary political spectrum. Where a Communist Party is numerically too small and of insufficient electoral appeal (as in Britain or the USA), however, 'the constitutional path' means principally infiltrating a wide range of 'front' organisations, placing key men in the media or in the factories, having friends in parliament and so forth; so that at all times, communist views are expressed not only by men and women carrying party membership cards but by others, preferably no further to the left than is implied by the profession of vaguely liberal or progressive views on such subjects as Vietnam or the Portuguese territories in Africa.

There are thus two kinds of 'front' involved: the 'united front' or 'popular front', meaning an electoral alliance or governing coalition; and the 'front organisation', purporting to stand for 'peace' or to represent trade unions, or women, or youth, or any of a wide variety of opinion groups, which the Communists control but in which they are not necessarily in a majority.

The most illuminating recent example of the 'front' technique in an attempt to take over a normally democratic and pluralistic State was that of Chile. The Chilean presidential elections of 1970 brought a Socialist President (Salvador Allende) to power on a minority vote of 36 per cent in a three-cornered contest. There were six parties in the winning electoral coalition (*Unidad Popular*, or Popular Unity), including the large and well-disciplined Communist Party and the revolutionary extreme Left (*Movimiento de la Izquierda Revolucionaria or MIR*). Politically, by the conventional measuring rule of Left and Right, Allende's own Socialist Party stood to the left of the Communists and indeed included an extreme left wing, under Senator Carlos Altamirano, that favoured revolutionary violence.

At no time in Chile's history had the Communists won more than 16 per cent of electoral votes. But as their share of the 1970 bargain, they were given the ministries of Labour and Finance; the ministry of Economics went to an independent Marxist, Pedro Vuskovic, who worked closely with the Communist central committee although claiming not to be a party member.

I have termed the communist strategy for revolution in Chile the 'Santiago model',[1] as distinct from, say, the Prague model (1948) or the Peking model (1949). The party moved with extraordinary swiftness to gain control over the economy by forcing the private sector out of business. The main weapon used by the Communists was a 1933 law, previously invoked only in exceptional cases, which provided for the appointment of an official administrator—an *interventor*—in businesses that could be shown to be losing money. Three techniques were used to force businesses to show a loss and 'justify' the use of the 1933 law.

One was the seizure of factories by the workers, who locked the management out; after a week or so, the business was assumed to be 'in recess' and an *interventor* was appointed. This technique was

[1] In an article issued in London by Forum World Features on 30 Jan. 1971.

facilitated by the fact that the Communists controlled not only the Ministry of Labour (which refrained from normal arbitration) but 80 per cent of organised labour through the main trade union organisation, the *Central Unica de Trabajadores*.

Another technique consisted of sending revenue auditors and inspectors to investigate banks and businesses. Any irregularities discovered, even if of a purely technical nature, provided a pretext for the appointment of an *interventor*. A longer-term technique was available through the Finance Ministry's fiscal powers and control of prices and incomes. For instance, at the outset all firms were ordered to grant an immediate rise equivalent to the previous year's inflationary rise in the cost-of-living index—36 per cent. At the same time, all prices were frozen. The effect was to drive many small firms out of business; larger firms held on longer. On the fiscal side, 21 new taxes were imposed, designed primarily to finance a projected increase of 33 per cent in State expenditure.

With these drastic measures went an officially encouraged breakdown of law and order. Soon after his election, the President banned the use of force by the security forces, dissolved the riot police (*Grupo Móvil*) and released MIR terrorists who had been gaoled under the previous (Christian Democratic) administration. Incredibly, the released *Miristas* were later formed into a Palace Guard for the protection of the President.

The President also encouraged, or tolerated, large-scale seizures of land, especially in the southern province of Cautín, where the Minister of Agriculture, Jacques Chonchol, trained in Cuba though a former Christian Democrat, worked closely with the MIR in the organisation of strictly illegal land grabs. Not unnaturally, farmers dispossessed or threatened with dispossession organised their own resistance movement, and an incipient civil war developed, for on the other side, guerrilla training camps were set up. Improbable though it may sound, training facilities for Altamirano's Socialist extremists were provided by the Cubans and North Koreans, and for the Miristas by the Soviet KGB.[2] Indeed, Chile became a major subversive centre and place of refuge for revolutionaries from all over Latin America. The new Cuban embassy's personnel largely consisted of members of the Soviet-controlled *Dirección General de Inteligencia* or of Fidel Castro's rival *Dirección de Liberación Nacional*.

It should not be thought that the Chilean Communist Party ap-

[2] See Brian Crozier, *Soviet Pressures in the Caribbean* (*Conflict Studies* No. 35, London, May 1973).

proved of such developments, or that they were insincere in their frequent denunciations of the MIR's 'left-wing adventurism'; still less that they were kept informed of the clandestine Soviet role in the training or financing of extremist groups. From all that is known of Soviet objectives in Cuba and Latin America as a whole, it must be inferred that the Russians aimed at bringing the wilder elements in Chile under their control. If so, however, they were signally unsuccessful. In pressing for the rapid seizure of the economy and the creation of mass support for their work, the Communists were strictly following Moscow's line of 'the constitutional road to power'. In the end, the activities of the MIR, and of Altamirano's extremists, together with President Allende's tolerant irresponsibility, brought to nought the highly skilled strategy of the Communists. The strategy itself was not unintelligent; but it demanded order and discipline, not revolutionary excesses.

As inflation tightened its grip on the economy, household items became scarcer and queues lengthened. Strikes that had not been planned by the Communist ministries took their toll, the most damaging of them, in the State-owned copper mines, from 19 April 1973 costing the country about $1 million a day. Clashes between activists of the Right and Left became more frequent.

Seeking both to reassure the unenthusiastic and to remove temptation from the normally non-political armed forces, Allende brought some high-ranking officers into his government—a move which the Communists strongly advocated. But in the end, the armed forces, finding that they were being made to share the blame for the descent into anarchy, withdrew. On 11 September 1973, a four-man *junta* representing the army, the navy, the air force and the para-military *Carabineros*, seized power. Allende lost his life, probably by his own hand. Marxists of all shades became hunted men and on being found, many were shot.

The collapse of the Allende experiment in blood and tears held interesting lessons both for Communist parties everywhere and for upholders of parliamentary democracy. For Marxists, the lesson appeared to be that the 'constitutional road to power' was less promising than it had seemed. The experiment might well have worked if the disciplined Communists had been allied only with reasonably well-controlled Socialists, but from the start the extreme Left had been out of control and its violence precipitated counter-violence from the Right. Perhaps after all, Lenin had been proved right in that those with interests to defend were going to defend them. From a Marxist–Leninist standpoint, the left-wing adventurism of the *Miristas* and the Altamirano Socialists wrecked the experiment. Lenin had always maintained that there could be no revolution without violence, and he was probably right; but *Mirista* violence was the wrong kind. What was needed was the controlled violence of the vanguard party, then of the State once the Communists had gained control. But that was not the way things worked out.

From a democratic standpoint, there was one major lesson to be drawn (although public opinion in Europe, whether because it was ill-informed, or because it allowed its hatred of military intervention to blind it to the facts, was curiously unwilling to draw it): that Marxism is incompatible with democratic pluralism. It should not be forgotten that Allende had come to power on a minority vote. He had a mandate to take office as President, but none to impose Marxism upon an unwilling majority. From the beginning, he had strained even the letter of the law, with his harassment of private business and above all of the press and other media. He had sought to bring down the long-established conservative newspaper *El Mercurio*, by depriving it of government advertising, by seeking to divide management and workers, by squeezing newsprint supplies, by continuous prying and searching for evidence to justify criminal charges. All congressional attempts to challenge the legality of Allende's actions through the *Contraloría* (the highest court of appeal) and the Supreme Court were vetoed or ignored. Nor would the President, at any stage, act to restrain the arbitrary violence of the extreme Left. The image of a 'democratic socialist' experiment in Chile was a myth.[3]

[3] For a full account of the Allende regime, see Robert Moss, *Chile's Marxist Experiment* (London, 1973).

FOUR

CONFLICT AND
THE CONTEMPORARY STATE, I

PREVENTION

The ground covered in this chapter

Good and bad government—the prevention of conflict—three post-war examples: France, Formosa and Britain—early warning signals and indicators of insurgency—description of indicators: theft of explosives and medical supplies, revolutionary talk, temporary disappearance of students or lecturers, etc.—early warning signals: presence of revolutionaries or their journeys—Ho Chi Minh and Belkacem Krim—Paris 1968—transitional terrorism—sins of omission and commission in Ireland

GOOD GOVERNMENT prevents conflict; bad government fosters it. Strong government discourages conflict; weak government makes it inevitable. Totally repressive government—for example, Stalin's—makes dissent almost impossible, since any sign of it is continually and ruthlessly suppressed. The issue of dissent, including revolutionary dissent, is therefore a more lively one in democratic and pluralist contexts than in others, and in this chapter and the next I concentrate upon such contexts.

Can conflict be prevented? The question, though fascinating, is by definition unanswerable, since it is impossible to know for certain that a situation that seemed to be working up to a climax and was then defused would in fact have led to uncontrollable violence if the right measures had not been taken in time. Some possible examples do suggest themselves, however. I have in mind the situations in France, Formosa (Taiwan) and Britain at the end of the Second World War. (I place Britain last, not because it was less important than the other two, but because the situation there was certainly not as explosive as in France or Formosa.)

Allowing for considerable differences of degree, the situation in France and Britain were in some respects similar. Both had emerged from war and deprivation; in both, public opinion had moved sharply to the left; and popular feeling on both sides of the Channel was ready to blame Conservative policies in the 1930s for the misfortunes and sufferings that had followed. There, I think, the comparison ended. In fighting terms, the French had had a comparatively short and easy war, but France, unlike Britain, had been occupied by an enemy who at first behaved relatively well (in comparison with his behaviour in Eastern Europe), but whose rule became progressively harsher as the war years went on. The Third Republic had collapsed with the humiliation of defeat. The war-time Vichy regime was discredited, and it too had fallen.

De Gaulle's Provisional Government was back in the seat of power —Paris—and the Free French forces had liberated the capital. But de Gaulle had not yet secured international recognition, and in France his authority was powerfully challenged by the Communists, who dominated the Resistance in several regions. Indeed, they were planning an insurrection in Paris, while a number of provincial cities were cut off from the capital and its authority. The Gaullist authorities had not yet had time to assert themselves; in many places, the local leader of the Communist-controlled Partisans carried more weight than the officially appointed local Commissioners of the Republic. Collaborators or 'class enemies' were being tortured and executed. Boldly, de Gaulle had declared the National Council of the Resistance dissolved, but so perilous was the situation that he had no confidence of being able to maintain order, and appealed to General Eisenhower, the Allied commander-in-chief, to lend him a couple of American divisions. These the supreme commander could not spare, but he agreed that two of the American divisions then on their way to the front would take part in a march-past on the Champs-Elysées, in the presence of General de Gaulle.

All this happened in a few tense days at the end of August 1944. By sheer authority and personality, de Gaulle saved the situation. He followed up his Parisian victory with repeated trips to the provinces, where he renewed his personal triumph.

Two other things helped him, however. One was a deal he made with Stalin, the Soviet dictator, to allow the former leader of the French Communist Party, Maurice Thorez, who had spent the war years in Moscow after deserting from the French Army, to return to Paris under a guaranteed immunity. In return, Stalin ordered the French Communists (as he then had the power to do) to respect the General's authority and abandon their revolutionary plans. Thorez fell in with this scheme without the slightest difficulty, since it enabled him to re-assert his own authority over the Communist Party, which had come to follow other leaders during the Resistance days.

The other element in this situation is of more direct relevance to this theory of conflict. Contrary to popular legend at that time, de Gaulle was in no sense a figure of the political Right. During the war, he had gained the confidence of the Resistance, including the Communists but with special reference to the important Socialist group, by pledging himself to introduce a broadly socialist programme of reforms after the liberation of France. In so doing, he was simply recognising political realities. For the discredited and fallen Vichy regime was identified with 'big business', and the Resistance with the parties of the Left.

Generally speaking, de Gaulle kept his pledges, by creating a French Welfare State, and nationalising the *Banque de France* and various credit institutions, and the sources of energy: coal, gas and electricity. The great State-controlled airline, Air France, owed its existence to this socialist programme.

I am not here concerned with absolute judgments on the value o these reforms. I simply record my view that if such measures had not been adopted, France might well have become a communist country within a year or two of the liberation.

Then as now, an important political difference between France and Britain was that the British Communist Party was relatively very weak. Nor did the government of Clement Attlee, which replaced Winston Churchill's wartime coalition, face an insurrectionary situation in a liberated capital. There is no doubt, however, that the Labour Party's victory at the polls in 1945 reflected a deep popular wave in favour of socialist reform. The Conservative Party, which had ruled England for so many years before the outbreak of war, was held to blame for many recent misfortunes: the Baldwin government was charged with culpable failure to prepare for war; and the Chamberlain government for appeasing Hitler and Mussolini. By association, 'capitalism' was widely held to share the Conservative discredit.

Many British workers had emerged from the depression and unemployment to see the country heading for war and to serve in the armed forces. The socialist *Daily Mirror* had become the Forces' favourite, and played a leading part in bringing Attlee his over-whelming victory and defeating Churchill, despite his overwhelming prestige and personal popularity, because he happened to be the leader of the Conservative Party. And Attlee responded to the public mood by giving the British what they so clearly wanted: a Welfare State and massive doses of nationalisation.

Again, I am not here concerned with the intrinsic merits or defects of Attlee's programme. I simply record the view that if his government had failed to do what in fact it did, it would probably have faced grave social disorders in the ensuing years. Instead, the war-weary British people settled down to the austerities of peace in a remarkably pacific mood, and the country entered a prolonged period of social calm.

Although the circumstances of the Formosan experience were so different, the situation that emerged was not in all respects dissimilar from the European examples I have given. Under the Cairo and Potsdam Declarations, it had been agreed that Chiang Kai-shek's National government should restore China's sovereignty over the island, which had been under Japanese occupation for half a century. And indeed, the National government took over Formosa immediately after the Japanese surrender on 15 August 1945. General Ch'en Yi was appointed 'Administrator-General and concurrently Supreme Commander in Taiwan Province'—Formosa being regarded as simply an overseas province of China proper.

The Nationalists were greeted as liberators, and in the prevailing euphoria could have had the loyalty of the Taiwanese for the asking. But Ch'en Yi, a brutal and insensitive man, chose to treat them as though they were a conquered people. Not unnaturally, the local mood changed. The Nationalists systematically looted the wealth of Formosa; output plummeted; and rice was short in the markets and shops. Health and education were neglected. To compound these sources of grievance, Ch'en Yi announced that the new Chinese constitution would not apply to Formosa until the end of 1949.

An ugly incident in which a woman was killed for hawking cigarettes on which the tobacco monopoly tax had not been paid sparked an orderly demonstration by the Formosans in February 1947. The Nationalist police opened fire, and the demonstration turned into a riot, in which the Formosans attacked Chinese from the mainland. An apparent peace was restored when Ch'en Yi met representatives of the Formosans and agreed to concede their demands for certain reforms. In return the Formosans ceased their riotous violence. But

Ch'en Yi had no intention of sticking to his side of the bargain. He sent to China for reinforcements, and when they arrived he broke his word and ordered widespread massacres. At least 10,000 Formosans were killed, including many of their leaders. Some estimates range much higher. When the American Embassy in Chungking protested, Chiang Kai-shek recalled General Ch'en Yi, and declared his 'pacification'—the current euphorism for the massacres—to be over. Formosa was made one of the thirty-five provinces of China and the local inhabitants (the great majority of whom were ethnically Chinese) were given a share in the administration of the province.

The situation calmed down, but not for long. Towards the end of 1948, it was becoming clear to Chiang Kai-shek that his forces were heading for defeat at the hands of the Communists in China's civil war. Faced with eviction from the mainland, Chiang sent his closest associate, General Ch'en Ch'eng to the island to take over control. As soon as he arrived, Ch'en Ch'eng re-established martial law. The island was teeming, or thought to be teeming, with Communist sympathisers. A further wave of arrests and executions followed.

A year later, in the chaotic and humiliating days of December 1949, the government of the Republic of China began to function on Formosa. Constitutionally, it was, and remained, a confusing situation. For on top of the local Provincial Government, the Chinese Central Government (in theory responsible for the whole of China) asserted its authority. Nearly a million civilians and more than half a million troops came over. At that time, the island—about half the size of Scotland, or about the size of the American State of Maryland—had a population of about 8 million.

Against this discouraging background, and in a mood of bitter self-analysis, the Generalissimo pondered the reasons for his defeat. Rather late in the day, he admitted to himself that his ruling Kuomintang party had not paid enough attention to the welfare of the people, and that corrupt officials had been more concerned with lining their pockets than with fighting inflation. Throughout the civil war, Chiang had made the profound error of thinking of China's problems and his own in strictly military terms. And now, from the mainland, came disturbing news of a massive land reform programme, carried out with ruthless precision but in the end successfully—at least from the standpoint of the Communist leadership, headed by Mao Tse-tung. Chiang had lost the mainland, although he could not bring himself to admit that the loss might be more than temporary. But if he were ever to regain the mainland, he would have to secure his Formosan base. And to do this, the first essential was to gain the confidence of the Formosan people.

Greatly helped, it is true, by massive American economic aid, the Nationalist government embarked on a sweeping programme of reforms and economic development. By far the most important aspect of these reforms, however, was an extraordinarily successful land reform programme. Land rents and prices were drastically lowered, government-owned lands were sold on easy terms to the tenants who were working them. The final phase, the government imposed limits on the acreage of land that could be owned, then purchased the excess and sold it to the tenants. An original feature of the programme was that land was not expropriated: by an ingenious device, the landowners were in effect turned into capitalists, by being compensated in industrial shares and farm commodities. By 1953, when the programme ended, some 75 per cent of the peasants owned the land they tilled. From that time forward, the Nationalist hold upon Formosa was secure. Rebellion had been averted.

It is obviously not easy to draw firm conclusions from these examples. The British and French cases might suggest that socialism was the way to avert revolution. But the Formosan example, despite the inevitable government intervention, would suggest the opposite. The long-term outcome of the reforms of the Nationalist administration of the island between 1949 and 1953 was a booming economy and a showpiece for Chinese capitalism and native ingenuity. There was one thing in common between the three examples given, however: in all three, a situation of actual or incipient social unrest was averted by reforms. Not all governments are intelligent enough to see where the trouble lies, sensitive enough to gauge the public temper, or courageous enough to act and push through a programme of reforms in the teeth of inherited inertia.

Failures

It is of course easier to spot failures than successes, when it comes to the prevention of rebellions. The failures indeed are legion and make a dismal and lengthening record. In only one of the examples we have just considered—France—was there evidence that an insurrection was actually being planned. In Britain, the threat was merely one of social unrest. In Formosa, there had already been violence, and the Formosans had found leaders to express their grievances. But even there,

there was not—as far as I am aware—any evidence that a sustained campaign of rebellion or revolution was being planned. The French circumstances were unusual, in that wartime conditions and a special role in the Resistance had given the French Communist Party an opportunity unlikely to recur in the foreseeable future. But there are countless examples of rebellions being planned under the noses of the authorities and in the end erupting into violence with the fatality of a Greek tragedy. In all of them, there were specific grievances of one kind or another—social or political, racial, ethnic or religious— which the authorities knew about and could have dealt with, but neglected. In most of them, too, there were early warning signals known at least to the intelligence or security services. As I have suggested, the grievances alone, such as social conditions, do not necessarily make rebellion inevitable. But where rebels are known to be plotting, and it is patent that they have grievances to exploit, inaction is unpardonable. Yet contemporary history suggests that official inertia and inaction are the rule, not the exception. I deal later with the difficult problem of subversion in an advanced society. I deal now with a related but not identical problem: the early detection and prevention of an armed insurrection—the important preparatory phase which we briefly considered in the preceding chapter in the light of terrorist aims, and which we now look at from the government side.

It is a disheartening fact that even 'good' governments are not necessarily immune to insurrection. For the techniques of revolutionary war, which we have already examined, are designed to create grievances where none previously existed, to provoke the authorities into unpopular excesses and to cause a breakdown of law and order. It is probably true, however, that an insurrection is more likely to be successful where genuine grievances exist than where they are artificially whipped up. But note the 'probably': there is no absolute certainty or invariable rule about such situations. How, then, can the authorities be sure that an insurrection or insurgency is being planned? Much, of course, depends on whether the government concerned has or lacks a good intelligence and security service. Without one, it is playing blind man's buff.

This is not a manual of counter-insurgency, and I shall not attempt to deal with the subject in any detail. The principles, however, are worth mentioning. No matter how careful the revolutionaries are, they are bound to leave some evidence of their activities. In the first instance, this evidence is likely to be circumstantial. Such circumstantial evidence is termed, in the security jargon, 'indicators of insurgency'.

An increase in bank robberies, especially if the robbers are apparently young and educated people, can be such an indicator. So can thefts of guns or other arms and ammunition, of explosive materials, of pharmaceutical supplies and the like. There may be other signs, such as the appearance of leaflets signed by new and apparently revolutionary groups; but this is usually a later development. The universities are a breeding ground for such movements. If students or faculty members become elusive or secretive in their movements or travel round to excess to other universities, it may well be that they are engaged in incipient revolutionary activities (although such signs do not in themselves constitute proof: verification is necessary before any action can be taken).

If the indicators strongly point to the existence of a clandestine revolutionary group, what is needed next is positive proof and the identification of the ringleaders. Verification of this kind is a highly skilled security operation, which inevitably involves the use of whatever detection devices are available—including 'bugging'—and the organisation of a network of reliable informants. Clearly, the aim of the revolutionaries is to escape detection until they are ready to strike. Conversely, the aim of the authorities is to detect the existence of the movement and identify the leaders before they have had time to put their plans into operation. Initially, it is the revolutionaries who enjoy the advantage of secrecy. The task of the security services is to deprive them of this advantage.

In many rebellions, perhaps in most, there are other 'early warning signals' besides the circumstantial 'indicators' we have listed. The most important are the presence and journeys of known revolutionaries. As a general rule, political agitators and extremists tend not to be taken seriously enough until it is uncomfortably late. In the Western colonial era, 'early warnings' often came very early indeed, but political action rarely ensued. To some extent, this was due to the administrative dichotomy between the police and security departments on the one hand, and the political ones on the other. The activities of Ho Chi Minh as a Comintern agent, or of Belkacem Krim as an Algerian nationalist, were known for many years before the insurrections in which each was a key figure broke out. Yet *preventive* political action was not contemplated, either in French Indochina or in Algeria, until it was too late.

There is almost invariably a long period (though 'long' is itself a variable) when police action seems both simpler and more likely to be effective than political measures. That it is simpler is self-evident:

political action may involve offence to vested interests or pressure groups, and the case for delay may seem overwhelmingly strong until it yields to the case for the utmost urgency. In recent years, the length of the warning period has shrunk alarmingly in many cases, in some almost to vanishing point. For example, the Palestine National Liberation Movement (Al-Fatah) emerged during the months after the Anglo-French 'Suez' expedition in 1956, but the Arabs as a whole were hardly aware of its existence for about nine years. When Al-Fatah's military wing, Al-Assifa, first went into action against Israel at the end of 1964, the fact went largely unnoticed; as late as after the June War of 1967, when Al-Assifa lost half its small force on the West Bank of the Jordan, the fact of its defeat certainly drew attention to its existence, but few people took it at all seriously.

A case in which there was scarcely any 'early warning' was the important one of the revolutionary riots in Paris and other French cities in May 1968. The various Maoist groups that played so active a part in these events had been formed only a few months earlier, and May was virtually their 'debut' in revolutionary action. In fact, the French government—and General de Gaulle in particular—were taken completely by surprise by the size and virulence of the explosion. The General had planned a State visit to Rumania and (still underestimating the danger) went ahead with it.

In this instance, however, there had indeed been early warnings, but of a different kind. The rapid expansion of the student population without a corresponding increase in the number of teachers and buildings, 'reforms' which imposed great strains on students obliged to switch from one curriculum to another, formalities that made it impossible for, say, a *licencié* in Psychology to take a Master's degree in Sociology—such conditions inevitably led to pent-up frustrations and resentments that were bound, some time or other, to explode. But it was nobody's business in particular to see that genuine student grievances, coupled with the emergence of violent revolutionary groups, were bound to form an explosive mixture.

As we have seen (Part III, 2) 1968 marked the beginning of the phenomenon I have described as 'transnational terrorism'. Agitators or terrorists began moving from one country to another, seeking or bringing arms, training or new techniques of revolution. Awareness that such people were indeed moving from country to country rapidly became known to individual police forces or security services. In some cases, where such services or forces had built up long habits of co-operation, some kind of concerted action soon became possible. But there were difficult cases, not least that of the Arab terrorists, who were harboured or in other ways aided by certain Arab governments. As these governments were members of Interpol, that admirable institution —so valuable in the apprehension of 'ordinary' criminals—virtually lost its usefulness in cases involving Palestinians or their friends.

It is easy to criticise, and I shall try to make my criticism constructive. By definition, any study of conflict is bound to pay more attention to 'bad' government than to 'good'. Faced with incipient revolutionary challenges, most governments tend to be guilty of both sins of omission and sins of commission, on the following lines:

(a) *Sins of omission:*

The disregarding of early warnings, the failure to take preventive action in the political and administrative (including police and security) fields.

(b) *Sins of commission:*

Actions or measures that aggravate, instead of improving, a situation; policies that defer the day of reckoning, while merely ensuring that the price to be paid will be higher than it need have been.

The extraordinary case of Ireland, both dismal and tragic, so clearly illustrates both types of administrative 'sins' that it deserves a few paragraphs to itself. The complexities of the Irish situation are notorious, and are inherent in: the stormy relations between the island and England; the 'plantation' of Ulster (Northern Ireland) in 1608 with Protestant settlers from the Scottish lowlands and England, and the expulsion of the native Catholic and Gaelic-speaking people to the poorer lands of the south and west; the oubreak of a guerrilla war against the British power, following the overwhelming victory of the Nationalist Sinn Fein party in 1918; the establishment in 1921 of the six counties of Ulster as a separate entity under the government of Northern Ireland, against a background of continuing civil war and sectarian disorder; the establishment in 1922 of the Irish Free State; and the proclamation of the Republic of Ireland in the south in 1949 —which Britain regarded as placing Southern Ireland outside the Commonwealth.

The situation in Ulster has been described as 'colonial', 'semicolonial' and 'quasi-colonial', and there is a strong element of truth in such tags, but they do not tell the whole story. Likewise, the struggle there has been described as a religious or sectarian war, and that too is no more than an aspect of the truth. It has also been described as a struggle for independence, but what the terrorists and guerrillas of the

Irish Republican Army (IRA) wanted was not the independence of Ulster as such, but the unity and independence of the whole of Ireland. There is a sense, too, in which it might be said that the Ulster troubles constituted an attempted social revolution by the less privileged citizens of Northern Ireland. The fact that not one of the foregoing descriptions is the entire truth illustrates the complexity of the situation. It is only by putting all these separate elements together that one may arrive at a reasonably rounded and realistic image.

Nor should a further complicating factor be overlooked: in the mass, the Protestants of Northern Ireland were fiercely, indeed passionately, attached to the British connection—more fiercely and passionately, no doubt, than the British themselves were attached to their Ulster province. Moreover, the facts of political history have produced unfortunate anomalies. If the island as a whole is considered, the Catholics were in a comfortable majority; but in Ulster considered separately, the Catholics constituted less than 35 per cent of the population, the remainder being divided between Presbyterians and members of the Church of Ireland.

Broadly speaking, the Catholics of the North were poor, politically deprived and anxious to break the British connection. The Protestants, though not all were equally fanatical, saw their own safety as being guaranteed solely by the British connection. They had no wish to exchange a long-standing situation of dominance (reflected in the phrase 'the Protestant Ascendancy') for possible oppression in a united and predominantly Catholic Irish Republic. Indeed, the polity of Northern Ireland was conceived *with the object* of denying political power to the Catholics in perpetuity.

I am not concerned here either to trace the history of the more recent struggles, or to propose solutions, or even to dispense moral judgments. My aim is simply to pinpoint the sins of omission and commission on the side of the British and the Unionists (that is, the Protestant majority).

Leaving aside Ireland's long history of brutality at the hands of the English soldiery, of being treated by the English as a slave people, or at any rate an inferior one, the first major error, on the British side, was probably in the drawing of the dividing boundary in 1920. If the southernmost counties of Northern Ireland had been included in what is now the Irish Republic, the proportion of Catholics in Ulster could have been no more than 10 per cent. This would have been manageable. Instead, the Catholics constituted 35 per cent of the population— an altogether more intractable figure.

A second error lay in the greed and sense of dominance of the descendants of the planted settlers after the First World War. The polity that had been devised to look after their interests did the job too well. It was never going to be possible for the Catholics to be adequately represented, let alone to have or share political power. It was probably only a matter of time before this permanent grievance exploded into violence.

And yet—in politics even a grievance does not necessarily perform to order. As in so many other majority-minority situations, everything depended on the political will of the Protestant–Unionist majority. So long as the Protestants were determined to keep the Catholic–Nationalist minority in its place—that is, as second-class citizens—the situation never threatened anything worse than occasional disorders. But in 1965, the autonomous Unionist government at Stormont (the district of Belfast containing the administrative buildings) yielded to a potent twinge of the liberal conscience. The Premier of the Northern Irish government at that time, Captain Terence O'Neill (later Lord O'Neill) was an able and honourable man. He decided to liberalise and give the Catholics a better deal.

It was a fatal miscalculation, for in Protestant eyes, Catholic grievances could be remedied only at the expense of the British connection and the Protestant Ascendancy.[1] Long and careful preparation and statesmanship might have produced the climate of opinion in which liberalising measures could gradually have been introduced. But once the first steps were taken, the situation snowballed. The Protestants were alarmed, and the Catholics sensed that this was their chance. Violence was inherent in this situation, and it is fair to attribute it to the liberalising policy of the O'Neill administration. Once again, events were to prove the truth of Alexis de Tocqueville's famous observation on the discontent that preceded the French Revolution: 'Patiently endured so long as it seems beyond redress, a grievance comes to appear intolerable once the possibility of removing it crosses men's minds.'

This does not end the list of sins of omission or commission in Ireland, but the other items on it mainly concern repression, which is the subject of the next chapter.

[1] See Iain Hamilton, in 'The Spreading Irish Conflict', *Conflict Studies* No. 17, Institute for the Study of Conflict, London, Nov. 1971).

FIVE

CONFLICT AND
THE CONTEMPORARY STATE, II

REPRESSION

The ground covered in this chapter

Stalin and total repression—repression inevitable when violence breaks out—principles of counter-insurgency—emergency legislation to be temporary—fairness before the law—advantages and drawbacks of detention—information and psychological war—morale and the strategy of reforms—a classic example: Malaya—errors in Cyprus— need for secret services—the meaning of Watergate—techniques of interrogation—the Ulster example—is torture ever justified—a morality versus statecraft—torture and bombing compared—ruthless methods paid in Turkey, Brazil, Uruguay—a code for interrogation— sins of omission and commission in Ulster

REPRESSION, I once wrote, is indivisible. Stalin knew this very well. Since his power was limitless and his willingness to use it utterly ruthless, it was never seriously threatened. One difference between Stalin's regime and the Soviet Union of his successors was that in his day intellectual and other dissidents vanished without trace, whereas today the outside world and even fellow-citizens, hear the protests of a Sakharov or an Amalrik.

But even in a totalist system, Stalin was a monstrous exception. Few rulers, even if they are dictators, are willing to deport whole peoples, to put millions to death, to practise deceit and inflict torture and death on a limitless scale. Yet many rulers, no matter how mild and well-intentioned they may be, are faced with the necessity for repression of one kind or another. Indeed, once systematic violence has broken out —whether in microcosm, as in a single university, or in macrocosm, where law and order are endangered in large administrative areas—the authorities have no choice: they *must* repress, even if they later decide to concede the demands that led to violence in the first place. But once the inevitable decision to repress has been taken, a fair variety of options are open to the authorities. It must be remembered that the hour is now later, prevention having failed or not having been attempted. At this stage, nearly all official measures are drastic, their severity varying only in degree. In democratic countries, repressive measures are exposed to public scrutiny and criticism: the conspiratorial group that is promoting revolutionary violence knows no such restraints. Having sown the wind, it may reap the whirlwind. For in the last resort, no State can afford to give up its power without a struggle. The men in power may hesitate and procrastinate. But in the end, they must act.

To be effective, however—and assuming that the authorities are not going to attempt to emulate Stalin—repression needs to be selective, in the towns or the countryside, and whatever its degree, the aims of the authorities are, or ought to be, basically similar. The population must be protected from terrorism, and given (if they lack it) a political stake in the future of their country; the terrorist must be isolated—that is, deprived of intelligence and supplies; the subversive apparatus of the revolutionaries must be detected and destroyed. All else, including firepower, is subsidiary to these central aims.

Many excellent studies, and some of less value, have been written upon the new art or science of counter-insurgency. I can do no more in this space than to summarise some of the main principles. It is one of the paradoxes of revolutionary action that it is marked by a defiance of a country's laws, but can only be countered—when violence has actually broken out—by the suspension of normal legal processes on the official side. If a state of insurgency is seen to exist the government should prepare emergency legislation. It is essential to act quickly. The draft laws should be easy to grasp and the entire population should be made aware of them. It is very important to make it clear that the emergency legislation is *temporary* in nature; that it is being introduced only because a group has taken the law into its own hands; and that the measures introduced will be revoked as soon as possible.

Another principle is of great importance: it is that of fairness. In Malaya and Cyprus, during their respective emergencies in the 1950s, collective punishments were inflicted upon villagers who had helped the rebels. This was grossly unfair to the innocent among the guilty and was inevitably counter-productive. In time, such laws were revoked.

A major legal and moral problem inevitably arises with the introduction of detention without trial. In authoritarian, or relatively primitive countries not much trouble need be expected. But in advanced and pluralist societies, detention without trial is bound to provoke an outcry, as it did when it was introduced in Northern Ireland in August 1971. At a time when violence is rapidly escalating, however, when witnesses and even juries and judges may be intimidated by terrorists, and when there may be no time to prepare evidence to support formal charges within a period statutorily laid down, there may be no other way. But again, the principle must be that detention is a *temporary* condition. The main point is to take dangerous men and women out of circulation, and to sort out from the mass those against whom formal evidence may be forthcoming, leading to charges in open court. As soon as possible, those likely to be found guilty must be tried; and the others released. But 'as soon as possible' cannot be precisely defined: if the situation grows worse, the period of detention and that of special powers to detain may have to be prolonged.

It must be admitted that such procedures carry enormous drawbacks, especially in an open society. Criticism will be widespread and sustained; and where the possibility exists, the media will be alerted and will tend, unless impeded, to be against the government. Public opinion abroad, too, will be alerted, and such promising platforms as the United Nations will not be neglected. From the rebel standpoint, detention without trial thus brings important bonuses. But these are subject to the law of diminishing returns. If the leaders are detained for prolonged periods, the organisation is bound to suffer. The revolutionaries know that they have every advantage in whipping up public opinion against detention without trial in the early stages, so that the government may be forced to yield to the critical clamour and release the detained leaders, even if they are really believed to be guilty.

Another and most important area of counter-insurgency is Information and Psychological War. The two are not identical, though they overlap. The objective of both, and indeed of the revolutionary enemy, is the loyalty of the people. If a government faced with an insurgency lacks an information department, it will have to create one. The purpose is not only to present the official version of events, but to counter the claims of the rebels. Inexperienced or unsophisticated governments often seek the answer to their current problems in a blanket censorship or punitive measures against the press; nor do they scorn to outdo the revolutionaries in the extravagance and mendacity of their claims. Governments that so act in the long run do themselves a deep disservice by discrediting their own effort. A fully censored press is rarely believed; but the people will normally accept the need for some restrictions in the interests of security. And credibility must be preserved: to claim that three people were killed in an incident that was seen to bring death to many more merely exposes the authorities to the corroding effects of rumour. Restraint in the presentation of the news is essential. An excessively vituperative and condemnatory tone may merely create sympathy for the revolutionaries. And it will be construed as a sign of weakness and lack of confidence on the part of the government.

When reforms are initiated—as they will have to be if the government is to win the confidence of the public—then it must be careful to present them as the outcome of its own policies, and not of revolutionary pressures. In information and psychological war, it is not sufficient simply to react to events: the government must have a strategy. It must aim at putting across certain basic messages. The most important of these undoubtedly concerns morale. The government is going to win and the guerrillas are going to lose: this is inherent in the long-term strength of the government, of its greater resources and of its concern for the people's welfare. This last point is perhaps the most essential of all, for the government will not necessarily win unless it can indeed convince the people that it has their interests at heart.

Any information programme must therefore be accompanied by reforms, even if they are overdue and even if the revolutionaries may argue that they are simply the consequence of their own actions. Even if well founded, this argument will come to seem irrelevant when something is actually being done. The revolutionaries may promise paradise of a kind, but their promises are hypothetical, while the government's are taking shape before the eyes of the public. If this basic message can be put over, then a subsidiary one follows: since the government is winning, and is doing something about the public welfare, it is therefore in the true interests of the people that victory should indeed go to the official side. Ordinary people should therefore help the government, even at some risk to themselves, for in the long run the risks will have been worthwhile in that they will have speeded the return of peace and order. Perhaps the ultimate message is one that is inherent in the preceding ones: that there is a fundamental unity between the government and the people: the odd men out are the guerrillas.

In conducting an information campaign, the authorities should austerely resist the temptation to argue with the guerrillas on points of ideology or policy, through the press, television or radio. To do this gives the people the impression that they stand outside a struggle of little concern to them—in effect that they are neutral witnesses to a settlement of accounts between the revolutionaries and the State.

Despite the passing of the years, the Malayan Emergency still stands as a classic example of a successful psychological warfare campaign. The aims were highly practical. There was no question of indulging in ideological debate about the respective merits and draw-backs of Communism and Democracy. Instead, the appeal was to the terrorist or guerrilla as a man or woman, as somebody who, often for misguided reasons of idealism, had strayed from the path of common sense. To do this it was essential to find out as much as could be dis-covered about the identities, personalities and life histories of indi-vidual members of the terrorist organisation. It was necessary to have their photographs, to know where they were hiding (at least in general terms), to know which of them had mistresses, and so forth.

To mount such an operation requires time, patience and painstaking attention to detail. Teams of men, including many Chinese working on the government side (since the overwhelming majority of the terror-ists were ethnic Chinese) or highly trained police or civilian members of the administration who had acquired the necessary standard of proficiency in both the written and the spoken Chinese tongue—especially Cantonese, the dialect most frequently spoken in Singapore and Malaya. Scraps of information were built up, from captured docu-ments, from careless gossip, from chance encounters and supplemented by police files where these existed. Armed with such information the 'Psywar' specialists could draft their surrender leaflets—addressing terrorists by name, reproducing their pictures or letters to friends that had been intercepted.

These leaflets were not written in a tone of moral superiority. Boasting was out of place. The sole object of the exercise was to induce terrorists to surrender. Surrender they did, by the hundreds. In the end, the communist and terrorist challenge in Malaya was defeated by a combination of things—the clear political objectives of democracy and independence; patience and efficient organisation; the devoted work of the security forces; and information and psychological war. I am inclined to think that the last-named was the most important.

In all forms of revolutionary war, intelligence and the protection of the population are closely linked and equally important. Initially, all the advantages are with the terrorist. He has the initiative. It is he who is taking action. His numbers are few, and he can bully or terrorise people into providing him with food and shelter, to hide him when he is being pursued, to treat his wounds when he is hurt. In the panic-stricken early days in Malaya (and later in Cyprus) there was much counter-productive emergency legislation. A special regulation made 'consorting with terrorists' punishable by death. But the Chinese in the villages could hardly avoid consorting with the terrorists, who would not leave them alone. In these conditions, the law seemed to give them a choice between death for consorting, and death for not consorting, with the terrorists. The temptation to see, hear and speak nothing must have been overwhelming.[1]

In Cyprus, there was a similar but slightly less onerous choice at one stage of the campaign to defeat Grivas and his EOKA terrorists: the choice between a share in a collective fine imposed by the British authorities, or of a bullet between the shoulder blades, administered by the terrorists. The terrorist side cannot help winning when the authorities make it that easy for them.

The people, then, must be protected from the terrorists, which essentially means that the terrorists must be isolated and prevented from having free contact with the local population in their operational area, whether in town or country. Unless the people can be protected from terrorism, they will not co-operate with the authorities; which means that they will not provide the intelligence that is essential to find and arrest or shoot the terrorists. I have described the incidence of terrorism as a barometer of the success or failure of the terrorists at any given time. Similarly, the flow of intelligence is a barometer of the success or failure of the authorities. If the flow is rapid and unimpeded, the authorities are beginning to win, for the clear message is that people are giving information because they no longer fear immediate terrorist reprisals. The organisation of an efficient intelligence service is there-fore of the utmost importance. Lucky is the country that already has one, either for foreign information or for the needs of internal security, or preferably for both. No State can do without one, and this applies no less to democratic and pluralist States than to authoritarian or totalist ones.

The problem for the open society is how to have, build up and preserve this essential tool of defence—which in the long run is in-dispensable for the protection of ordinary people—and not so outrage the liberal conscience that the legitimate exercise of State power is frustrated. The Watergate affair, which blighted President Nixon's second term of office, was a perfect illustration of the dilemma. Essen-tially, what happened was that the White House set up its own internal

[1] Brian Crozier, *The Rebels* (London, 1960), p. 211.

security organisation because in certain areas it had lost confidence in the Federal Bureau of Investigation. It is indeed impossible for *any* government to conduct its business unless it can enforce the secrecy, or even the confidency, of its normal communications. In a situation that enabled a former public servant to steal and publish documents of the Department of Defence, and a journalist to fill his column with State secrets, the frustration of the administration was total. No government deserves to be placed in such a situation. It was unfortunate that the men who sought to remedy it on the President's behalf bungled the job. Nor was Mr. Nixon's handling of the consequences better than inept. In very similar circumstances, President de Gaulle—whose associate Jacques Foccart ran a very similar clandestine service, but more efficiently than the Haldeman–Ehrlichman team—was able to ride successive resulting storms by a superb combination of prestige and magisterial disdain, together with a ruthless readiness to get rid of bunglers.

This is not the place to pursue a discussion of Watergate, which I cited only as an example of a fundamental requirement of the State. If this is a trained intelligence service, then, how is it to proceed with its work? Much of intelligence work inevitably consists of the painstaking collection and collation of facts—where guerrillas were seen on a certain day and at a certain time; what individuals may look like; biographical details about them; personality anecdotes; and so forth. It is obviously of great importance that the security forces should have as complete a file as possible of the leaders of a revolutionary movement, so that the information may be used to psychological effect, or to make an arrest at a suitable time. But when all is said and done, by far the most vital element in any security intelligence operation will come from the lips of captured terrorists or 'surrendered enemy personnel'.

The treatment of revolutionary detainees, and methods and techniques of interrogation, are therefore of crucial relevance. Despite the complaints about the rough treatment of detainees being interrogated in Northern Ireland, the British tradition is considerably more humane than that of most other countries. Certainly, the guiding philosophy is that captives should be treated fairly—on the ground that if the police or army have a reputation for brutality, this will inevitably discourage guerrillas or terrorists who might otherwise have been minded to give themselves up.

In any revolutionary movement that has gone into the active phase there is a minority that has been coerced or intimidated, or has joined for adventure or 'kicks' and has later found the glamour wearing thin.

All such people are candidates for surrender. Through leaflets or through advertising in the press, the government can offer reasonable conditions—not only good treatment and protection for those who wish to come back within the law, but generous rewards for information leading to the capture of other guerrillas or terrorists—especially for the capture alive of the real leaders. Some captives, ready to collaborate freely and still willing to take risks, may agree to act as agents for the security forces, returning to their colleagues and carrying on as though nothing had happened. Obviously, this is a risky process—not only for themselves but also for the police or security people who may be deceived into thinking that a man is going to help them and later discover that they are being fed with false information. Clearly again, a man who returns to the revolutionaries after detention must have a convincing story to tell, such as an escape that sounds genuine. In some cases, however, detention may have been so short that there is no need to explain anything.

There remain the cases of detainees who have nothing to contribute, and of the occasional top leader who is captured but resists all the pressures of interrogation in line with the fanaticism that made him turn to violence in the first place. In the former case, the arrested man should be charged, if at all possible, under the normal criminal law for whatever offences may fit the case, such as armed robbery, illegal possession of arms, thefts and so forth.

The capture of a leading figure in the terrorist movement raises problems of a different kind. If the capture occurs when the tide has turned against the revolutionaries, it may well be that the man may be prepared to talk in return for certain guarantees. If he shows no such willingness, it is sometimes thought best to conceal the fact of his arrest from the world. In the absence of news, his former comrades may well suppose him to have defected; and this will contribute to the demoralisation of the leadership.

It is a firmly established British principle that interrogation need not be accompanied by brutality. It is argued that the skilled interrogator, and preferably a team of two or three interrogators, by probing for weak points and cross-checking information received from several prisoners and confronting a new detainee with facts which he thought were known only to the revolutionary side, can obtain the desired information. This is not to say that brutality never occurs in British counter-insurgency campaigns. In Malaya, in Cyprus and in Ireland there have been cases of excessive force on the side of authority. In most cases, the force used is unauthorised and may simply be the almost unavoidable reaction of police or troops provoked beyond human endurance and yielding to the temptation to get their own back.

The specific allegations of ill-treatment during interrogation in Ulster were clearly different in kind. It was alleged, in an article in the *Sunday Times* of 17 October 1971, that detainees under interrogation had been made to stand for hours with their hands raised above their heads against a wall, that they had had hoods put over their heads and that they had been subjected to a continuous high-pitched whistling noise. Moreover, while the interrogation lasted, they were kept on a diet of bread and water, and deprived of sleep. Two separate Committees reported on these allegations. The first, a Committee of Inquiry under Sir Edmund Compton, had been sitting when the *Sunday Times* published its allegations, and reported on 18 November that some of the techniques mentioned had inded been used, to a degree amounting to ill-treatment.

The second Committee, under Lord Parker, a former Chief Justice, reported on 2 March 1972 that the technique of 'interrogation in depth' had been used on fourteen of the 342 people arrested. Its conclusions included these: 'There is no reason to rule out these techniques on moral grounds'; and 'It is possible to operate them in a manner consistent with the highest standards of our society'. One member of the second Committee, however, Lord Gardner (a former Labour Lord Chancellor) expressed a minority view in that he did not consider the techniques to be justified and was of the opinion that the information could have been obtained by other means.

In this, he differed from his colleagues, who had pointed out in their majority report that the fourteen men interrogated in depth had given information including the identification of the authors of about 85 hitherto unsolved incidents, and the discovery of more arms, ammunition and explosives than at any previous time. They went on to record that the interrogated men had given information about 700 other members of the IRA, both Provisional and Official. And they expressed the view that this valuable information could not have been obtained by any other means, and that it had probably saved many lives. The majority report concluded that normal techniques were not effective in an urban guerrilla situation. Though necessary in their view, the techniques should be permitted, however, only when it was essential to obtain information quickly and even then only under strict safeguards, including the presence of a doctor with psychiatric training. In the event, the government took greater notice of the Compton Report and of the dissenting view of Lord Gardner than of the majority Parker Report. It decided to continue with interrogation in depth, but to cut out the techniques described by the Compton Committee as constituting ill-treatment. An end was therefore made to hooding and noise, excessive wall-standing and deprivation of sleep, and those being interrogated were given a more interesting and nutritious diet than bread and water.

The question of ill-treatment, even of torture, in interrogation is an agonising one, but it would be cowardly to ignore or evade it. Does the end ever justify the means in counter-insurgency? Wars create such moral dilemmas, and revolutionary war is a form of warfare. The British philosophy of interrogation is humane and civilised, but it can hardly be claimed that it brings quick results. The Malayan Emergency lasted twelve years. At the time of writing, four years had already elapsed from the beginning of the Irish disorders in 1969, and no end was yet in sight. The Parker Report made it clear that the rough but concentrated interrogation of fourteen men had brought unprecedented results and had probably saved many lives. The government bowed to public pressure—that is, especially, pressure from the media; and after all, the use or manipulation of public opinion is an important weapon of revolutionary war. The terrorists used it (with the help of the *Sunday Times*) and it was shown to be effective. But who is to say that it was more important to stop treating others as the fourteen had been treated than to save many lives and appreciably reduce the duration of the conflict, with all that it entailed in wasted money and resources, fear and the disruption of people's lives?

It was a dilemma similar in kind, though on far smaller a scale, to that which President Truman faced in the last months of the Second World War when he decided to use the atomic bomb against Japan. Tens of thousands of Japanese were incinerated, and many more suffered serious and prolonged consequences of radiation. On the other hand, a vast but unaccountable number of American and Japanese lives were spared, as the destruction of two Japanese cities brought the war to an unexpectedly sudden end. On the basis of a fanatical record, the Japanese would have fought heroically and possibly to the last few people in defence of their homeland.

These are dreadful balance sheets. On the one hand, there is a known and recorded offence against humanity. On the other hand, there is nothing more than a hypothesis, but a reasonable one. For my part, I am convinced that Truman took the right decision. Equally, I believe with the majority of the Parker Committee that the methods of interrogation in depth used on the fourteen men were justified.

But what if the ill-treatment used by interrogators goes far beyond the relative mildness that so distressed the *Sunday Times*? What if it extends to the grim horrors reported during the Battle of Algiers and during terrorist outbreaks in the early 1970s in Turkey, Brazil, Uruguay and other places? That torture, including the selective use of electricity, was used during the Battle of Algiers in 1957 has indeed been confirmed by the then French commander of the élite Paratroop Division, General Massu.[2] The torture was a fact. But it is also a fact that by such ruthless methods, Massu smashed the FLN organisation in Algiers and re-established unchallenged French authority. And he did the job in seven months—from March to mid-October. It is relevant to recall that by January 1957, two months before Massu was given the job of cleaning up the city, the rate of civilians killed had reached 200 a month.

The other cases I have mentioned were no less striking. In Turkey, widespread riots and violence fostered by the Turkish People's Liberation Army (TPLA) had brought fear and suffering and forced the closure of the Middle East Technical University in the latter half of 1970 and early in 1971. The military intervened in April 1971, to force the creation of a government determined to restore order. A state of emergency was proclaimed. The use of ruthless interrogation methods undoubtedly helped to provide the security forces with the intelligence they needed and by mid-1972, the TPLA had been smashed as an effective instrument of revolution. In Brazil, similar methods rapidly restored order after the initial successes of a gang of urban terrorists led by the late Carlos Marighella, who was killed in a street battle in 1969. The terrorism went on, but had been brought under control by late 1971.

The case of Uruguay is perhaps the most interesting of all. During a period of about four years, from 1968, the Tupamaros terrorists gained so complete an ascendency that they were able to operate with impunity, kidnapping officials or foreign diplomats, robbing banks, escaping if captured—all as their will dictated. They were unable, however, to prevent the Presidential elections of November 1971, which returned a Chief of State, Juan-María Bordaberry, who was determined to stamp our terrorism. A *state of internal war* was proclaimed, civil rights were suspended, and the army given a free hand to restore order. Once again, ruthless interrogation methods were used. Between April and August 1972, the Tupamaros movement was smashed. By the end of November, 2,600 people had been jailed and 42 killed.

[2] In Jaques Massu, *La Vraie Bataille d'Alger* (Paris, 1971), pp. 169 et seq.

Bases and hide-outs had been uncovered, some equipped with air-conditioning, food storage, books and television. Among the places overrun were an electronics laboratory, a laboratory used for forging equipment, a foundry with a furnace, and a hospital complete with operating table and x-ray equipment.

In moral terms, the dilemma remains absolute and insoluble. But in terms of statecraft the figures speak for themselves and are indeed unanswerable. The British philosophy of interrogation—so highly suited to a country with a long tradition of tolerance—is thus answered by the dramatic results achieved by more determined methods.

Such facts do not, and cannot, dispose of the debate about torture. It is important to get this highly emotive subject in perspective. It is generally recognised that it is immoral to inflict suffering and death upon the innocent and the defenceless. If a terrorist is caught 'in the act', he cannot be considered innocent (although it might be difficult to establish his guilt in a court of law), but he is thereafter defenceless. If it is conceded, as it must be, that there are degrees of immorality just as there are degrees of guilt, then it follows in logic that it is less immoral for the captured terrorist to be tortured than for the uncaptured one to torture innocent people to enforce obedience and strike fear in a neighbourhood.

Although any revelations of the official use of torture inevitably provoke a public outcry denouncing such methods as repugnant to the civilised conscience, or degrading to those who use them, I do not think that the fact of torture as such is any more tolerable on moral grounds if imputed to members of a gang or political group than to the interrogators of a properly constituted authority. But the circumstances are crucially important.

In *The Rebels* (1960), I expressed views on the relative morality of terrorism and bombing in a passage which I now requote without apology, to save the reader the trouble of a search:

Terrorism is a weapon of the weak. This is a factual observation: it does not exonerate those who use terrorism as a weapon from any moral blame that may be put on them by their victims or by outsiders. Nor, on the other hand, does it imply that the weak are morally inferior to the strong. All acts of violence are open to criticism on moral grounds. The violence of the strong may express itself in high explosive or napalm bombs. These weapons are no less discriminate than a hand-grenade tossed from a roof-top; indeed, they will make more innocent victims. Yet they arouse less moral indignation around Western firesides. The terrorist is an outlaw and —except when he deposits a time-bomb—he is physically close to his victims. The airman is an agent of established order and may be thousands of feet above the roof-tops of those to be blasted by high explosive or seared by fire. Often enough, the victims of terrorism are 'us', whereas the victims of bombing raids are 'them'.

There will never be complete agreement about the morality or immorality of specific political or military operations. The terrorist justifies his use of torture and his maiming of the innocent by his conviction of the absolute righteousness of his cause. The authorities justify their use of bombing by the absolute necessity to win a war. Those who dispute the righteousness of the terrorists' cause or dismiss the relevance of the war that is being fought will disagree with the subjective judgments of those whose actions they disapprove. But a regime may indeed be tyrannical and oppressive, and there may indeed be a case for overthrowing it with whatever means are at hand. And a war may be 'just': it may be a war for national survival, or at any rate a war of legitimate self-defence.

The State, I have said, has a right to defend itself—implicit in the absolute necessity of the State. A properly constituted government, enjoying initially the overwhelming support (even if it is only tacit) of the population may nevertheless be threatened with extinction by the methods of revolutionary war. In Uruguay in 1972, the decision to use ruthless methods, once it was taken, brought about the defeat of an apparently invincible terrorist organisation within a matter of months.

It is fair to add that in the process of using such methods and entrusting its salvation to the armed forces, the country lost—perhaps temporarily—its remarkable tradition of parliamentary democracy. But is it fair to ascribe that loss to the government's ruthless methods? Is it not fairer to blame it on the ruthless methods of the terrorists that had almost brought about the collapse of the State? It could be argued that if the authorities had had the courage to take the decision earlier, they might have spared the population much unnecessary suffering—and saved the democratic tradition as well. There are no moral winners —only losers—in this kind of competition.

Repression in Ulster

In many ways, the Irish situation in the 1970s was a classic case of insurgency, and the British response was conducted on classical counter-insurgency lines. That is, security and suppressive measures of one kind or another had to be balanced at fairly regular intervals by political initiatives designed to deprive the terrorists of popular support for their action and make it unnecessary; and if possible to produce a reconciliation between the communities and a new and viable polity. In terms of logistics, the proximity of Ireland to Great Britain made it easier to deploy the army there than in such distant places as Cyprus or Malaya; on the other hand, there was virtually no army available in Britain itself and the troops had to be brought over from Germany.

Against this relative advantage, there were serious disadvantages. For one thing, the proximity of Ulster and the fact that it was constitutionally part of the United Kingdom meant that the full glare of publicity was permanently trained upon events in the province. Any departure from the exacting British official standards of behaviour was immediately criticised. Moreover, for the first time in a situation of this kind involving British forces, television coverage played a major part in the determination of public opinion. As I have remarked elsewhere, television is never impartial in a situation of this kind: it invariably favours the terrorists and places the security forces at a disadvantage. A further disadvantage was the proximity of the sovereign Republic of Ireland which, at least in the early stages, the terrorists could use with impunity for sanctuary and training. Yet another factor was the willingness of foreign terrorist groups—notably the Palestinian ones—and certain governments—notably that of the Soviet Union and Czechoslovakia—to provide arms or training for the IRA Provisionals. The excessive and unrestricted publicity in which operations were conducted was undoubtedly a grave handicap to the security forces, as any such publicity always is in a situation of this kind. Moreover, the undoubted need for political initiatives on several occasions reduced the momentum of the security drive, giving temporary advantages to the terrorists.

It is never difficult to be wise after the event, and in a situation of such ferocious complexity, severity of judgment is perhaps inappropriate. In retrospect, there is a case for saying that (a) the troubles might have been nipped in the bud; and (b) on a later occasion, the Provisional organisation might have been smashed beyond repair. As in all hypothetical arguments, however, these propositions are not susceptible of absolute proof. The troubles began in the autumn of 1968 with violent clashes in Derry City between Civil Rights demonstrators and the Royal Ulster Constabulary. During the next eighteen months, the violence escalated, with protest demonstrations, rioting and burning and killing. It was during this time that quick action on the part of the police, supplemented if necessary by the British Army, could perhaps have broken the incipient terrorist organisation: thereafter, political reforms could have been implemented in a climate of relative calm. Instead, on the political side, commissions of inquiry proliferated and reforms were rushed through the Stormont legislature under growing pressure from Westminster in a climate of increasing violence that ensured they would be irrelevant to a developing situation.

It is in the early months of an incipient insurgency that swift and decisive action is most required; and it is during this period that it is least likely to be forthcoming. All governments—but especially democratic ones, subject to the pressures of a free parliament and press— —are reluctant to face evidences of mounting discontent and impending guerrilla war. Neither in Ulster itself nor in Great Britain was public opinion at that time prepared for a new outbreak of Irish troubles. On the contrary, there was at that time ground for optimism both in Northern Ireland and in the Republic. Some kind of reconciliation seemed round the corner—indeed it was partly this feeling that caused the northern Protestants to harden their feelings in the face of liberal reforms proposed by the then government of Captain O'Neill and the militant Catholics to organise for a further show of violence, which they were convinced in the prevailing climate of compromise might give them what they wanted: unity and independence for all Ireland.

It is against the British tradition to send in the troops until more pacific and constitutional methods have failed. It has also, throughout history, proved difficult for the English to understand the unreasonableness of their Irish neighbours. The English way is a commission of inquiry; the Irish way is resort to the gun. In the midst of such incomprehension, the British government wasted time that should have been devoted to swift suppression. Had the initiative been taken at that time, it is at least likely that the violence would have ended and that reforms could have been introduced with some chance of success. Instead, the violence got out of hand and the reforms were abortive.

The second proposition is no less controversial. In March 1972, the British government deprived Stormont of its power to legislate and rule in Ulster, and imposed direct rule from Westminster. 'Low-profile' tactics by the Army allowed the terrorists to expand their organisation and consolidate their hold on certain areas. In Catholic parts of Belfast (Andersonstown) and of Londonderry (Bogside and Creggan) the Provisionals held local sway in the so-called 'no-go' areas—a gesture of defiance both to the Army and to the Protestant majority.

Then came 'Bloody Friday', on 21 July 1972, with the explosion of twenty bombs in Belfast, killing nine civilians and injuring at least 130. In the ensuing public revulsion, it was politically possible for the security forces to adopt harsher methods. On 27 July, 4,000 additional troops arrived in Ulster, bringing the total to 21,000. On the 31st the security forces launched 'Operation Motorman'—the invasion of the no-go areas of Londonderry and Belfast. No attempt at secrecy or concealment had been made. On the contrary, the Army had published details of its massive build-up, to discourage the IRA from resisting.

Psychologically, the calculation was accurate: the gunmen moved back across the border to the South, and the Army simply removed the barricades, freeing the no-go areas. Within a fortnight, ten leading Provisionals in Belfast had been arrested, and by the end of November the tally had risen to 150 gunmen, at least 100 of whom were 'officers' of the IRA Command in the North. There was a dramatic rise in intelligence collected, and a similar drop in bombing attacks in Londonderry's city centre. Large hauls of arms and ammunition were made: they included 14,000 rounds of ammunition and more than two tons of explosives.

That was the moment. Could the Army have gone further, crossing the border into the Republic and over-running the training camps? Could it, in a swift and dramatic move, defy the United Nations, and the outraged cries of the liberals in many countries? Could it have sealed off the border, with barbed wire, electronic devices and traps of one kind or another? The questions are hypothetical. British governments do not behave like that—at least, they have not so be-haved since the gigantic fiasco of Suez in 1956. Nor could they, as had happened half a century earlier, send in the dreaded Black and Tans to clean up recalcitrant regions. Nor would it have been possible, even in that moment of triumph, to persuade the Irish Government of Mr. Lynch to collaborate fully with Westminster in wiping out terrorism once and for all. True, that government was well aware that in the long term, the IRA constituted a threat to its existence. But its hold on political power was too precarious for Mr. Lynch to take many chances.

His successor, Mr. Cosgrave, was in a stronger position. In these circumstances and understandably, the British government prepared further political initiatives. In September, six months after the an-nouncement of direct rule, a conference was held at Darlington to which all seven of the parliamentary parties of Northern Ireland had been invited, although only three attended. The views put forward were published in a Green Paper and in March 1973 new constitutional proposals were published. They had been preceded, however, by a referendum on 8 March in which an overwhelming majority of those voting expressed a wish to remain citizens of the United Kingdom: but the Catholics had boycotted the poll so that it could not be regarded as a true expression of the will (or the divided will) of the people of Northern Ireland. The point, however, had been to pre-empt any Protestant attempt to proclaim independence unilaterally. As such, it was a success. As a result the British government confirmed that the current status of Northern Ireland as part of the United Kingdom would continue for as long as a majority of its people desired. Moreover, the province would continue to return twelve members to Parliament at Westminster, which in turn would retain the power to legislate on all matters in the province.

The political effectiveness of these proposals—which in any case were scarcely revolutionary—was marred by a vicious outbreak of sectarian murders, many of which appeared to be the work of criminals rather than ideologically motivated people. It was too early—even early in 1974, when these lines were written—to see whether Ireland was heading for any kind of a political solution. The brief opportunity of 31 July—if opportunity it was—had come and gone, yielding important successes but not decisive ones. The terrorism went on.

PART IV

The Price of Revolution

ONE

'SPONTANEOUS' UPHEAVALS

The ground covered in this chapter

Rarity of spontaneous revolutions—bloodless ones also rare—revolutions as catastrophes—the English Revolution: money, the divine right and religion—revolution inevitable, but not civil war—the French Revolution: bankruptcy and feudal privilege—parallels with English Revolution—the revolution out of control—the Russian Revolution: autocracy and corrupt bureaucracy—reforms and repression—a short-lived revolution—Lenin takes over—extreme hazards of revolutionary upheaval

WE ALL know, or think we know, what we mean by 'revolution'. Yet the concept lacks precision and the word means different things to different people. Great spontaneous upheavals, such as the French or Russian Revolutions, or the abortive Hungarian uprising of 1956, are relatively rare in history. Most of the examples I have cited in this book are of protracted and highly organised attempts to disturb the public order—in other words, to stir up 'revolutions'. The outcome, in the end, may be no more than the exchange of one set of masters for another. Such, too, is normally the outcome of 'palace' revolutions, which are more properly termed 'revolts'.

Nor is a revolution necessarily violent. England's 'Bloodless' or 'Glorious' Revolution of 1688–9 was as far-reaching in its consequences as many more sanguinary episodes, but cost no lives. Other upheavals may be costly in blood and treasure but fail in the end, leaving things much as they were, only worse: the classic case, again, is Hungary.

Such is Man's natural abhorrence of anarchy that even the rare spontaneous upheavals I mentioned do not stay spontaneous for very long. Soon enough, a leader or a group of determined men will appear, seize the advantages of opportunity and try to steer in a precise direction. But they will succeed only if the central authority has irretrievably broken down; and even then, they may be unable to control events. (This was true of the French Revolution, for some years, and of the Russian for some months.) If some vestige of the original authority remains, or if its loss of power is purely local, then the upheaval may turn out to be no more than a more or less severe breakdown of law and order: a mere riot, not a revolution. The American Negroes who set fire to whole quarters (their own, ironically) of United States cities in the disorderly summers of 1966 to 1968 were out of control, but not for long: the government of the USA was in no way threatened.

If spontaneous revolutions are rare, so too are bloodless ones. Revolution is a costly business, causing much human suffering, hardship, loss of blood and and lives, destroying property, emptying treasuries, in the worst of cases graduating to civil war; and yielding in the end something different, for certain, but not inevitably something better. For revolution is the bluntest of all political tools: it sweeps away the good with the bad, and offers no guarantee of improvement. Nor indeed, even in the premeditated revolutions or the planned seizure of revolutionary opportunities, can the people, whether participants or helpless spectators, be certain that the new men will even carry out their revolutionary promises—let alone bring about an absolute improvement in conditions.

Nor can the leaders themselves, whatever their fanaticism or self-confidence, have any such certainty. The passions stirred by events are now seen, if the evolutionary biologists are right, as pure manifestations of the reptilian brain, over which the neo-cortex of the leadership may have no control if indeed they can control their own primitive passions. Nor do revolutionaries act in an international vacuum. Both the French and the Russian Revolutions provoked massive foreign interventions, which in the end the revolutionaries turned to patriotic advantage. The late President Allende's attempt at a 'constitutional' Marxist revolution in Chile after his minority victory in the 1970 Presidential elections did not provoke an American military intervention, but it would be untrue to say that there was no American intervention at all.

At its worst, then, revolution is a disaster, comparable in its suddenness and far-reaching effects, to some natural cataclysm, such as an earthquake or a tidal wave. At best, it is an adventure, exciting to its leaders, exhilarating for their followers, but deeply disturbing to the mass of ordinary people, who have no more control over events (except in a restricted sense, for instance when rioting or looting) than the denizens of flooded homes have over the rising water level or the victims of a conflagration over the speed and intensity of the spreading flames. It may be unavoidable (as indeed an earthquake was, in the state of seismic science of 1974), but it promises nothing with certainty except death, wounds and hardship.

To say that an upheaval is spontaneous does not mean that it is without cause, or even that there was no way of knowing that it was about to happen. When I say that it is spontaneous I mean only that it was not the planned outcome of the activities of a revolutionary party, but happened the way a fire happens if a lighted match falls upon inflammable material. The fire-prone material may, however, have been stockpiled over a period of years. The violence that characterises most revolutions may have started suddenly, but the causes may have been maturing for many years.

The English Revolution

So it was with that least typical of revolutions, the Great Rebellion, also called the English Civil War and also (especially by non-British historians), the first English Revolution—as distinct from the Bloodless Revolution which they term the second. Although a library of books has been written on the first of these events, and rather fewer on the second, it is conceptually absurd, from the standpoint of a student of conflicts, to consider the one without the other; since the second so clearly complemented the first. Similarly, it would be absurd, from the same standpoint, to write about the first years of the French Revolution *in vacuo*, as though they had not been succeeded by the Directoire or Bonaparte's *coup d'état*; or to stop an examination of the Russian Revolution before the events of November 1917.

Although in the end the consequences of the Great Rebellion were political and constitutional, the causes were concerned at least as much with economics and religion as with politics. An imbalance had been maturing for years, for generations even, so that by the 1620s, economic and political power no longer coincided in England. The merchants and bankers had been growing rich, and so had the farmers who farmed their own land intensively. But the King and some of his nobles leased out their land at rents that had become uneconomic, so that they were growing poorer while the business men were growing richer. When Charles I came to the throne in 1625, he turned to Parliament for money; but Parliament sought to extract political concessions that would have reduced the monarch's power in return for the grant of taxes. Thereupon the King, who believed in the doctrine of the 'divine right of kings' first proclaimed by his father James I, dissolved Parliament, ruling without it for a period known as the 'Eleven Years' Tyranny'. Freed from constitutional restraints, the King raised money by various means that lacked legality, such as the sale of monopolies or by Ship Money—a tax previously confined to ports which he extended to inland towns.

The initial quarrel between King and Parliament, then, was about power and money. But there was an aggravating factor in religion. The King was a High Churchman and suspected of favouring the Catholics. The Parliamentarians, broadly speaking, were Low Churchmen, or Puritans. Although the Stuarts were Scots, Charles was intolerant of their puritanism and presbyterianism and allowed his adviser, William Laud, to impose the English Prayer Book upon the Scots. In the end, this ill-starred move, perhaps more than any other, was the King's undoing.

For the Scots revolted and were not mollified even when the King withdrew the Prayer Book. The army he raised showed little inclination to fight and Charles signed the Pacification of Dunse (18 June 1638). Short of money, once again, the King summoned his fourth parliament, but almost immediately dissolved it when it refused to grant him anything until grievances were settled. As it had lasted only twenty-three days, it was known as the Short Parliament. Riots followed, and Laud's palace was attacked. The Scots took to arms again, and the King's men were defeated in what was little more than a skirmish. Under the Treaty of Ripon (26 October), Charles agreed to pay the Scottish army £850 a day, pending a permanent settlement. Yet again his weakness was demonstrated: he could not do without Parliament, and this time on 3 November 1640—the Parliamentarians dug themselves in—to such effect that they did not vacate their seats for nearly twenty years. Hence, the fifth Parliament of King Charles I, which was to outlive him, is known as the Long Parliament.

Sensing its power, Parliament forced the King to agree to the abolishing of the Star Chamber, a favourite monarchical power device, not to rule for more than three years without Parliament, and to raise no new taxes without its consent. Reluctantly, the King signed these demands and others. But he drew the line at the still more revolutionary demands presented to him in 1641 under the Grand Remonstrance. This time, instead of signing, he raised an army. And the Civil War began.

No story is more familiar than the one that ensued, which ended with the King's execution on 30 January 1649.

Was the Civil War inevitable? Certainly it could not be argued that it was spontaneous. The King was given several opportunities to give in to Parliament. Had he done so, in the end, he might have lost his pride, but he would have kept his head. Alternatively, he could have abdicated, saving both but losing his throne. He was a noble and dignified man whose real mistake was to believe in the divinity of his mission. But then, so did many of his subjects. He could have opted for a constitutional status and spared his country a civil war (though it is quite possible that Parliament would have had trouble of a sort from some of the nobles).

Conflict, though not necessarily war, was unavoidable in that the King wished to extend his power at the expense of Parliament, whereas Parliament wished to curtail the King's prerogatives and expand its own rights. In one sense, it was a crisis of modernisation at a time when the medieval system had ceased to be adequate to the needs of a country that had entered a world made 'modern' through the discovery of gunpowder, the introduction of the printing press and the circumnavigation of the globe. Had military genius been available to the Cavaliers instead of to the Roundheads, the King's side might have won and his divine right have been consolidated, at least for a time. But he lost and revolutionary change was made inevitable by his defeat. The conflict was inherent in the political impotence of the risen bourgeoisie and the King's penury and power. It was the King's blindness and folly that had made the conflict violent; it was Parliament's victory that brought constitutional change.

In the end, the price paid by the country was not great, compared with other revolutions and civil wars. The rival armies—Cavaliers and Roundheads—were small and the excesses few. The political price was higher, though impermanent. For the first and only time in British history, England became a republic, and in the end Cromwell—the Lord Protector—was her absolute dictator.

The divine right had gone for ever, but it was not for Cromwell's dictatorship that his model army had defeated the King's men. When the King's son, Charles, himself mounted the throne in 1660 as the second of his name in English history, the wheel had completed an ironical full circle. The country settled down happily to a period of elegance, wit, bawd and pleasure.

The business of revolution, however, was unfinished. It was the misfortune of Charles I's brother and successor, James II, that he was both a Catholic and of a despotic nature. Neither was tolerable to the Parliamentary temper in the 1680s. His throne, left vacant when he abandoned it, was offered to William of Orange and his consort Mary, daughter of James II, in February 1689, but there was a 'condition of sale': their joint acceptance of the Declaration of Rights, which permanently reduced the power of the sovereign and transferred the real power to Parliament. Thus in a real sense the Bloodless Revolution completed the Long Parliament's 'English Revolution', the Civil War and the sovereign's execution. It was by no means the only revolution in two phases, but it was singular in the relative cheapness of the changes wrought.

England was lucky, whether in the placidity of her people or the wisdom of her politicians. But one is driven, once more, to reflect on the adventurous uncertainties of political violence. As in other such upheavals, the situation had thrown up a leader of genius in Cromwell. But who knows where he might have led a country which asked no more of its leadership than that it should curb the power of its King, if he had lived; that is, if that tiny grain of sand which Pascal wrote about had not lodged in his urethra, causing his premature death at 59? We can no more answer that question than could the French philosopher.

The French turmoil

The uncertainties and turmoil of the French Revolution were infinitely greater than those of the English counterpart. The causes were, however, in some respects similar, and the manifestations included, as in England, a King's execution. One should note in passing that the French Revolution, although more violent and prolonged than elsewhere, was in fact only one of a series of convulsions beginning with the American War of Independence (1775–83), and continuing with disorders in England, Holland, Belgium, Switzerland and Poland. There were some common factors in all these outbreaks, especially in the ideas of liberty that were being disseminated at that time. But the French Revolution had autonomous causes, some of which paralleled those of the English Revolution more than a century earlier.

It has been said that France in 1789 was a fairly prosperous society with a bankrupt government. The new middle class had been growing richer, but was politically powerless, even and especially in local affairs. To its members, the ideas of the *Philosophes* were heady. The peasants, too, were more prosperous than they had ever been, and few of them suffered from servile restrictions. They were, however, heavily taxed, and the nobles (who along with the clergy, did not pay a fair share) made a determined attempt, towards the end of the 18th century, to collect dues from them. Resentment at this 'feudal reaction' was the outcome.

The government was inefficient rather than tyrannical, and the role of the infamous *lettres de cachet*, which sent people to dungeons without trial, has been exaggerated, their intent being more often to bring wayward sons to their senses than to silence firebrands.

Just as Charles I had summoned Parliament to raise money, so Louis XVI called the Estates-General to rescue his establishment from bankruptcy. And as with the Long Parliament, the Estates-General were more interested in reforming the State wholesale than in meeting the King's pleasure.

The ingredients of a revolutionary situation were all there: a bankrupt and irresponsible government; a peasantry discontented not by deepening poverty but by the expectations aroused by increasing prosperity; an unrepresented bourgeoisie; the survival of feudal privileges and of inequities which the unprivileged could not be expected to bear any longer. The National Assembly (17 June 1789), formed by the 600 breakaway members of the Estates-General, provided a platform for the discontented or those who spoke in their name. Their power was enormously increased when their refusal to conduct business forced the King to send the clergy and nobles to join their Assembly.

But the violence, when it came, was unexpected, giving every sign of spontaneity. The mob that gathered in the streets of Paris on 14 July 1789 was searching, it is said, for arms with which to defeat the rumoured plots of the aristocrats, the most prominent of whom was the King's conspiratorial cousin, the Duc d'Orléans. It was not a particularly proletarian crowd: indeed, artisans and shopkeepers predominated. That there were such plots seems likely; possibly the object was to provoke violence and justify armed intervention by the King's men to restore order.

Within the mob, too, there may have been agitators, possibly paid by the scheming duke, or even to serve the ends of the extremists within the National Assembly, who had not yet shown their hand. At all events somebody, at some pregnant moment, must have shouted '*à la Bastille!*', and that was where the mob converged. Spontaneous or not, the storming of the King's punitive fortress produced a lasting myth of revolt against tyranny and injustice, which even the most sober or the most reactionary of French governments continues to celebrate, along with the most radical or reforming.

The story of ensuing events has been told too often to bear repetition here, and I offer only a few reflections upon the course of events. Again, the Revolution offers a striking parallel with the events of 1640–1 in that during two relatively peaceful years (1790–2), the National Assembly was able to draft its revolutionary Constitution and pass other measures—such as stripping the Church of its lands and privileges—all apparently with the acquiescence of a weak but well-intentioned monarch. Montesquieu's ideas of proper checks and balances—between the King and the legislators, or between central authority and local government—were given the shape of law; the famous Declaration of the Rights of Man and the Citizen, with its insistence (notorious to socialists of a future generation) on liberty and the rights of property, rather than upon equality, except before the law (itself a tremendous advance) was approved. This was it: the Revolution.

And if this was it, was there any need for the successive waves of violence, for the National Convention and the Terror, for the execution of Louis XVI and his Queen, for the Directoire and Bonaparte's 18 Brumaire, for the Empire and incessant war? Once again, one is struck by the bluntness, the unpredictability, the adventurous surge into the unknown that is unleashed by the revolutionary process. The violence had begun in Paris, but it continued in the provinces where, in scattered places, the peasants rioted and stormed their lords' fortresses, burning the records that bound them to pay this or that in perpetuity. The King's weakness and his blunders contributed to his own downfall. He was misguided enough to attempt flight from France with his family in June 1791, and though forgiven, to encourage the plots of aristocratic *émigrés* to spark a foreign military intervention. The Assembly, too, had its blunders, not least the Church settlement which alienated the clergy and was soon shown to be unworkable. And the extremists, who wanted violence, and openly advocated it in their inflammatory tabloids, got their way. In the prevailing chaos, inflation took its toll, contributing mightily to public unrest.

Conceivably that remarkable orator and prospective statesman, Count Mirabeau, might have preserved the situation, had he not died in 1791, aged only 42. But that is hypothetical, and historians disagree upon the nature of his plans and ambitions and the value of the role he was playing when he died. But the point surely is this: once revolution has started, nobody can predict how it will develop and end, nor can any hopes be vested upon the advent of a providential man. It is this adventurous uncertainty that appeals to revolutionaries, whose extremism contributes to the violence they crave for. When the providential man came, his name was Napoleon Bonaparte and he led France along the path of conquest and empire. Without the Revolution, he would assuredly have achieved fame of a sort, but it was the Revolution that gave him his chance of supreme power. And before him, France had endured sanguinary monsters, such as Robespierre and Marat, and their favourite toy, the guillotine (to which Robespierre himself paid the ultimate obeisance, Marat's end being by the assassin's knife).

The parallels continue. In lieu of revolutionary reform, the English violence had produced Cromwell and the Commonwealth; in lieu of revolution, the French violence had yielded a conquering dictator. And yet, in France as in England, when the dust settled and the violence ended, something of the reforms of the National and Legislative Assemblies remained or was restored. The principle of equality before the law was established; the Church and the aristocrats had lost their privileges for ever; land had indeed been redistributed; and the ideas of liberty and representation, though temporarily stifled, found their way at last into permanent institutions. Some historians and critics believe all this could have been achieved without violence. But this again is hypothetical. As the great writer Alexis de Tocqueville put it:

... Chance played no part whatever in the outbreak of the Revolution; though it took the world by surprise, it was the inevitable outcome of a long period of gestation, the abrupt and violent conclusion of a process in which six generations had played an intermittent part. Even if it had not taken place, the old social structure would nonetheless have been shattered everywhere sooner or later. The only difference would have been that instead of collapsing with such brutal suddenness it would have crumbled bit by bit. At one fell swoop, without warning, without transition, and without compunction, the Revolution effected what in any case was bound to happen, if by slow degrees.[1]

Russia: a wrong turning

History was kinder to the English and French than to the Russians. In France and England—especially the former—revolution was accompanied by violence and unpredictable upheaval; but in the end things got back to something recognisably normal, and there were net gains.

[1] *The Ancien Régime and the French Revolution* (London, 1966), p. 51.

In Russia, the 'providential man' was a destroyer of genius who set his country and its subject peoples on a course of perpetual tyranny. History, as has been observed, took a wrong turning.

In Russia, the imbalance between society and government was even greater than it had been in France 128 years earlier. The Tsar still ruled Russia as an absolute autocrat, with a corrupt and inefficient bureaucracy to do his bidding and an army and secret police to enforce it. In class terms, the only support he had came from the wealthy landowners, who were few in numbers. Although Alexander II (1818–81) had emancipated the serfs and attempted to reform local government and the judiciary, he had taken alarm at the violent activities of the Nihilists and turned to repression. He himself was their victim, and his son Alexander III, who succeeded him after his assassination, suppressed all revolutionary activity, restored the pre-eminence of the nobles, persecuted religious minorities and discriminated against the non-Russian peoples of his empire. The last of the Tsars, Nicholas II, was weak of will, as Louis XVI had been in France, though more intelligent than the French king. His government was discredited by Russia's defeat in the war with Japan in 1905, and disorders followed, in which, for the first time, the factory workers in St. Petersburg and other cities played an important part. The culmination of the abortive revolution at the end of that year was the insurrection of the workers in Moscow.

At the end of October 1905, the Tsar had granted Russia a constitution, with extended franchise, a duma with real legislative powers and guaranteed civil liberties. But after the disorders had been crushed, he reaffirmed his autocracy under the Fundamental Laws of May 1906. The social–political imbalance remained entire.

There is less room for hypothetical speculation about the Russian Revolution than about the English or French. Given peace, the Tsar would have had a better chance than he did of forestalling revolution by reform, but the repression of 1906, in its absoluteness, favoured the revolutionaries. In Peter Stolypin, Nicholas II had an able reforming Prime Minister. But Stolypin was assassinated in 1911 and his successor, Kokovtsev, lacked comparable will-power and prestige.

The outbreak of the First World War less than three years later sealed the fate of the Russian monarchy. Soon the Russian armies were in deep trouble and the great defeat in Galicia in May 1915 stirred public opinion into outspoken criticism of the inefficiency and indeed the criminal negligence of the government in failing to supply the armies. The Tsar's decision in September to dismiss his commander-in-chief and take command himself merely made matters worse, for it meant his absenting himself from the capital. It was during the next phase that the Tsarina fell under the nefarious influence of the adventurer Rasputin. Amid rumours of high treason in high places, economic chaos deepened and the assassination of Rasputin at the end of 1916 solved nothing.

The revolution happened, as spontaneously as a revolution can, in March 1917 (February, by the old Russian calendar), with strikes and riots in Petrograd (St. Petersburg), a general mutiny of the forces in the capital and the refusal of the Duma to obey an imperial decree ordering its dissolution. On the 12th, a provisional government was proclaimed, and on the 15th the Tsar abdicated. The old regime was dead.

But the new one was to live only eight months. The provisional government proclaimed the civic liberties and removed all discrimination on grounds of social origins, race or religion. Independence was granted to Finland and Poland, and autonomy to Estonia. A far-reaching land reform programme was announced, but deferred for consideration by the proposed Constituent Assembly.

By the end of March 1917, then, the Russian Revolution had reached a stage that curiously paralleled events in England in 1640 and in France in 1790. The old regime had been defeated or swept away, and the Revolution had given the people the reforms for which the revolutionaries had agitated. So much had been accomplished by the blind and impersonal forces of history, and by the follies of inadequate leaders.

But now, in living disproof of Marxist determinism, a leader of genius was about to transform the situation, snuffing out the brief light of freedom that had flickered during the early days of the Provisional Government.

Lenin had played a minor role in the 1905 disturbances, then gone abroad, living mostly in London. He was in Switzerland, however, when the 'February' Revolution took place. With a small group of his associates—including Zinoviev, Radek and Lunacharski—he had taken no part in the 'capitalist' and 'imperialist' war in which their country and Germany were the antagonists. He turned to the Germans as the only way to get into Russia and the Germans obliged with the famous sealed train that conveyed the little band of revolutionaries from Sweden to Petrograd. Instead of praising the men of the revolution, Lenin castigated them for allowing events to take control and for failing to see that while the war went on, capitalism was digging itself in. The real revolution, he proclaimed, was still to come; and it had to be *planned*.

Lenin's own programme called for a separate peace with the Central Powers, immediate seizure of the land by the peasants without waiting for a decision by the Constituent Assembly, and control of industry by committees (soviets) of workers. Although the Socialists had already set up the Petrograd Soviet of Workers' and Soldiers' Deputies, Lenin's programme was not immediately popular.

The original Prime Minister of the provisional government, Prince Lvov, resigned in July and his place was taken by the liberal Socialist, Alexander Kerensky. The new premier was given no chance to settle down. From the left he was challenged by Lenin's Bolsheviks; from the right by the new commander-in-chief, Gen. Lavr Kornilov, who marched on Petrograd with the aim of destroying the Soviet. Many of his soldiers defected, however, and he was defeated. Kerensky released Trotsky and other Bolsheviks from gaol and soon found himself powerless in their hands.

On 6 November (24 October), Lenin, judging the time was ripe, launched his *coup d'état*. The timing was perfect. The revolutionaries stormed the Winter Palace, captured the government offices and arrested the ministers. Kerensky himself escaped and went into exile. The Revolution was over; the long night of totalism began.

It was the Bolshevik *coup d'état*, above all, that demonstrated the extreme hazards of a revolutionary upheaval. In Russia, as in England and France, events had got out of control. In all three, a leader of genius had seized his opportunity, setting up a dictatorship. But the special polities of Cromwell and Napoleon had been tailored to the needs or measurements of those exceptional men in forms that made their survival unlikely. Lenin alone, however, had lived and planned revolution all his life. He alone had set up a small, fanatical party of the revolutionary vanguard. His talk of the withering away of the State was not necessarily insincere. But the roots of a self-perpetuating autocracy were in the vanguard party he had created. Stalin was his unwitting gift to Russia and the world.

TWO

THE MANDATE OF HEAVEN

The ground covered in this chapter

The vulnerability of pluralistic rule—misguided autocracies and irresponsible democracies—causes of the Chinese Revolution (1911) —failures of Chiang Kai-shek: corruption and brutality of regime— the communist challenge—how Mao Tse-tung achieved mass support —Sukarno's 'guided democracy'—corruption and irresponsibility— monumental failure of the Spanish Second Republic—the parliamentary game in Greece—demagogy and the Aspida affair—the Colonels strike—the myth of Allende's social-democratic experiment

IT IS a law of politics that those who achieve power will henceforth devote the major part of their time and energy to keeping it. It is unfortunately not a law—although it ought to be an obligation—that they will try to rule well. Yet the two are in close correlation: to rule well may help to keep a man or a team in power. To be well-intentioned is insufficient; to rule badly but autocratically is a more likely recipe for the maintenance of power than to rule in a well-meaning way but with excessive benevolence—even though the evil autocrat invites rebellion. For elevation of sentiment does not compensate for weakness of execution, and the autocrat, however evil, has the power to repress.

These aphorisms may seem obvious, but are not always understood. Alternatively, some may be accepted but not others, and this partiality can lead to dangerous confusion. It is not always appreciated, for instance, that a wise and benevolent despot, who not only maintains order but tries to, and succeeds in, ruling in the interests of his people, is preferable by far to a weak, corrupt and inefficient democracy. For the short-term enjoyment of tolerance is liable, under the second, to be succeeded only too soon by the discomforts or actual sufferings inherent in anarchy, inflation and the loss of popular esteem. In other words, with the exception of modern totalism (which offers neither hope nor choice), the system is less important than the way it works, or is made or allowed to work.

This proposition is not readily acceptable to ideological liberals who automatically assume that a democracy, however bad, is self-correcting and by definition better than a despotism, however benevolent. They are, however, mistaken, and the fallacy of the assumption lies in the extreme vulnerability of pluralistic rule that falls into corrupt or irresponsible hands.

The century offers many striking examples both of misguided autocracies and of irresponsible democracies, and of the fates to which either are prone. Among the many, let me suggest the years of Kuomintang rule in China, the Spanish Second Republic, the Sukarno regime in Indonesia and the Greek and Chilean parliamentary regime.

It will be seen that the examples alternate: whatever the outward constitutional forms in either case, Kuomintang China and Sukarno's Indonesia were basically autocracies; and the Spanish Republic, Greece and Chile were democracies.

The Chinese Revolutions of 1911 and 1949 offer some parallels with, but also striking dissimilarities from, the examples considered in the last chapter. The most interesting parallel, from our standpoint, is that once again, here was a revolution (if the period is considered as a whole) in two phases: Nationalist in 1911, and Communist in 1949. But the gap of thirty-eight years between the two events weakens the parallel: the corresponding gap between the two Russian Revolutions was only eight months, and the second resulted from a *coup d'état* and was followed by a civil war. In China, there was no *coup d'état* and the civil war preceded the second Revolution. There were other major divergences between the Russian and Chinese Revolutions, the most important of which was that although Mao Tse-tung was a Marxist–Leninist and a founder-member of the Chinese Communist Party, he based his revolution not upon the working class, as ordered by Marx and Lenin, but upon the peasantry.

In this chapter, however, I am less concerned with Mao than with the man he defeated, Generalissimo Chiang Kai-shek. Chiang's story, from 1925 (death of Sun Yat-sen) to 1949 is that of perhaps the most gigantic failure of the 20th century—a failure on so colossal a scale as to be almost beyond imaginative grasp. It is worth inquiring into the causes of that failure.

It must be admitted that there was mitigation in the daunting circumstances that faced him. Although China's was the oldest continuous civilisation in the world, the country had sunk by the middle of the

19th century to a condition of unprecedented misery and national humiliation. A major factor in this situation was a tremendous population explosion, carrying the population from 150 million to 430 million in the 150 years to 1850. In 1700, the Chinese way of life had been viable and the condition of the peasantry was not particularly miserable. But the population had soared while farming methods remained almost static. During the first decades of the 19th century, the peasants were gradually reduced first to subsistence, then to less-than-subsistence, agriculture. Or to put it another way, whereas they had previously produced enough to feed themselves, with a surplus to feed the nobles and the mandarinal bureaucracy *and* support the continuing feudal society and the Chinese State, the situation now was that there was little or no surplus, so that the exactions of tax-collectors and absentee landlords ate—literally—into the food needed for empty bellies.

Natural calamities exacerbated human failings, and the predictable outcome was the great T'ai P'ing Rebellion (1850–64), which further devastated China, wrecking the communications that were blood-vessels of the vast country, and damaging the flood control and irrigation systems painstakingly built and maintained by generations of muscle-power. It is thought that no fewer than 20 million lives were lost during the Rebellion, which in the end was abortive after initial rebel successes, but left the country not only impoverished but a prey to widespread banditry and plunder.

The foreign humiliations reflected the weakness, disarray and technical backwardness of the Chinese empire. The national myth saw China as the centre of the world and foreigners as barbarians—the second part of the proposition, at least, having been essentially true for much of recorded history. As late as 1805, Christian literature had been banned, and a Catholic missionary was strangled in 1815 by official edict for having dared to be present in China without permission. A year later, the Emperor still felt strong and disdainful enough to send a British ambassador home without receiving him. The rot began with the illicit trade in Indian opium in the 1820s, and it seems monstrous in retrospect that the British should have made war upon the Chinese (1841–2) to legalise the opium trade; and still more monstrous that the British and French, not content with occupying Peking in 1860, should find it necessary to burn the Summer Palace to punish the court for the seizure of envoys. Britain, France, the United States and Russia all imposed 'unequal treaties' on an impotent China between 1842 and 1860. This history, recent by the scale of Chinese annals, does much to explain, though it cannot justify, the anti-foreign excesses of the Great Proletarian Cultural Revolution, from April 1966 on.

The culmination of this humiliating process came in 1895, after the Sino-Japanese war, when China, under the Treaty of Shimonoseki, recognised the independence of Korea and ceded Formosa and other possessions to Japan.

Every now and again, the Chinese turned round and, as it were, kicked the foreign devils. On 21 June 1870, for instance, a mob in Tientsin massacred a French consul and missionaries. And in 1900, the Boxer militias, spurred on by a xenophobic faction in the Manchu court, killed or harassed foreigners in many areas. The outcome, however, was the further humiliation of the Boxer Protocol, providing for costly indemnities to the aggrieved powers. It is relevant to the revolutionary situation that was developing to point out that the Boxer uprising came two years after the so-called 'hundred days of reform' (11 June–16 September 1898), in which the Emperor, under the guidance of a group of radical advisers, introduced measures designed to expand and westernise the educational system. The Empress Dowager, Tzu-hsi, put a stop to this progressive nonsense by gaoling the Emperor and revoking all measures contrary to the interests of the Manchu court and of the official classes. (There is a parallel there with the Russian repression of 1906.)

It will be noticed that three main elements composed the situation on the eve of the overthrow of the Manchu dynasty in 1911–12: the failure of the dynasty to protect China from foreign depredations; the need to modernise the country; and the desperate condition of the peasantry. The first two were closely linked, in a mirror-image relationship. The 'foreign devils' had humiliated China, and the Manchus had proved helpless: to remove them therefore became a nationalist rallying cry, which was equated with the creation of a strong China able to stand up to the foreigners.

At the same time, one of China's weaknesses was educational and technical backwardness. To catch up with the powerful Western countries, and Japan, therefore, the Chinese would have to borrow from the West. To some extent, modernisation was equated with westernisation, and the lesson of Japan's rapid assimilation of Western techniques and weapons was not lost upon the young revolutionaries. It was China's tragedy, however, that the enormous social problem of peasant poverty was almost overlooked in the prevailing struggle for power.

To a large extent, this was a tragedy of missing leadership and ill-luck. The outstanding personality among the Nationalist leaders was Sun Yat-sen, founder of the Kuomintang (Nationalist) Party. Dr. Sun, a Cantonese, was a man of ideas and vision, a convert to Christianity; the slogan of his party was 'the three principles of the people' —Nationalism, Democracy and Social Progress. He was not blind to the condition of the peasantry, and saw the remedy in the creation of a fertiliser industry, in flood control and the building of roads and railways. But he was never given a chance to implement his plans.

It was his misfortune to be abroad (as Lenin was) when the hour of Revolution struck. In consequence, power was seized by a disgruntled Manchu official, Yuan Shih-k'ai, who had been dismissed two years earlier. Returning to China at the end of 1911, three months after the outbreak of revolution, Sun (unlike Lenin) was unable to impose his leadership, except in southern China. He died in 1925 after a period of national confusion marked, *inter alia*, by two abortive attempts to restore the monarchy.

Dr. Sun's mantle fell upon Chiang Kai-shek, who had first come to public notice as Commandant of the Military Academy of Whangpoa (1924). Although Chiang was, as one would say nowadays, a charismatic leader, his genius was almost purely military. He had little understanding of social and indeed of political problems. He was unfortunate, moreover, in inheriting not only the enormous problems I have mentioned, but a decision that was to have far-reaching consequences for China and the world. Sun Yat-sen and his party had hoped that China would regain lost territory in the peace settlement after the First World War. But President Wilson's promises of self-determination were seen not to apply to China. Japan, having seized Chinese territory formerly grabbed by Germany, was not in a dispossessive mood, and the European victors were no more interested than the Americans in supporting the claims of the Chinese Republic. The Kuomintang thereupon turned to the young regime of Lenin's Bolsheviks, admitting Communists to their party and accepting Soviet advisers.

This was in many ways a fateful decision. The chief Soviet adviser, Michael Borodin, who arrived in China in September 1923, reorganised the Kuomintang on Communist lines. Chiang Kai-shek, though initially in favour of this link, turned against it after his visit to Moscow some months later and expressed himself forcibly on the issue in a private letter.[1] Soon enough, he was to start hunting and killing Communists. His first preoccupation, however, was to establish the

[1] Chiang Kai-shek, *Soviet Russia in China* (New York, 1957), pp. 23–4.

authority of the central government over areas controlled by the war-lords. His campaign against the northern war-lords in 1926 was a success. His first break with the Communist members of the KMT came in March 1927 when the latter took advantage of the seizure of Nanking to burn and loot foreign houses and kill some of their owners. Chiang turned on the Communists and managed, according to some of the conflicting reports of this confused period, to kill some thousands of them.

A more serious challenge to him soon came. It took the form of the establishment of Russian-style Soviets in the provinces of Kiangsi and Fukien. A formidable leader had launched this experiment, promising and apparently giving land to the landless peasants, ready to defend them against their landlords and against all attempts by Chiang's government to enter the Communist areas. The name of that leader, at that time hardly known, was Mao Tse-tung.

By 1934, however, Chiang's forces had managed at last to evict the Communists, but not to force their surrender: instead, with Mao in command, the Communist guerrillas trekked thousands of miles to the caves of Yenan in a legendary feat known as 'the long march'.

On paper, at all events, the situation in 1935 was that Chiang Kai-shek had broken the incipient power of the Chinese Communist Party and smashed Mao's Soviet experiment. Yet fourteen years later, Chiang was in his Formosan exile, and Mao was the fountain-head of power in the new Chinese People's Republic. How had this extraordinary reversal of fortune come about?

This is not the place to attempt even an abridged version of some of the most complex events in contemporary history, but some comments can be offered. Many allowances can be made: for the overwhelming problems Chiang inherited; for the fresh and ghastly challenges of the two Japanese invasions (1930 and 1937); for the further complications brought by the Second World War; and in the end by Russia's last-minute decision to invade Manchuria (on 8 August 1945, two days after the first atomic bomb had been dropped on Hiroshima, and two days before the Japanese offer to surrender). Credit, too, should be given where it was due. At the height of his power in 1937, on the eve of the second undeclared war by Japan on China, Chiang had indeed much to be proud of. China had been given a uniform and stabilised paper currency; new railways and roads had been opened; radio and telephone communications had been modernised; and most import-antly, there had been an impressive expansion of educational facilities.

None of this, however, percolated down to the great, inert and long-suffering mass of the peasantry. Inevitably, the KMT was the party of the gentry and the mandarinate, and increasingly, as the war with Japan took its toll, it became a party that existed largely for the private enrichment of its leading members. Nobody has suggested that Chiang himself was corrupt; but he was surrounded by corrupt people. And the Second World War progressed, and as American money and arms and supplies of all kinds, including medicaments, came on the habitually generous scale, they contributed not to the war effort but to a gigantic black market. Deficit financing on a reckless scale was the primary cause of the great Chinese inflation of the 1940s—the only rival of which was that of the Weimar Republic in Germany.

To make matters worse, Chiang seems to have taken a purely military view of his war against the Japanese. Given China's acute shortage of modern weapons, and Japan's plenitude, he decided to do as Tsar Alexander I had done in the face of Napoleon's invasion of Russia: to trade space against survival, drawing the enemy even further inland, avoiding a possibly fateful confrontation while preserving his forces intact; so that in the end, Chiang was forced to set up his capital in the Far West of China, at Chungking, beyond the rugged Yangtse gorges. The social and political consequence of this policy of strategic retreat and attrition was that the people in the vast areas abandoned by the Nationalists remained unprotected, both against the Japanese and against the Communists.

Not that the Communists, at that stage, were oppressors of the peasantry. On the contrary, Mao had grasped that power in the long run would be his if he could gain the support of China's teeming millions. And he set out, successfully, to gain it, by promising and distributing land, by helping with the harvest, by the avoidance of soldierly excesses. Moreover, whereas Chiang was avoiding battle with the Japanese (for sound military reasons, as I have argued), Mao's guerrillas harassed the Japanese, visibly fighting a 'patriotic war' as well as relieving the peasants of immemorial oppression. (The peasants were not to know, at that time, that one of the Communist government's first policy objectives, on gaining power, would be to collectivise the land that had been distributed to those who tilled it; but by that time, the policy of land redistribution had served its purpose, and doctrine could take over.)

The end of the war found Chiang Kai-shek recognised as one of the 'Big Four', along with Stalin, Churchill and Roosevelt. But the China over which he presided was a shell. The Communists controlled most of Inner Mongolia and Manchuria, and had been given the vast stocks of arms and ammunition seized from the Japanese by the invading Russians. The approved Kuomintang version of the Chinese Civil War attributes the Nationalist defeat to this late gift from Stalin, who had neglected Mao's highly unorthodox agrarian Communist Party until then. True, the gift proved decisive in the sense that Chiang might well have won if the Communists had had to make do with rudimentary arms. But the argument is hypothetical. The hard reality is that the Kuomintang regime was deeply unpopular, whereas Mao had gained mass popular support. With that *and* the arms, he was invincible.

Fate was unkind to Chiang Kai-shek. But he cannot be exonerated from responsibility for presiding over a brutal, corrupt and inefficient regime.

I have described Sukarno's Indonesia as an autocracy, and this had become true some years before his downfall. But from the proclamation of independence in 1945 until, say, 1959 (when President Sukarno introduced 'guided democracy'), it had been a pluralistic regime and even (on the basis of general elections held in 1955) a parliamentary democracy of a sort.

Sukarno naturally cast himself in the role of 'guide' in his guided democracy. It was time, he said, to do away with 'wasteful debates' and opposition parties. Borrowing (though not explicitly) from the principles of Mussolini's corporative State, he established a Council of People's Representatives, which included not only members of political parties, but representatives of 'functional groups', such as farmers, professional people, and the armed forces. Guided democracy was supplemented by a 'guided economy' under a National Planning Board.

These, at any rate, were the visible lines of the State. In terms of power, Sukarno's base rested upon 'Nasakom'—a portmanteau word composed of the first syllables of Indonesian words meaning 'nationalism', 'religious forces' and 'communism'. Although all three of these components were indeed powerful currents in the mainstream of Indonesian awareness, they were not a suitable power base, in that they did not correspond with the real centres of power in that vast and scattered island country. The real factors in the power equation were in fact Sukarno himself, the Communist Party (PKI) and the Army.

In his precarious balancing act between the last two, Sukarno made the mistake of leaning increasingly upon the enormous PKI, the membership of which reached 3 million. This was his undoing. The President collapsed on 30 September 1965 while addressing a big audience in Djakarta stadium. Believing him to be dead, the Com-

munists launched a well-prepared *coup d'état* involving the murder of
eight leading anti-Communist generals. Only six were killed, however,
the other two escaped, and one of them—a virtually unknown soldier
of cool disposition and calm judgment, named Suharto—took control
and eventually dispossessed Sukarno of his office and privileges. The
PKI was broken and its members or sympathisers were massacred on
a fearful scale: about half a million people were put to death.

In personality, Sukarno was the antithesis of Chiang Kai-shek, but
there were similarities between the regimes over which they presided.
Chiang was austere and it has never been seriously suggested that he
was personally corrupt. He was, however, surrounded by corrupt
people, and since these people manipulated the KMT party for their
own ends, it could scarcely be said that the Nationalists ruled in the
interests of the people. Moreover, the Kuomintang programme which
Chiang had inherited from Sun Yat-sen provided for a period of
'tutelage' of the Chinese people (of indefinite duration) before the
introduction of full democracy, in which a parallel can be found with
Sukarno's 'guided democracy'.

Sukarno was a gay and irrepressible personality, and an orator of
hypnotic power. He was also irresponsible and flagrantly debauched.
He discredited the public service and the press, poisoned public opinion and bankrupted the State. He had a taste for costly follies, such as
grandiose buildings to his own glory, and by habit gave precedence to
shows of magnificence over the boring routine of dealing with real
problems, such as agriculture, the balancing of trade and the budget,
or the ill-balanced overpopulation of Java. His foreign policy was a
vainglorious shambles, based upon demagogic rhetoric and seeking,
by pressures on neighbouring countries (especially Malaysia and
Singapore) and 'anti-colonialist' actions against the Dutch, to justify
recurrent appearances in the world's headlines as the champion of the
Third World and 'Nefo' (another of the portmanteau slogan words
which were used increasingly as substitutes for policy-making, and
meaning 'new emerging forces'). Long before his overthrow, Sukarno
has lost whatever Mandate Heaven might, in an absent-minded mood,
have conferred upon him.

Misgovernment is by no means the prerogative of autocrats. From
the Weimar Republic on, modern history provides many examples of
the mismanagement of parliamentary democracies. There are always
penalties in store, and their severity varies in direct proportion to the
extent of governmental failure. A change of regime; defeat in war;

collapse of the State; a *coup d'état*, followed by the imposition of either an authoritarian or a totalist regime, whether of the Left or Right; civil war, even – these, singly or in combination, await the politicians who fail to put the public or national interest above their private advantage, who prefer the *game* of politics to the hard work of facing problems and governing, or who, though well-meaning, are simply incapable of coping with a deteriorating situation. Defeat in war and the collapse of the State awaited the men of the French Third Republic. The Weimar Republic yielded to Hitler. Profligate or adventurous presidencies in Brazil, marked latterly by a singular tolerance for the drift towards revolutionary anarchy, were rewarded by a military *coup d'état* in 1964. The list could be extended.

One of the most striking failures of modern times was that of the Second Spanish Republic. The mythology of the Left, and the misconceptions of more than a generation of ordinary citizens, have held the men of the Second Republic to be guiltless and righteous, the helpless victims of a polarisation of politics and of a right-wing military conspiracy, aided by the Nazis and Fascists. But this is a very one-sided picture. Whether by inexperience and lack of democratic tradition, through national temperament, or obstinacy, the Spanish politicians of the 1930s did not make a go of the parliamentary process. Their failure was monumentally costly and cannot be primarily ascribed to circumstances beyond their control.

It was, at the outset, a failure of judgment and even of common sense. The King of Spain, Alfonso XIII, had left the country, though without abdicating, after the victory of the Republican parties in the *municipal* elections of April 1931. The Provisional government that took over was faced almost immediately with serious disorders, which included the burning of churches and convents in many cities. As an act of policy, however, it decided to do nothing to restore order, and the Civil Guard were ordered to stand by. The dominant personality was Manuel Azaña, a distinguished writer and, by political conviction an anti-clerical and anti-military Jacobin. Still lacking any more precise legal mandate than the municipal elections, he rushed through anti-clerical and anti-military measures which, whatever their intrinsic merit, were bound, by their indecent haste and their indifference to the feelings of large sections of the population, to produce deep resentment.[2]

By the end of 1933, the gaols were full, armed police were everywhere, unemployment was rife and strikes were constant. The right-

[2] See Brian Crozier, *Franco* (London, 1967), pp. 114 et seq.

wing parties that came to power with the elections of November 1933 fared no better and were soon faced with a separatist rising in Catalonia and an insurrection of the Asturian miners, which were suppressed —especially the second—with great brutality. Corruption scandals further marred the record of the 'two black years' (*Bienio negro*) as the Left dubbed the right-wing interlude. During this period and especially after the victory of the Popular Front in February 1936, the inflammatory speeches of the Socialist leaders, Largo Caballero and Indalecio Prieto, greatly contributed to the climate of violence and the polarisation of Spanish politics. Street battles and assassinations, especially between the small Communist and Fascist (*Falange*) parties were rife. By the spring of 1936, Spain was gripped in an orgy of riots, strikes and arson, the culmination of which was the kidnapping and murder of the right-wing deputy Calvo Sotelo, by *the police*. It is one aspect of the truth to say that the civil war began because a section of the army had plotted to rise against the Republic. But it must be admitted that the conspirators had something to plot against. The record of the Republican politicians from 1931 to 1936 is one of venality, irresponsibility and folly on an appalling scale. And the folly was sustained to the bitter end, for in February that year, the government declined Franco's offer to restore order, and in June it left unanswered Franco's warning of disaffection within the army.

The situation in Greece in the four years before the successful military coup of 21 April 1967 bears various similarities with that in Spain before the Civil War, although the descent into anarchy was less rapid. Indeed, it was presumably forestalled by the coup. So much sentimental nonsense has been written about Greece as 'the cradle of democracy' that it may be worth recalling that it was also, for that matter, 'the cradle of tyranny' and indeed of many other political or philosophical concepts. The 'democracy' of the Greek city-States in any case bore little resemblance to the mass democracies of contemporary society, and the country's recent experience of it was spasmodic and inconclusive. To the extent that it flourished, it was, to an even greater degree than in France, essentially a game in which power was held more or less ephemerally by the man best able to do his parliamentary arithmetic and replace one coalition of votes by another in time to avoid defeat. At all times, the brilliance and wit of Athenian society was remote from the realities of rural life in an arid land.

Between the world wars, the practice of democracy was interrupted for several years by the military *coup d'état* of General Metaxas

(August 1936) and by the German occupation, from 1941 on. After the war, the country was gripped by a civil war (May 1946–October 1949) in which the protagonists were the elected government and the self-proclaimed Communist 'First Provisional Democratic Government of Free Greece'. After the defeat of the Communists (whose party was outlawed in December 1947), Greece enjoyed—if that is the appropriate word—a period of democratic rule, marked by a multiplicity of cabinets. By far the most successful of the Greek politicians was Constantine Karamanlis, who held office as Prime Minister between 1955 and 1963. After inconclusive elections in November 1964 and a succession of caretaker governments, fresh elections in February 1964 yielded a solid majority for the Centre Union party of the veteran politician George Papandreou. The headlong decline of a system which, whatever its faults, had demonstrated its resilience under an able leader—Karamanlis—began with the advent, or return, of Papandreou. Or rather, with the advent of the Papandreous, for George Papandreou, who was 75 when elected in 1964, brought with him into the cabinet his son Andreas (born in 1919). By all accounts, the son was at least as active as the father in most of the events that followed.

Andreas Papandreou had gone to America as a young man, and become an academic, teaching at various universities. He went back to Athens at his father's invitation and renounced his American citizenship before the 1964 elections, which returned him to Parliament. He became Minister to the Prime Minister (his father). Most previous holders of this unexalted post had found themselves doing odd jobs, such as dealing with inquisitive gentlemen of the press, or sorting out archaeological claims and counter-claims. But his interests and ambitions outstripped this narrow compass, and it was said that his hand was visible in other matters, including Economic affairs.

In November 1964, however, Andreas Papandreou resigned when a friend's husband secured a contract. Back again in April 1965, and promoted to Deputy Minister of Co-ordination, he was soon, it was said, doing the Minister's job.

During the next period, a number of fellow travellers of the Greek Communist Party (KKE) were appointed to positions in the Greek Central Intelligence Service (whose duties covered domestic security as well as foreign intelligence). In January 1965, the government, though it did not lift the ban on the KKE, released many Communists or sympathisers from gaol. This was in line with the general encouragement the Papandreous had given to the legal 'front' party known as the United Democratic Left (EDA) behind which the banned KKE had sheltered since 1951. Indeed, during the Papandreou administration, the EDA's membership approximately doubled, to 90,000.

There were widespread complaints in the spring of 1965 (anticipating Watergate) that the security and intelligence machinery was being used to spy on Ministers who had expressed doubts or criticisms of the Papandreous, whose homes were bugged.

Next came the Aspida affair. Aspida means 'shield' in Greek, and it was said to be the name of a secret political organisation within the army; though what it was plotting was at first obscure. The Prime Minister appointed a Judge-Advocate-General to look into it.

The repercussions were far-reaching. Rumour linked Andreas Papandreou with the plotters. In July 1965, his father called on King Constantine to dismiss the Defence Minister, Mr. Garouphalias, and appoint him (George Papandreou) in his stead. The King refused and Papandreou resigned.

The Aspida trial did not begin until October 1966, and in March 1967, 13 of the 28 army officers in dock were acquitted; the other 15 were gaoled for terms of two to 18 years. By now the purpose of the Aspida organisation had long been public knowledge, for the charges included plotting to overthrow the monarchy and set up a republican regime modelled on Nasser's in Egypt. What of Andreas Papandreou's supposed link with the conspirators? The question was never clearly answered, for the public prosecutor failed—though not for lack of trying—to get his parliamentary immunity lifted so that he could be tried before a civilian court on a charge of treason.

While the Aspida trial was proceeding, the democratic process was breaking down. A prolonged ministerial crisis had followed Papandreou's dismissal by the King. The EDA, with the clandestine party apparatus behind it, organised anti-monarchist and pro-Papandreou marches and demonstrations, and in Parliament the Papandreou supporters set out to howl down the government of defecting Centre Union deputies that has succeeded his own. Parliamentary rowdyism increasingly became habitual, the Papandreous' campaigning against the King grew shriller and the public grew more and more nervous.

When Colonel Papadopoulos and his fellow-plotters struck on 21 April 1967, they rationalised their *coup d'état* on the ground that Greece had become a 'pit of political corruption' and that the Communists were about to launch an insurrection. The first of these charges was undoubtedly well founded. The second was not. The true danger was of a Centre–Union–Communist coalition, with Andreas Papandreou as the prime mover. It was indeed plausibly reported at that time that the Communists themselves were becoming apprehensive at the possible consequences of the younger Papandreou's courtship of their support. What they feared was a coup in which they would be the first sufferers. And their apprehension was well founded, for when the Colonels struck, the Communists clearly had no idea of their plans and thousands of them were rounded up and interned within a few hours.

The Parliamentary regime had become a farce in Greece. The politicians, who had long lost the confidence of the public, had lately earned its contempt. Their responsibility for the deprivation of freedom from which they themselves were to suffer was heavy.

From a distance, in the intellectual armchairs of the great cities and capitals of the West—in London, Paris, Rome, New York—there is normally an instant readiness to heap blame upon soldiers who intervene to save their countries from the follies of the politicians, and a curious unwillingness to see the follies for what they are.

Of no country and situation was this truer than of Chile and the Allende experiment. Misconceiving the headlong rush towards Marxist totalism as a democratic exercise, misinterpreting arbitrary and high-handed actions as constitutionally justified, and entirely ignoring the President's tolerance of left-wing violence, the press in various countries (with a few honourable exceptions) was swift to condemn the 'murder of Chilean democracy'—as though its corpse had not already been dragged through the streets.

A simple transposition may help to clarify the situation. Imagine, then, that a British Prime Minister on reaching Downing Street by a minority vote in a split contest had publicly declared his lack of confidence in the police. Imagine further that he should release terrorists of the Angry Brigade and the IRA from gaol or detention, give them arms and constitute them into a Prime Ministerial Guard. Do not stop there. Imagine that the new Prime Minister, ignoring all votes of censure, should send an army of official snoopers to pry into private business and that he should encourage his Ministers to foment strikes and disorders; that he should embark on a reckless programme of nationalisation and finance it by printing money so that after three years in power inflation runs at *400 per cent*. But that is not all. Imagine that the Prime Minister should invite not only the IRA, but trained Palestinian terrorists, the German Baader–Meinhof Gang and similar groups to settle in Britain, and call in the KGB and the North Koreans to train them.[3]

Mutatis mutandis, Allende did all these things. The wonder, surely, is not that the armed services intervened, but that they did not intervene much sooner. Wherever Allende's mandate came from, it was not from Heaven.

[3] Similar transpositions can easily be made to suit French, American, German or Italian conditions.

PART V

The Containment of Dissent

ONE

THE PROBLEM OF SUBVERSION

The ground covered in this chapter

Authoritarian and totalist regimes contrasted—What Mill did not foresee: the failure of liberalism—normality of dissent—subversion the abuse of freedom—subversion in the open society—identifying subversive groups—subversion within and outside the law—containing subversion within the constitution—need for moral courage—publicity for alternative facts and views—attributable and unattributable information—obsolete dividing line between 'home' and 'foreign'—need for 'Departments of Unconventional War'—the concept of 'internal war'

TOTALIST GOVERNMENTS are the ultimate political horror. Since they reserve the 'right' to invade every area of privacy, they cannot by definition be really endangered by subversion, for at all times they hold the decisive remedy of total repression within their hands. Authoritarian governments, too, can look after themselves: unless they are traditional to a given country, they are likely to have come to power as the result of a *coup d'état* made necessary, or at any rate inevitable, by prevailing chaos—itself possibly the consequence of misgovernment or subversion, or both. By restoring order, they at least provide the social foundation for economic expansion which cannot co-exist with anarchy.

The price they exact for this service to the public good is the impoverishment of intellectual life implicit in the suppression of free debate and inquiry. It is, in the long run, a high price to pay, but in the short run—apart from the intellectuals, who will suffer persecution and possibly physical injury—it is a price that the great majority of the people seem normally willing to pay. To the frustrated dismay of liberal observers, especially in countries that have not suffered a dictatorship, such regimes are not necessarily unpopular. (This appears to have been true of the Greece of the colonels, for instance.) On one point at least, as I have noted, the authoritarian solution is the anti-thesis of the totalist: instead of ramming politics and ideology down people's throats, it confers upon them a benefit not to be despised—the freedom to opt out. If subversion is a non-problem for totalist govern-ments, and a controlled problem for authoritarian ones, it is a real and continuing one for democracies. They alone are truly vulnerable.

The tolerance inherent in a pluralist society is a form of intellectual pacifism. John Stuart Mill did not make the error of supposing all opinions to be of equal value: on the contrary, he argued that in a free market-place of ideas, the good would inevitably drive out the bad. There was a touch of innocence in his optimism. He envisaged free debate among men as civilised as himself—a common failing of lib-erals before and since. He could not foresee that a free market-place of ideas could rapidly degenerate into a free-for-all, in which the intellec-tual bully is at an advantage over more honest opponents. He could not foresee the invasion of universities by Marxist musclemen of various shades, elbowing the timid out of the way and gaining control of faculties as well as student bodies. In his day, the press may have been staid and prim, but editors wrote in a vigorous literary and intel-lectual mould. The mass circulation press lay in the future, and nobody had thought of television. It could not have occurred to him that groups of journalists, or even individual writers, could wish to pool their talents with the aim of destructive criticism of the society in which they flourished. The concept of an 'agent of influence' lay entirely outside his experience; as did that of 'disinformation'.

Is it seriously suggested that Locke and Mill would have approved, in the name of free debate, a situation in which the cause of freedom from censorship has been so abused in the commercial cinema that pornography and violence have become inescapable, to the extent that scarcely a film is free from either, and violence reigns on the television screen, while in every major Western city a growing number of cinema theatres are reserved for the pornographic output? Among the 'free-doms' that did not occur to these far-sighted men was that of ordinary people to be spared, for themselves and above all for their children, the universal public display of pornography in the streets, the hoardings and the bookshops.

The failure of liberalism, which by now must be sadly acknowledged, lies not in the incapacity of liberal intellectuals to discern and dis-tinguish between good and bad, or better and worse, but in the intellec-tual pacifism I have mentioned. Tolerating intolerant doctrines, or uncritically accepting inferior work in various spheres, they contribute to the general impoverishment of life, and the perversion of values. A first consequence of their timidity is the disappearance of the free market-place of ideas: all ideas become equal. Soon, however, some ideas are seen to be more equal than others. Equating progress with egalitarian social doctrines, they more readily tolerate the Left—even the extreme Left—than even the moderate Right, which soon they will denounce as 'fascist'. In the end, the bad drives out the good, and yesterday's liberal, no longer timid or impotent, but by now a *de facto* convert to intolerance, blesses the prevailing barbarism with his enthusiasm.

And what, it may be asked, has all this to do with subversion? In fact, 'all this' is central to the issue. What, then, is subversion? In what way does it differ from normal dissent? The second of these questions is crucially related to the first, and it will be seen that basically it is of interest primarily to democratic and pluralist societies. No dissent can be tolerated in totalist regimes; and in authoritarian ones, only within a narrowly defined set of options, and sometimes not even that. In pluralist societies, however, dissent is not only normal but essential. Without it, such societies would cease to be what they are. There is no virtue in tolerating opinions that are broadly similar to one's own: the virtue lies in tolerating those with which one disagrees. Moreover, the benefit of dissent is twofold: it acts as a safety valve to prevent frustrations from exploding into violence; and also, to the extent that it is expressed coherently, it may well make an important contribution to the pool of ideas without which a society becomes stagnant.

I define subversion as: a systematic attempt to undermine a society. It can never be easy—though it is vitally important—to distinguish between legitimate dissent and subversion. It seems to me that the distinction lies in the dividing line between use and abuse. In an open society, the law guarantees freedoms, and tradition protects them. These freedoms include those of speech, the press and assembly. The use of such freedoms is so normal that we take it for granted. The abuse of them is not easy to discern, for it does not follow that abuse transgresses the law—so tolerant is the law in pluralist societies.

Perhaps the point may be made clearer by analogy. Taken in moderation, alcohol can relieve tensions and contribute to social amenity. Taken to excess, it will lead to that unpleasant condition known as a hangover. And a true dependence upon alcohol can wreck a home, kill a marriage and disintegrate a personality, leading in the end to illness, madness and premature death In the first instance, we have use; in the second, abuse. The ingredient consumed is the same in both cases. It is the same, I submit, with speech, the press and assembly, and the dividing line between use and abuse is clear enough in the case of activities that transgress the law.

To use the editorial columns of a newspaper, or the sound waves of a broadcasting station, or the widely available images of the television services, to advocate the removal of a prime minister or president and his replacement by somebody considered more suitable, is normal use of the medium. At least in democratic countries. But to use such facilities to advocate, say, the ritual murder of all children under the age of five, or the public scalping of Jews or Negroes, would rightly be considered an abuse of such facilities. In some countries—especially Great Britain—derogatory references to an individual, even if accurate in some cases, and even if the author is convinced that such references are in the interests of the public—may be considered libellous and heavily punished accordingly. Although English law is notably illiberal in this particular respect, there is no difficulty, once again, in distinguishing between use and abuse.

Let us vary the metaphor. A brick may be used as a modest contribution to the building of a house; or to batter an unwanted spouse to death. It would not occur to anyone to blame the unfeeling and uncaring brick for the abuse, nor to praise it for its constructive use. The option of using or abusing lies with the individual.

It is surely the same with the freedoms we are discussing. An open society is inconceivable without a free press. But to use the freedom of the press is one thing; to abuse it, quite another. There may be abuse when the cumulative effect of articles in the press, broadcast talks or television programmes, is seen to be subversive, in the sense that the authors or producers or speakers apparently aim at bringing a regime into disrepute, causing a loss of confidence on the part of the ruling establishment, institutions and government; still more if the object appears to be to provoke a breakdown of law and order and even, in the final analysis, to bring about a total collapse of the State. In itself, each item or article, programme or talk, may be well within the law and defensible as a legitimate exercise of the rights of free speech and comment. Subversive intent may lie in the repetition of themes and arguments, involving a consistent denigration of the values or institutions of the open society, or systematic praise for totalist systems, or a one-sided presentation of events with the bias permanently in favour of revolutionaries, terrorists or other extremists.

Since the dividing line is often so tenuous, diagnosis can never be easy, but two guiding principles may help to reduce the risks of error:

intent and *organisation*. Although ultimate intent is almost impossible to detect in isolated items, it may emerge beyond doubt with the re-iteration of subversive themes. One advantage of the open society, however, cuts both ways—benefiting both subversives and the ordin-ary public. In a country such as Britain, or the United States or Hol-land, it is not necessary for revolutionary groups to hide their views to escape prosecution. To that extent, they have less need than under an authoritarian system to resort to clandestinity. When they do, how-ever, it may be assumed that their purpose is to transgress the law—for example, by planning violent action.

On the other hand, it is correspondingly harder in an open society to uncover a clandestine conspiracy, and politically far more difficult to make use of any discoveries, in the light of public opinion. Any group, whether of the Left or the Right, which advocates violence for political ends, must be defined as subversive. But violence does not necessarily accompany subversion. The object of international sub-version—for instance from the Soviet Union—is not necessarily to provoke a violent revolution. In the 1970s, the objects have appeared to be more subtle: to weaken and demoralise a government, and to create a climate of opinion conducive to the public acceptance of Soviet foreign policy objectives, by undermining the will to resist, or to face up to the realities of Soviet intentions.

It is legitimate, therefore, to ask whether a group or movement, even when it does not advocate violence, is in fact advocating objectives that are in themselves revolutionary or that consistently serve the policy objectives of a foreign power. Since it is not necessary, in an open society, for groups or individuals to hide ultimately revolution-ary intentions (although it may be prudent not to mention a violent intent), it is not difficult to decide whether a group is or is not sub-versive. One way of ascertaining whether it serves the interests of a foreign power is to study the press or radio of that power and find out whether the group or its objectives are regularly praised therein.

It is open to informed members of the public to do these things for themselves. But security services—essential for the defence of the State —will have to go further. They will have to seek evidence of clandes-tine meetings with agents of a hostile or totalist foreign power. They will have to seek evidence, too, that members of a group have received money, arms or training from a foreign power, or whether they have gone abroad to receive such advantages. And they will have to link such evidence with circumstantial matters such as thefts of arms and ammunition, or evidence of raids on banks by members of a politically motivated group.

Let us postulate that certain groups or parties or movements are regarded as subversive because they are engaged in the advocacy of subversive objectives, or indulging in subversive actions. Such groups, whatever their names, may come under various familiar general labels, such as Marxist, Communist, Trotskyist, Anarchist or simply National-ist. But if a group is subversive, then it follows logically that each of its members, taken individually, is also subversive.

Moreover, since it is open to individuals to leave such groups by agreement with the leadership, while continuing to support its objec-tives, and indeed to work actively on its behalf, then individuals, even if they are not members of a subversive group, but are seen to work for similar objectives—must also be considered subversive. Either as individuals, or as members of a group, such people may have secured positions in a broadcasting or television company or organisation, or in the press, or in the trade unions. Although the usual presumption of innocence must prevail, should they be charged with a crime or offence against the law, they cannot benefit from any such presumption where *political* objectives are concerned. Their motives in writing an article, or commissioning it, or organising a programme, or selecting speakers or witnesses in a television occasion must be closely questioned.

Similarly, trade union leaders who call strikes, often in defiance of official union policy, for apparently political purposes or in furtherance of long-term revolutionary aims, must also be credited with subversive intent. These aims may include the general debilitation of industry (that is, of the 'capitalist' system), and the weakening of the currency, for instance by the creation of an inflationary spiral. In some Western countries (for instance, Britain, France and Italy) industry is indeed a main target for the subversive groups. But they are also active in the universities (and latterly even in the schools) in the countries named, and perhaps even more in the United States, West Germany and various Latin American countries, with aims that include the dis-semination of Marxism and other revolutionary ideologies; the dis-crediting of 'capitalism', 'imperialism' and the democratic system; the denigration of national achievements and history; the encouragement of praise for Communist or 'progressive' regimes; the organising of protest demonstrations (for instance, against American action in Vietnam before it ended, or the British Army's intervention in Ulster), and of sympathy for terrorist or revolutionary organisations (such as the Palestinian guerrillas or the 'freedom fighters' of Africa, especially in territories regarded as colonial or oppressive, such as the Portuguese dependencies in Africa).

In previous chapters, I have described in some detail the phases of a revolutionary war, and the dangers of a world in which Soviet power (and, to a lesser degree, Chinese, or still less North Vietnamese or Cuban power) supports or benefits from subversive activities. The ultimate peril remains the same: the victory of a totalist group dedicated to the elimination of all opposition. A relatively more tolerable (if only because less permanent) alternative to a democracy under threat is the authoritarian solution—which many people in Western countries would find (for reasons that escape me) even less tolerable than the totalist one. But the real problem, for a pluralist society, is how to contain subversion while maintaining the freedoms and avoiding the alternative dangers of the authoritarian solution or the totalist horror.

Is it possible to contain subversion within the existing legal and constitutional system, and to preserve or restore liberties temporarily suspended? I believe that it is, and that the real danger lies—as so many examples mentioned in this book demonstrate beyond doubt, in the reluctance or inability to see subversion as a problem until it is too late. The first and most pressing need is for governments and politicians to take the time to study and grasp the problem, and then to find the moral courage to lead public opinion and to take action.

Moral courage is exactly what is required, for at every step a government determined to act in the field of subversion will be running the gauntlet of carefully orchestrated attacks from those who have been doing the subverting and those who, often out of misguided idealism, support them or—in the name of free speech and freedom from censorship—their right to be heard undisturbed. That they have this right is not denied, but those with the courage to act will immediately find themselves branded as illiberal or 'fascist'. They should have the moral courage to take such accusations in their stride and not to be deflected from what needs to be done. For the issue is not whether to drop democracy and abandon liberalism, but how best to defend both against attacks from within and without.

The alternatives may be authoritarian rule (the 'Right-wing backlash' so often threatened and often so much more dreaded than the ultimate evil to which it may be a poor solution) and the long night of totalism. The nature of the threat, the dangers ahead, and the alternatives to firm action before it is too late need to be explained and interpreted—not once in a single magisterial speech, but repeatedly and through all available means—parliament or congress or assembly, the press and radio, and not least television. For the box of images—so potent in the dissemination of falsehood—can be equally strong in the spreading of the truth. If this were done, and done skilfully, with confidence and repeatedly, there is little doubt that public opinion—the sane if silent majority at the heart of most nations—would respond.

When opinion is bewildered and misled, assailed on all sides by images, sounds and words purporting to show that everything in the system is rotten, it can hardly be expected to support authorities too timid to take action against forces intent on destroying it, and with it a way of life. But give it a chance and observe what happens.

In the early stages of a subversive campaign, and when subversion remains primarily verbal—that is, non-violent—the best remedy in an open society is *maximum publicity for alternative facts and opinions*. Too often, subversive words, biased or distorted presentation of the news, and one-sided debates, go unanswered because the subverters are organised and self-confident and because the defenders—the overwhelming majority of the population—are unorganised and unled, and lack self-confidence. Thus the subverters have things their own way. The best way to stop them is to allow sounder voices to have a hearing.

The abuse of the freedoms by potentially totalist groups or individuals, or by agents, conscious, or unconscious, of hostile or totalist foreign regimes, constitutes a threat to those freedoms. The defence of the open society implies an obligation upon that great majority of citizens who enjoy the benefits of the existing way of life and would like to preserve them. Still more, however, does it imply an obligation upon that majority of politicians—still—who reject the totalist challenge but have hitherto been too timid to do anything about it.

Democratic countries may or may not have departments or ministries of Information. There is something slightly repugnant to the liberal conscience in such devices, which smack of totalist thought-control, but it can hardly be denied that the State is entitled to present the official version of the facts and as entitled to a public relations office as an oil company or the film industry. But more than that is needed. Too often, the government's version of events is leaked in a haphazard way to chosen journalists. The principle is not necessarily wrong: not all journalists can be trusted, alas, nor can it be said of all of them that they are responsible public citizens. It is the haphazard way of getting leaks into the press—particularly, perhaps, in the United States—that I am criticising.

All governments should have a department, or even several departments, specifically charged with authoritative but unattributable information. It should be the function of such departments to correct misleading or subversive allegations—not by distorting the truth, but by giving trusted journalists access to supporting evidence, under seal of confidence, and to trust them to write their own stories unaided. It is not a question of censoring the news, but of making sure that one-sided versions of events that serve no other purposes than those of the totalist groups and their foreign supporters do not go unanswered.

In the fight against subversion, to the extent that it is joined, all governments, and certainly all Western ones, are handicapped by the traditional dividing line between 'home' and 'foreign'—or 'the interior' and 'external affairs'. The dividing line has a long and honourable history, and in many respects is still valid. But it is totally obsolete and irrelevant to the needs of subversion. The conventional wisdom has always been that subversion is something that foreigners do—either to each other or at home as part of an exercise conducted from abroad. This may be true still, but it is now quite inadequate as a concept. In fact, subversion is often, and indeed usually, conducted by home-grown revolutionaries who may or may not accept foreign help, but who wish to subvert, undermine and eventually overthrow the system from within.

In such a situation, there is no place for the traditional dividing lines, and the old departmental jealousies. And yet, security services still jealously guard their secrets from intelligence agencies working in the foreign field—just as home or interior ministries guard their prerogatives against foreign ministries, while defence ministries (which self-evidently have a foot in both camps) face the difficulty of deciding what is home and what is foreign. In normal circumstances (and outside such countries as the Soviet Union), what contacts is a police force expected to have with a foreign ministry? Yet subversion involves both, as it involves defence, home affairs, security and foreign intelligence. The subverters know no boundaries; and neither should the defenders.

For all democratic countries taken individually, and for alliances between such countries, I advocate the rapid creation of 'Departments of Unconventional War' or of 'Irregular Warfare' (the name is less important than the notion). Let me explain. A Department of Irregular Warfare would bring together in conditions implying a permanent career, men and women who normally work in different departments, often with little or no contact between each other except at times of emergency. Thus security specialists and Special Branch men would be needed; and so would intelligence experts. Civil servants trained in the techniques of information would be there, and specialists in psychological warfare. Skilled interrogators would be essential and so too would imaginative practitioners of special operations. Bomb disposal experts; linguists and anthropologists; soldiers experienced in fighting terrorists and guerrillas in the cities, the mountains and the jungles. And beyond all these, highly-trained armed forces with all the conventional skills and the best weapons available through modern military technology.

It is a curious and in a way touching commentary upon the natural optimism of authorities that each subversive emergency is assumed to be the last. The special range of talents I have mentioned have been brought together on many occasions, because the situation dictated togetherness. The British in Malaya, Cyprus, Kenya and later Ulster. The French in Indochina and Algeria. The Americans in the Philippines; many Latin American governments, sometimes with outside help. But once these situations are over, once the emergencies to which the co-operation of talents was a response have been declared finished, the men or women involved disperse to their respective departments or services. What I am saying is that they should not disperse: on the contrary, that a conscious effort should be made to keep them together in a special service, and to train new generations of people with an understanding of these problems, so that when the next emergency comes round, the country that faces it will be equipped so to do.

In the age of trans-national terrorism, and of nuclear stalemate, such organisations are necessary as they never were before. Between emergencies, the Department of Irregular Warfare would run courses on revolutionary war techniques, on subversion, terrorism and guerrilla war, and on the wide range of appropriate counter-measures now available.

Nor should the process stop there. It would be highly desirable for each member country of existing Western alliances to set up similar departments, and for each alliance to have its own Department of Irregular Warfare, to be composed of personnel seconded from the various national departments. This proposal would call for a major re-examination of the terms of reference of the alliances. This re-organisation and re-appraisal would be enormously to the benefit of NATO, CENTO and SEATO. It might even be necessary to re-negotiate the alliances, which were all conceived in static situations that have vanished, to enable them to face up to the fluid, mobile and deceptive 'peace' of today. Eventually, each alliance, equipped with its own Department of Irregular Warfare would be able to respond to appeals for help from any country, whether or not a member of the appropriate alliance, that felt itself threatened by subversion, terrorism or revolutionary war. It is not hard to see how departments of this kind could have helped such governments as that of Turkey (a member of CENTO and NATO) in its revolutionary crisis of 1971; Ceylon (not a member of an alliance) when student revolutionaries tried to seize power in the spring of 1972; or Uruguay in its prolonged agony.

The law

I have been writing about organisational changes that seemed to me to be necessary to contain subversion and its consequences on a long-term basis. But I have suggested that in the non-violent phase of subversion (which may indeed be long-lasting if the intention is simply to cause a general breakdown of confidence), the first answer in the open society should, as I have said, be the proper airing of alternative views. But the law, too, has an important part to play in a situation that ultimately threatens both law and order.

In this context, it is necessary to dispel a falsehood assiduously propagated by the subverters and their misguided or ill-intentioned supporters. The falsehood is that political motivation is a mitigating circumstance in the perpetration of a crime. The advantage of this sophistry lies in the opportunity it gives to defenders of terrorists to argue that they are being punished for 'political' offences. If the argument is conceded, it puts normally constituted courts in a democratically governed country on a par with the arbitrary administration of a penal code in authoritarian or totalist countries, or the complete disregard for written civil guarantees so often in evidence in the persecution of dissidents.

The argument is, however, specious. To kill innocent people is a crime even if political motivation is pleaded. To rob a bank is a crime even if it is claimed that the robbery was in a good cause. As far as possible, terrorists and 'urban guerrillas'—an unfortunate phrase, which seems to confer an aura of heroic imagery upon people whose 'heroism' may have consisted of posting a letter-bomb that could maim and kill recipients other than the addressee—should be brought to trial for specific common law crimes, felonies or misdemeanours. Political motivation does not modify the nature of a crime—even though 'crimes' of violence may be inescapable in justifiable rebellion against intolerable despotisms.

Here again, moral courage is required—the courage to invoke laws and statutes that already exist in most legislative systems, but which have tended to fall into disuse in a general climate of misguided tolerance. Most civilised governments have laws relating to riots, rebellions and treason. Some countries have laws against intimidatory picketing in industrial disputes. Again, some countries (most notably Great Britain, but with the United States as an extraordinary exception) have laws against the publication of official secrets. True, if such laws, regulations and statutes are abused by the authorities, the outcome may be a major step towards authoritarian government. But the dividing line between abuse and non-use is vast. If subversion is recognised to be a problem, most countries can cope with it in the early stages by a fair but determined use of existing laws.

If all else fails, there is usually the last resort (and it should indeed be a last resort) of introducing martial law. In this context, the concept of *internal war* deserves consideration. If it is allowed, the problems of counter-subversion (as distinct from counter-terrorism and counter-insurgency) will be seen in a clearer light. For there is general recognition of the fact that when a country is at war, it has the right—inherent in the greater right of legitimate self-defence—to adopt emergency regulations. During the Second World War, for instance, emergency regulations in Britain allowed the government to detain suspects without trial; military censorship was initiated, and was supplemented by voluntary restraints under the D-Regulations. The point is that the general public broadly accepted these restrictions upon their normal liberties. Recognising that there was a national emergency, they trusted the authorities—rightly, as later the circumstances showed—to rescind the exceptional measures taken after hostilities had ceased: that is, after the need for emergency regulations had clearly lapsed.

Is there not a parallel, peculiarly apt for the 1970s, between the situation of a country at war with an external enemy, and the country faced with a situation like Ulster, or Vietnam, or Turkey or Uruguay? Are not countries in such situations in the 1970s no less at war than Britain and her allies were between 1914 and 1918, or between 1939 and 1945? A sensible government will not introduce emergency measures until there is a real emergency; the danger often is that it fails to act when there is one, out of timidity or excessive deference to tradition. The concept of internal war therefore requires examination; and if it is thought to contribute to an understanding of the need for special measures in cases of subversion, steps can be taken to accustom the public to the concept, if only with the aim of encouraging understanding of the need for a more stringent application of existing laws in the early stages. For if the existing laws, courageously applied, do the trick, there will be no need for further action. But if they do not, there will be a real need for sterner measures later on. And there is much to be said for avoiding the shock to public opinion that is inevitable when a subject has been inadequately explored and explained.

TWO

THE PRECONDITIONS OF CONFLICT

The ground covered in this chapter

Conflicts and alternatives—fallacies in the prevailing orthodoxy—advocacy of non-alternatives exacerbates conflict—absurdities of 'peace research'—improbability of conflict resolution—non-agreements on Indochina and Cyprus—usefulness of face-saving—unattainable objectives, permanent frustration, total hostility—civilisation imperfect but worth defending—the point is not to resolve the insoluble but to win—moral crisis of the West—tolerance of the intolerable—decline of the Churches—sex, violence and technological change—the atom bomb and over-population—unnecessary aggravations—Marx and collective guilt—Freud and the removal of guilt—egalitarian absurdities—poverty and envy

CONFLICTS ARE usually not resolved: we have to learn to live with them. But there is no need actually to make them worse than they should be, which prevailing cultural attitudes in the 1970s tended to do. It is even possible to find ways that will reduce the likelihood of conflict, or at any rate its intensity. Let us explore these themes in these last chapters.

Conflicts and alternatives constitute the proper subject matter for a study of politics. A politician, whether on the way up or the way down, competes with others for the support of the voters. In an authoritarian state, or *a fortiori* in totalist ones, the competition may be less for popular support than for the support of the ruling group. When a leader has achieved power—which is one of the main things politics is about—he will struggle against rivals and detractors to stay where he is. All the time, the life of politics is ruled by conflict. The student of politics performs a useful function to the extent that he is able, with reasonable objectivity, to analyse the strengths and weaknesses of competing men, groups and policies, and assess probable outcomes. In wider conflicts, he will need to consider the causes, not with a view

212

to resolving the problems, but to help him in his reasoned assessment of probabilities.

The consideration of alternatives is only slightly less central to the study of politics. No assessment of outcomes is likely to be valid if the alternatives to men and their policies or courses of action are ignored. Objectivity, however, does not necessarily imply impartiality. It may well be that the facts of a situation point to the victory of a man or a policy of which the political student or analyst may deeply disapprove. But his partiality for the alternatives available should not blind him to the evidence. If he is to fulfil his primary function as a reliable guide, he will concern himself primarily with the question: who is going to win?

Thus stated, the study of politics must seem inescapably amoral; and indeed, since it is a study of the attainment and retention of power, it cannot be otherwise. But we have been talking about the *primary* function of political study. There is another function, which though secondary to the first, involves moral judgments. This secondary function is *advocacy*, which involves a choice between alternatives. Indeed, the advocacy of reasonable alternatives is itself, in an open society, a factor in the final political assessment of outcomes. But suffering humanity has the right to expect that the political advocate should know what he is talking about, and that the alternative leader or course of action he advocates is in fact a realistic one—that is, a true alternative, and not a fanciful, idealistic or Utopian one. It is in the nature of human imperfection that this reasonable expectation is more often than not disappointed.

Unfortunately, in most advanced Western societies, the prevailing orthodoxy in political studies, especially in the international field, is concerned with non-alternatives. There are innumerable examples, but a striking one, which illustrates the point perfectly, is the extraordinary persistence with which speakers and writers on both sides of the Atlantic refer to the urgent need, as they see it, to reduce or even close the 'gap' in income between the developed and the under-developed countries. Since it can be mathematically demonstrated that the gap is bound to grow, even if the under-developed achieve an economic growth rate many times that of the developed ones, the only effect of this advocacy of a non-alternative is to exacerbate frustration and envy —and thus to intensify conflict: the exact opposite of what the speakers and writers profess to want. This argument has no bearing whatever on what would be a *true* alternative to the current situation, in that it is realistic, and no doubt desirable, to aim at raising the standards of income and living in the Third World as quickly as possible.

It is hardly surprising that the argument is most frequently heard on the floor of the General Assembly of the United Nations, which is disproportionately packed with the representatives of the more indigent sovereign States; but it is a source of some impatience that it should be so frequently repeated in Western countries by writers or speakers who either know it to be a fallacy, or could work it out for themselves with the expenditure of a little time and elementary arithmetic.

Closely related to such unrealism is the advent of a new growth industry: using various names, the most common of which are 'peace research' and 'conflict resolution'. (The most recent variant is 'peace science', which is presumably designed to confer upon its exponents the additional aura of infallibility associated with the word 'science', in a field that is by its nature essentially unscientific.) Vast sums of money, countless man-hours of intellectual time, and measureless cerebration are expended on these pseudo-disciplines. Elaborate models of imaginary situations are constructed, and data are fed into computers, which obediently regurgitate non-answers, since few of the factors in conflict situations are quantifiable, and many are either intangible or infinitely variable. (Such as the most important of all: human behaviour). Occasionally—such are the rules of chance—the computer will oblige with a correct answer, for instance if fed with all the possible alternatives at issue in a set of negotiations. But the predictive value of such occasional successes is nil, for at any time the unexpected and unpredictable—the sudden death of a key negotiator, or a *coup d'état* in one of the negotiating countries—could nullify the most careful computer programming. Undeterred, the 'peace researchers' (or should one now say, 'peace scientists'?) and the 'conflict resolutioners' carry on. A point of departure for many of these pastimes is the saying, attributed to Gandhi, that a conflict should unite the parties to it, instead of separating them, because the one thing they have in common is their incompatibility. One school of conflict resolution advocates the need to turn our fights into games and our games into debates. A favourite activity of one school of peace researchers is to attempt to create areas of peace, and then to extend them, on the analogy of blobs of ink, so that in the end all the blobs join together and the whole world is at peace.

When it comes to revolutionary conflict of the kind that has been considered in this book, one group of conflict resolutioners spends part of its time drafting rules of behaviour, supposedly applicable to both sides, so that for instance the terrorists will agree, say, not to blow up babies or maltreat women; while on the side of authority, they would be undertaking not to hit captured terrorists over the head or torture them with electrodes during interrogation. The futility of such exercises is inherent in the fact that terrorists, by definition, are fanatics and often, whatever their stated political motives, psychopaths as well, who would not turn to terrorism in the first place unless they were indifferent to, or derived some pleasure from, the murdering of babies and the torture of women.

One of the leading peace researchers advocates an international rejection of the legitimacy of the institution of war, as Lord Keynes had rejected the legitimacy of mass unemployment. Such 'studies' bear about as much relation to the study of the real world of internal or international politics as behaviourism (so brilliantly demolished by Arthur Koestler[1]) to the study of human psychology.

Not that all peace researchers are equally unrealistic. Johan Galtung is sensibly aware that we are more likely to have to live with increasing conflict than to resolve it.[2] Indeed we do. Major conflicts of interest, especially if ideologically formulated, are unlikely to be resolved. In international relations, what appears to be a resolution is often no more than a device enabling one or more of the parties to a dispute (most normally an outside Power whose interests are only indirectly affected) to retire without too visible a loss of face. Examples are legion, but two or three will illustrate the point. The Laos 'settlement' of 23 July 1962 was widely hailed as an example of wise statesmanship, but it settled nothing. The fourteen governments that had been meeting in Geneva agreed to uphold and respect the neutrality of Laos and the integrity of its territory. The Americans withdrew their undercover advisers; the North Vietnamese, who had never admitted the presence, known to all, of thousands of their armed regulars, made a token withdrawal of a few men who, they said, might have strayed into Laos inadvertently.

Within a few months, the North Vietnamese were building up their forces to new high levels, and roaming at will over Laotian territory. The Americans returned, and the undeclared war, which the Geneva agreements were supposed to have settled, resumed as though nothing had been said or signed. Much the same, *mutatis mutandis*, could be said of the Geneva agreements of July 1954 halting the first Indochina war (involving the French), and of those of January and February

[1] Arthur Koestler, *The Ghost in the Machine* (London, 1967), pp. 5 et seq.
[2] See J. Galtung, 'Conflict as a Way of Life' in *New Society*, 16 Oct. 1969 (reproduced in *Survival*, the journal of the International Institute for Strategic Studies, London, Jan. 1970.) There is also much to disagree with in this article, but that is not my purpose.

1973 ending the American intervention in the second Indochina war, when the cease-fire agreements barely interrupted hostilities.

Similar hopes had been aroused by the 'settlement' of the multilateral dispute over Cyprus under the Zurich and London agreements of February 1959, which led on 16 August 1960 to the independence of the island. But the EOKA terrorist organisation of General Grivas had been fighting not for independence but for *Enosis*—the union of Cyprus with mother Greece, 560 miles away. The Turkish minority of the island had made it clear, however, that *Enosis* was unacceptable to it, and indeed that if there was going to be any *Enosis*, it would be with Turkey, only 40 miles away. The 'settlement' thus settled nothing, and violence flared up again in the 1960s and 1970s.

It does not follow from these examples that a search for an agreed settlement should not be made, or if attempted, that it should be abandoned. For it may well be useful for outsiders to be given a face-saving way of ending their intervention or cutting their losses. Equally, it may be to the general benefit that the parties directly involved should be allowed to rest, and that the mass of ordinary people to whom a conflict means personal suffering should be given a respite from violence. There may be a further advantage in persuading contenders to sign or publicly accept a settlement, even if it is not to their liking, in that the first to violate it may be exposed as a transgressor. But it is usually wrong, or mistaken, to suppose that a paper agreement, even if adorned with the right signatures, necessarily represents in any true or lasting sense a resolution of the conflict.

In situations of conflict, total frustration = permanent hostility. And total frustration results if one party to a dispute wants the one thing that is not on offer. In Indochina, the Vietnamese Communists wanted to control South Vietnam, Laos and Cambodia. The South Vietnamese, Laotians and Cambodians were trying to deny them this control. The war, therefore, was bound to go on until either the Communists had achieved their objectives, or they should weary in the endeavour and channel their energies and frustrations elsewhere.

In internal affairs, and indeed in personal problems, as in international affairs, the desire for the unattainable spells frustration and hostility. If militant trade unionists are on strike not to gain temporary goals in wages or conditions, but ultimately to weaken or destroy a system of which they disapprove, and the great majority of those who benefit from the system wish to preserve it and are ready to fight in its defence, the conflict is likely to be protracted and intractable. In private lives, suicide has many a time been the outcome of a hopeless love affair.

In revolutionary conflict and its strategic consequences, however, *no compromise is ultimately possible*, although expediency or temporary disadvantage may dictate a tactical cease-fire or an interim 'settlement', or limited agreements in which neither side suffers to excess. In the final analysis, what is at stake is the survival of civilisation. The case is not altered by pointing to the imperfections of that civilisation, to the cruelties that may still be practised or endured in countries that belong to it, or to the distance between aspiration and achievement; for the imperfections, the cruelties and the shortcomings are inherent in Man's nature and his evolutionary inheritance. Too often the astonishing intellectual, moral and cultural achievements of the neo-cortex are spoilt by brutal reminders of the still uncontrolled assertiveness of the reptilian ganglion. But imperfect or flawed though the civilisation may be, it conserves its capacity for improvement. However much those who live in democratic societies may disapprove of certain aspects of life in contemporary Spain, Greece and Portugal, they too belong to the civilised stream, along with Scandinavia, the United States, Brazil and Australia and all other States deeply touched by Roman law, English common law or Christianity, however residual.

And the alternative that is proposed is the long night of totalism, whether the revolutionaries win or sovereign States allow their freedom to be eroded to the advantage of a totalist super-Power. Between the imperfect present, flawed but correctible, and the irreversible future, there can be no compromise, and there should be no hesitation. *The point is not to resolve the conflict but to win.* All who adopt the neutralist stance between NATO and the Warsaw Pact, equating the two in the interests of a hypothetical 'conflict resolution', stand condemned of selling the pass. Equally, those who wish to compromise with the terrorists and fanatics who threaten a way of life from within are accepting the unacceptable. The internal enemy can be defeated; it may be beyond the present power of the West, under the nuclear stalemate, to defeat the external enemy. Nor can the attempt be made by military means, for extinction is an unacceptable price for a hypothetical victory, for one side or the other. But the great unspoken crisis of the 1970s was not being decided by military means, conventional or nuclear. The two threats, external and internal, were merging. Societies unwilling to defend themselves against the internal revolutionary threat or insufficiently resistant to it, were likely to find themselves incapable of standing up to the mixture of threats and blandishments with which the Soviet Union conducted its foreign policy. In the international context, to survive intact, to stand united, would amount to a tolerable approximation of victory.

The conditions of defeat

A number of Western countries, including the major ones, entered into a moral crisis in the 1960s, which reached a paroxysm in 1968, the maximum year of student revolts, thereafter marginally abating, but which, at the start of 1974, showed no sign of truly subsiding. In my view, the crisis was unnecessary and avoidable, and it remained correctible.

In this crisis, the young revolutionaries were both cause and effect. They had seized upon issues (most notably Vietnam, but the issues were pretexts and varied from time to time) to symbolise and canalise a general protest against society as they found it, or as it appeared to them to be. And their protests, often violent, always disturbing, served to deepen or intensify the moral malaise that was the true crisis.

The symptoms were many. The alarming growth in addiction to dangerous and even lethal drugs, especially in the United States; the flood of pornography, on screen and stage, or in print; the reiteration of images of violence on screen and television, and in the novel; the accompanying rise in violent crime in Western cities; the visible corruption of public life; the decline in standards of public service and the awareness and practice of duties, as distinct from the assertion of obligations; the emergence of hippy communities, the cult of the drop-out and the mass ritual of pop music. Yet the true malaise lay not in these symptoms, grave or disturbing though they might be, but in *the abject tolerance of them* by those who did not necessarily approve, much less practise, that which they tolerated.

In the last analysis, this was what the 'permissive society' really meant. In the name of a 'sacred' principle—freedom from censorship —liberals and progressives (and people who were neither but lacked the courage to say what they thought) tolerated the extravagant invasion of bookstalls, stage and cinema by a flood of pornography which inevitably drove out other forms of expression to the general impoverishment. The constant depiction of violence anaesthetised the public mind, and conditioned the young and the impressionable to the view that violence was normal. In the truest sense, these developments amounted to the advent of new forms of barbarism. Yet there was never a lack of prominent people ready to stand up and deny any

correlation between fictional and real violence or to defend pornography in many of its forms on a variety of grounds, each more spurious
than the last. The prominent British politician who publicly declared
that he preferred to call the permissive society the 'civilised society'
may well, in retrospect, be found to have written the epitaph of his
own generation.

Perhaps the most startling example of moral decay, disorientation
and collapsed self-confidence was the decision of the World Council of
Churches in 1970 to support terrorism in Africa. Indeed, most of the
Christian churches, but especially the Catholic Church and the Church
of England, were suffering from a general decline of authority and of
confidence in their own faith. The Catholic Church was deeply divided,
and it was a symptom of this division that priests, especially in Latin
America but elsewhere as well, had taken to supporting revolutionary
violence and even in some cases to participating in it. This decadence
yielded curious logical absurdities, such as the term 'Christian–
Marxist', implying a marriage of incompatibles between believers and
atheists. The causes of this state of affairs were complex. Let us leave
subversion aside, for while it is an important contributory cause, it
does not in itself explain the state of mind that made so many people
tolerate aesthetic and moral barbarism, and ready to heap praise
upon witless productions for fear of appearing old-fashioned, 'square'
or in general out of tune with the times.

Some of the causes were inherent in the facts of contemporary life,
and especially in the startling discoveries of science and the vertiginous
expansion of technology. Discoveries of spatial physics, of palaeonto-
logy and of evolutionary biology; the uncovering of some of the genetic
secrets of life itself; such things were bound to weaken the hold of the
Churches upon the faithful. It is impossible, in the light of modern
science, to accept the myths of *Genesis*; but dogmas come whole: if
one element of the affirmation is no longer credible, belief in the rest is
weakened. It became increasingly difficult to accept the dogma of the
Virgin Birth; and the discovery of the Dead Sea Scrolls weakened
faith in the uniqueness and divinity of Jesus Christ. It need not have
followed (but it did, human nature being what it is) that the Church's
moral message should also be disbelieved. And with the declining
acceptance of the moral authority of the churches went a corresponding decline in the authority of elders in general—whether parents or
teachers.

Some decline was inherent also in the conditions of modern industrial societies, especially at a time of accelerated technological change.

The increasing employment of women, whether in business or in industry, weakened the family ties; and the decline of the family stimulated the growth of urban crime. Exploding technology compounded these problems. More and more young people were coming onto the labour market. Fewer of them could expect decent employment. Populations were on the move: whether coloured immigrants into Britain, or Southern Negroes into the northern cities of the United States, or under-privileged labour from southern into northern Europe. Inequalities were glaring, and expectations higher than ever at a period of generalised affluence.

The unassimilated were the discontented. And among the idle young, inured to violence and no longer respectful of authority or even of normal family ties, was the potential consumer market of the great drug trade. Graduating from cannabis to cocaine, morphine and at the stage of the death-wish, heroin, the young ate out of the hand of the drug pushers, creating fortunes, contributing to the rising corruption of the police and public officials, and in escalating numbers, ensuring their own premature deaths. All, whether deprived or privileged, whether employed or idle, whether law-abiding or delinquent, were consumers. All were caught up in the rhythms and pressures of economic growth—producing more and more goods to contribute to a sometimes specious standard of living, and contributing by their purchases to the planned obsolescence of the goods on offer. All, too, were voters in the societies we are discussing, and all were called upon to choose at intervals between leaders and parties that seemed to offer too narrow a range of options and to be motivated less by the public good and the genuine search for solutions to such problems as were soluble than by gaining power or keeping it. Politicians, too, shared in the declining force of respect and authority.

There were other sources of tension or anxiety. The world had changed in a fundamental way with the first atomic bomb dropped in anger upon a city—with the destruction of Hiroshima in 1945. Years later, the first hysteria had died down, but subconsciously the general anxiety remained. It was a temporary consolation that great wars no longer seemed to happen as they might once have been expected to do. Small wars prevailed, but in the background was the knowledge, never to be assuaged, that man had found the means of totally destroying his planet and the civilisation he had created. Together with this irremovable cause of anxiety went fresh causes of worry: in the exponential curve of population growth, and the startling rise in the pollution of man's environment. At one end of the scale, people feared total destruction; at the other, they feared an over-population of the world so gross that humanity could no longer feed itself, even if it did not choke in its own filth.[3]

This almost exhausts the list of what I would call 'inherent causes', that is, causes arising out of the normal and unchecked growth of population and industry. But to these must be added a list of unnecessary aggravating factors. By removing the sense of personal moral responsibility, by ascribing all guilt to neurosis and all neurosis to the frustrated sex drive, the Freudian school of psychology powerfully contributed to the decline of moral standards (by no means exclusively in the sexual sphere) and provided a potent justification of mass pornography. By challenging the moral authority of the churches and of established society, and by introducing the class struggle and the concept of collective guilt, Marxism in all its phases powerfully contributed to discontent and to conflict. The advocacy of the class struggle in particular encourages aggression, hostility and malice. The curative value of psychoanalysis is dubious; and Marxism does not solve problems, while creating new ones. As Lord Halsbury has said: 'What revolutionary movements have achieved . . . from 1789 to the present day is the wrecking of Western society by envy, malice and guilt.'[4]

The concept of collective guilt is one that requires more critical attention than it normally receives. I would not deny that there can be such a thing. The law recognises the principle when it finds several defendants in a murder case equally guilty if all have conspired to kill, even though only one may have done the deed. But the notion of 'class guilt' or 'historical guilt' is irrational. It is essential to distinguish between true and induced guilt. If I have enslaved an African or murdered a servant, then I am guilty of the practice of slavery and of murder. But if these things were done by my forebears, or persons belonging to the same class as my forebears, then I am in no sense guilty. Guilt is essentially personal, and to visit the sins of the fathers upon their sons and grandsons is the mark of the barbarian.

Yet thousands of adults suffer from the induced guilt propagated by Marxism. They *feel* guilty for what their grandfathers did to Africans and Asians during the era of expanding empire, or even for having attended expensive private schools. And because they feel guilty they strive to deprive a newer generation of access to private education (or medicine, or whatever seems to them to merit destruction) and regard

[3] A chilling and brilliant account of the age of exponential growth is contained in A. Koestler, *op. cit.*, pp. 313 et seq.
[4] In his commentary on Schoek: see my Introduction.

racial discrimination as inherently more heinous than general crimes against humanity. Such attitudes are irrational, and by that fact difficult to eradicate. They contribute to conflict and solve nothing.

The rationale of egalitarianism has always eluded me; nor do the egalitarians necessarily agree among themselves in their stated reasons for supporting a doctrine so evidently doomed to failure. But a common line of reasoning equates inequality with injustice. By removing inequalities, it is argued, social justice will be achieved, or at any rate furthered. The eradication of poverty is often linked, as an objective, with the elimination of inequality; although in practice, more emphasis seems to be given to the eradication of individual fortunes.

For my part, I readily concede that poverty is a cause of suffering, and that its elimination is desirable both on moral grounds and as a valid objective of social policy. (Egalitarians would equate the two, but this does not dispose of the distinction.) But it does not follow that the impoverishment of the rich materially contributes to the elimination of poverty. Where wealth is traditional, inherited and static (that is, in the form of land and property, or large but unproductive bank balances), its confiscation and redistribution will do little for the poor except to the extent that it is part of a land reform that will give peasants the means and the incentive to improve their lot. Where wealth refers to the large incomes of enterprising people—indeed, of entrepreneurs, or of managers—the opportunities for redistributive income tax and welfare projects undoubtedly exist. But a penal rate of personal taxation merely inhibits risk-taking and the exercise of managerial skill, and may actually contribute to the further impoverishment of the less fortunate as of the community as a whole.

The real, though unstated, reason for egalitarianism appears to be envy. The poor do not necessarily envy the very rich, especially if the gap between them is so great that imagination does not easily comprehend it. But revolutionary, or merely progressive, intellectuals will make it their business to stimulate envy where none existed. In fact, in a large community of mainly poor people, the act of depriving a handful of the very rich of their ownership of a Rolls-Royce or a private yacht, will not of itself make any difference to the poor, whose individual share of a car might be as unsatisfactory as, say, a gear-box or carburettor. Still, it is reasoned (tacitly, for envy is not a popular subject for discussion), remove the evidences of wealth and you will remove a cause of envy, and therefore of frustration and potential violence.

In fact, it is by no means proved that poverty, in itself, is a cause of conflict; or even that one cause may be the visible ('glaring' is a favourite adjective) inequalities of wealth.

History offers many examples of poverty-stricken societies that are relatively free of conflict (in our special sense). Current anthropological studies do not establish any correlation between poverty and conflict. Schoeck quotes the fascinating example—well known to anthropologists because it has been extensively studied—of Dobu, a small island off New Guinea. Nobody would claim that Dobu is envy-free: on the contrary, it is ridden with envy, and everybody appears to be envious of, and maliciously disposed to, everyone else. Anxiety is universal since everybody is wondering what his neighbours are up to, and busy on his side procuring their downfall by spells of one kind or another bought, and counter-bought, from the local sorcerers— evidently a well-heeled lot. Yet Dobu was remarkably stable and the conflicts apparently never erupted into violence, since envy was balanced by envy, and malice by malice.

When one turns to more civilised communities, whether in the East or the West, one is struck by the fact that, regardless of poverty or wealth, societies that are hierarchical and religious are less prone to envy and conflict than those that are egalitarian and free of doctrinal beliefs. In India, and other Asian societies in which the Hindu concept of Karma prevails, envy is at a discount, since Karma is in effect the trading balance of all the good and evil deeds of the present incarnation and past incarnations. Karma, it is acknowledged, is bound to produce irreversible inequality, since whatever one is, and whatever situation one finds oneself in, it has been brought upon oneself in some past existence. In India, until the advent of Western and Socialist ideas, there was very little envy between the castes, whatever degree of it may prevail within each caste. I am not here concerned with whether the Indian social system, in absolute terms, is good or evil: I merely note that in a country of desperate poverty, and glaring inequality of wealth, there has been remarkably little social conflict. Such conflict as there is has taken the form of religious strife as between Hindu and Moslem, or latterly in revolutionary activities imported into India from alien societies, or fostered by non-Indian ideologies, especially Marxism and its Maoist variant.

Schoeck refers to the New Testament's 'achievement in freeing believers from . . . this primitive, pre-religious, irrational sense of guilt, this universal fear of one's neighbour's envy and of the envy of the gods and spirits.'[5] In his unpublished commentary, Lord Halsbury

[5] Schoeck, Envy, *op. cit.*, p. 257.

clarifies the argument. Since we are all the children of a loving God, we shall all be rewarded in heaven on the basis of the courage, patience, altruism and faith with which we face our handicaps. In this way irreversible inequalities are explained away to the satisfaction of the disadvantaged and on a basis free of anxiety and guilt for those with advantages.

Similarly in societies in which a leader, universally admired, holds sway (as distinct from a resented tyrant) envy is dissolved and admiration takes its place, for the leader is seen as 'one of us, only better'.

Schoeck makes the point that envy-ridden societies are static and backward: cultural backwaters. But they are free of conflict to the extent that their individual envy and malice cancels itself out. The envy turns to conflict only when a more educated minority attempts to stimulate the egalitarian mass into greater effort or more intelligent application of resources than they have been accustomed to.

One of the characteristics of egalitarian societies is the phenomenon which Schoeck calls 'envy-avoidance'. This, he notes, is as characteristic of advanced egalitarian societies as of more primitive ones. For instance, in the world-famous kibbutzim of Israel, which are technically advanced and consist of intelligent hard-working and well-educated people, the phenomenon of envy-avoidance had led to psychological problems, and extreme difficulty in finding managers, who are afraid of provoking the envy of other members by assuming functions of leadership.

In his commentary on Schoeck's book, Lord Halsbury writes: 'Britain as the most egalitarian and therefore the most envy-ridden country in the Western world is paying the penalty by becoming the most backward and least progressive, as envy-ridden communities do. Innovation is at a discount. Workers will not accept automation; rail-road-ship container devices, and so on.' And he points out that Britain has slowly slipped behind France, Western Germany and Eastern Germany; that it is now slipping behind Italy; and that Japan will soon have overtaken Britain in Gross National Product per head. I am not sure that I would go so far with Lord Halsbury, while recognising that the egalitarian society is the most likely to foster conflict. It could be argued, for instance, that France in the 1950s was as relatively backward in economic performance as Britain was to be twenty years later, but France was not at that time any more egalitarian than it now is. The cause of Britain's relatively poor performance must therefore lie elsewhere; although it may well be that the attitudes fostered by egalitarianism and universal welfare are a contributory cause.

The point to be made, however, was that poverty has no direct correlation with conflict.

The spectrum of envy, as dissected by Halsbury from Schoeck's book, is fascinating. Under *Undirected Envy*, he lists: blind violence (including vandalism); the grudge or grievance or self-pity; and *Schadenfreude*, meaning malicious pleasure in the misfortunes of others. Under *Directed Envy*, he gives: malice (the ugly girl throwing vitriol at the pretty one); resentment and dislike; and ingratitude. Of these, perhaps the most relevant to the study of conflict is *Schadenfreude*, and Lord Halsbury's commentary gives examples drawn from British experience—which could doubtless be matched in other countries, of the malicious pleasure taken by television commentators and interviewers in humiliating the distinguished people they interview by making them look foolish. In view of the enormous potential of television, this constant ridiculing of authority must be accounted as one of the major factors in the decline of authority which I mentioned as one of the symptoms of the prevailing malaise.

To sum up:

—Hierarchies are less envy-ridden than egalitarian societies. Envy tends to be confined to equals or near-equals.
—Faith explains away irreversible inequalities and promotes contentment.
—Marxism (which considers religion to be the opium of the people) has in part destroyed religion, but the ideology it proposes is not spontaneously acceptable and needs to be imposed: hence, permanent conflict.
—Egalitarianism breeds envy, anxiety and guilt; hence impotence, frustration and aggression.

To this list should be added the concept of the class struggle, which encourages aggression, hostility and malice.

THREE

THE REDUCTION OF CONFLICT

The ground covered in this chapter

The search for emollients—making pornography unprofitable— merchants of hate and violence—censorship a last resort—declaring the violence-content of films and plays—the case for harsher treatment of television—alienation in post-industrial societies—capitalism and the suicide-complex—the case for shorter hours and voluntary restriction of superfluous production—definitions of 'participation'— totalism the outcome of 'participatory democracy'—failures of the party system—a polity for industrial and post-industrial societies: the no-party State—the need for a 'public philosophy'

IF THE 'aggravants' analysed in the foregoing passages are valid, then a search for 'emollients' must lie in radically different directions. In 1974, the hour was late. It was late in two senses: both for the world as a whole, facing the explosive problems of population and pollution; and for the Western countries in particular, for the United States and Britain, France and Germany and Italy. But at all times the remedies were in the hands of people, groups and governments. We have already considered the problems of subversion and terrorism, and proposed ways of dealing with them. What we are concerned with here is *the pre-conditions of revolutionary conflict*, and *the general vulnerability of Western societies*. Specifically, the need was for remedies to the following: the encouragement of hate, violence and pornography; the alienation of the industrial worker in the technological age; the foster-ing of induced guilt through egalitarianism; and the decline in public and private morality.

The long debate about pornography in various Western countries has been singularly unrealistic. In Britain and the United States, it has concentrated upon legal definitions of obscenity which can never be anything but subjective and arbitrary. It has never been difficult to find 'experts' ready to stand up in court and declare that what a judge or magistrate may have found obscene did not, in his or her view, constitute obscenity. Let us be quite clear what the issues are. The question is not whether to abolish pornography: the real issue is to reverse the recent trend whereby the pornographic trickle has become a flood, and a mass industry of pornography has grown up to meet an artificially stimulated demand, so that pornography has become inescapable, even to those who do not want it, or who are actively offended by it. It used to be a recognised principle of public morality that children, for instance, should be spared pornography: but even they cannot escape it when it surrounds them in bookstalls and is thrust upon them from public hoardings in the street.

If one realises that this is the real issue, then the remedy is fairly simple: it consists of depriving the pornographic industry of its market outlets. To do this, there is no need for either censorship or abolition. All that is needed is restrictive legislation, making it a punishable offence to display certain parts of the body in public, either in the flesh or in books, the screen or television. This ban should be absolute, and its infringement should be punishable by heavy fines and/or imprisonment. However, there would be no ban on pornography as such—merely on the public display of it. Each large city should have a declared area in which pornography, whether in the shape of books or the screen or the theatre, should be available to those who actively want it and request it. But establishments providing it, under special licence, would be required to deny access to children below a specific age. Even in such establishments, the ban on public display would be enforced. In large metropolises, such areas would probably be those traditionally associated in any case with this kind of trade: in London, it could be Soho; in New York it could be the area of 42nd Street and Times Square; and so forth. The effect of such legislation would be almost immediately to reduce the flood to a trickle, to remove the real problem of cultural pollution, to drive the pornographic industry largely out of business, and to restore critics to a sense of proportion, while again widening the public choice of entertainment, and protecting minors.[1]

Under such legislation, there need be no censorship of the printed

----

[1] I first put forward these proposals in a letter published in *Encounter* of June 1972. At about the same time, rather similar proposals were outlined, independently, by Sir Frederick Catherwood (a member of Lord Longford's committee on pornography) in a letter to the *Financial Times*. The Conservative government that fell in February 1974 had introduced a bill—unsatisfactory in other respects—to ban the public display of pornographic material of every kind.

word, of the moving image or even of the live theatre. And the judges and magistrates would be rescued from their insoluble dilemmas about the definition of obscenity.

The fostering of hate and violence is a more intractable problem, but not necessarily insuperable. It is obviously much harder to be specific about scenes of violence than about public displays of nudity. It would be absurd, and impossible, to ban the public display of specific acts of violence, for where would one draw the line? A blow on the head? A kick in the face? Scenes of torture? The machine-gunning of civilians? The burning of witches? There is no end to the potential list, and a ban based on specifics of this kind would be unenforceable. But here again, it is important to be clear about issues and objectives. Not all violence is necessarily objectionable. As a child, I doubt whether I was ever adversely affected by the mutual brutalities of cowboys and Indians or the spectacle of battles fought long ago. The same may not necessarily be true of cops and robbers in a contemporary setting.

The real problem, it seems to me, is one of quantity, quality and intent. As with pornography, modern Western societies are faced with a saturation by images of violence, or by accounts of it in fiction. It is not difficult to establish that a vast gulf exists between the bulk of today's cinematic productions and those of twenty or thirty years ago, since these are regularly shown on television screens in various countries. The difference is striking. The occasional act of violence did, of course, occur in older offerings. Today, there is so much of it that in most cases, it goes unnoticed and unrecorded by the critics: it is only the film of quite exceptional savagery that seems worthy of comment in this regard. Moreover, the extraordinary technological advances of the camera and projection room have made it possible to provide, in enormously magnified close-up, the most persuasive images of the physical disintegration of violence. The camera dwells gloatingly upon such scenes, and once again, the total effect is a form of pollution and a denial of choice to the public.

It used not to be exceptional to be offered dialogue of wit and intelligence, and acting of charm. In the 1970s, the voyeurism of sex, hate and violence had swept such luxuries away. This would be bad enough, in itself, but we the public were being invited by the critics and the legion of young and not-so-young producers and commentators to admire the poverty-stricken productions on offer, and to associate ourselves with their supposed 'social message'.

The remedy is not easy, nor is there much that legislation can do. It is difficult to legislate against a mood or in favour of the improvement of public taste. The unspeakable horrors of the ancient Greek tragedies took place off stage; in the 1970s, audiences or readers were required to witness explicit descriptions or enactments of events. Imagination was at a discount. Sadism replaced catharsis. We lived in an age of barbarism. It was hard to see how the swelling input of hate and violence could be reduced, still less eradicated, without some form of censorship. I am as aware of the evils of censorship as anybody, and the great problem has always been to limit its application. It may well be simply a question of degree. Self-censorship is obviously the best remedy, but there would be self-censorship only if the public outcry were sufficient to warrant it. The commercial purveyors of hate and violence would cease to pour out their offerings, only if faced with a dwindling market. The public—alas—tends to be apathetic, leaderless and helpless. However, the producers and distributors of hate and violence were unlikely to act to mend their ways if unprodded. A lead had to come from somewhere, and in the circumstances was unlikely to come from anybody except governments. To them, therefore, and to politicians whether in office or not, I offer the following thoughts and suggestions.

Censorship should not be ruled out entirely, but should, in the first instance, be kept in reserve as the ultimate sanction. It should be made clear that it has not been ruled out, as this in itself would be a form of pressure upon the purveyors to reduce the quantity of the stuff they peddle. In the meantime, a legislative start should be made by forcing publishers, bookshops, cinemas and theatres, and television stations, to make a public disclosure of the contents of the goods on offer. There are respectable precedents for such a course of action. In many countries, the manufacturers of pharmaceutical products are required to publish the formulae of their pills or potions. In some countries, public advertisements for tobacco wares are obliged to publish a warning notice about possibly injurious effects on health. Similarly, I suggest, the hate and violence content of a film, television programme or book or magazine should be publicly displayed. A typical notice concerning a new film, for instance, might read as follows: 'Screen time: 120 minutes. Violent content: 20 minutes. Rapes: 2. Torture: 1. Violent deaths: 10. Close-ups of violence showing blood: 15.'

Although I make this suggestion, I am by no means certain about the results that would be achieved. Any casual glance at the hoardings advertising violent films would show that the distributors considered it worthwhile to display, in the largest possible type, any quotations from the press notices dwelling upon horrifying details. It was evidently thought that this added to the attractions of the film. But it was possible that this kind of appeal to sadistic instinct would be considerably mitigated by the almost clinical formula I have proposed. At all events, legislation of this kind could be given a trial run. It might well be successful in stimulating public awareness of the problem and sales resistance to the product offered. At the very least, it would give people a warning of precisely what to expect after they had paid their money; and specifically, it would constitute a warning to parents. In the event of failure, however, the next legislative step would be to limit the screen time, or even conceivably the book space, devoted to explicit scenes of violence. I cannot imagine that a restrictive device of this kind would deprive the world of many great artistic masterpieces. It would certainly reduce the flow of violence, and its harmful effects upon the public—a more worthy objective, I think, than to protect the absolute right of producers and writers to cater solely for the voyeuristic minority. And if all else failed, censorship would be the last resort.

All the foregoing applies with particular force to television, which enters public homes by the million. The case for a collectively much harsher treatment of television than other media is overwhelming. It is true that the ultimate self-censorship lies in the hands of the viewers, who can, if they so wish, turn the box off. Many do. But the mindless and hypnotic propensity of the medium is notorious. Countless families sit in front of it regardless of what is on offer. The public good, whether or not they recognise it, requires that they should be better served. A start could be made by totally banning all violent material until a fairly late hour—say 11 p.m. in countries that eat fairly early, and 12 midnight or 1 a.m. in certain Hispanic countries where the last meal is consumed very late. In most countries, television is State-controlled, and the problem of eradicating or greatly reducing the hate–violence content of screen matter should be relatively easy. In Britain, the British Broadcasting Corporation competes with various commercial companies. The competition has not always been to the public benefit. In the United States, the situation is one of competitive anarchy. In all countries, whatever the system, there should be greater awareness than there now is of the need to regulate the content of programmes, not only in the sense of the hate, violence and pornography that are offered, but of the arrogance and presumption of programme organisers (unelected but wielding enormous power) to undermine public morality, to discredit the pluralistic system, to subvert the way of life, and to contribute in general to the problem of conflict.

Another problem that needed to be faced, especially by supporters of 'capitalism', was that of alienation in the industrial and post-industrial society. There was probably little to be done about the former. Not all countries that enter the industrial era need go through such suffering as Britain did during the Industrial Revolution or for that matter the Russians during the period of the early Five-Year Plans and Stalinist State terror. But industrial production, for those entering upon it, is unlikely ever to be of idyllic pleasantness. The problems of the post-industrial society were upon us, in a number of countries, and needed to be faced. It was already possible, and it was soon going to become a rule, that all the needs of the mass consumer, including food, could be satisfied by an ever decreasing labour force. Was mass unemployment to be the inevitable social consequence? Wedded to economic growth, and dreading the idleness of industrial equipment, egged on by the economists, the banks and the politicians, industry in the post-industrial era of mass consumerism faced ever sharpening problems of turnover.

Essentially, the problem was what to offer to consumers who were already sated. The 'solution' had been sought in planned obsolescence and the artificial creation of consumer needs through the mass advertising industry. Herbert Marcuse and others who criticised the absurdities of this state of affairs were not necessarily wrong because they happened to be Marxists. It was possible to be right about the diagnosis and wrong about the remedies proposed. One of the great successes of several generations of Marxist propagandists was that, by and large, 'capitalism' had become a dirty word, even among that great majority of the people in Western countries that enjoyed the benefits of capitalist abundance and was not in the least convinced of the truth of the Marxist case for the abolition of capitalism. But the solution did not lie in the abolition of the instruments of abundance, and the substitution of an inefficient State monopoly (with its proved propensity towards political tyranny) for the inestimable benefits of industrial competition. The correlation between modern capitalism and abundance for all was patent; so was the correlation between modern capitalism and the political liberties. (That was one reason for supposing that the authoritarian regime in Spain was bound, before too long, to yield to a more flexible system as economic abundance spread.)

In most Western countries (but not in the United States to anything like the same degree as elsewhere) 'capitalism', perhaps labouring under an induced guilt that stemmed from the reiteration of Marxist propaganda and was in no sense necessary, was extraordinarily timid. It was reluctant to venture into public affairs, shy of being seen to support parties that were against excessive state control, or to find money for organisations willing to defend the 'capitalist' system, as an indispensable element in the pluralist society. They were not alone in suffering from the collective suicide complex of the West; but they were in a position to carry the process further than most by the eagerness with which they rushed to build up the bankrupt economic system of the Soviet Union (as Lenin said, the capitalists themselves would provide the rope with which to hang themselves).

The captains of industry should be bolder than they had shown themselves hitherto, and readier to defend themselves against their detractors—especially against those who sought the total abolition of a uniquely flexible system that had shown itself over the decades to be highly amenable to improvement of one kind or another. But they needed also to face the fact that the Marxist criticisms of consumerism were not necessarily baseless. Unbridled advertising was also a form of environmental pollution, and the artificial stimulation of needs and planned obsolescence and waste—although essential to the system as it stood in the 1970s—were social absurdities, which cried out for revision. The solution to the social and political problems of the post-industrial age might well lie in the direction of drastically reduced working hours and weeks, with a tremendous extension of the shift system. It was surely better that thirty million people should have a twenty-hour week than that fifteen million should have a forty-hour week and the rest be unemployed.

This principle would permit the voluntary restriction of production of unnecessary lines. Abundance may be desirable; a superfluity of goods is redundant and absurd. The application of the principle of drastically reduced working hours would of course create an unprecedented problem of the use of leisure. Too little thought has been extended upon such issues. It is beyond the capacity of any single person to analyse the problem and propose acceptable solutions. But the studies needed to be done, and only industry was likely to have the money to finance such studies, which in the end might be essential for its own survival.

In recent years, much has been heard of 'participation' as a proposed remedy for the evils of the industrial and post-industrial society. As always, definitions are important. Participation can mean either profit-sharing in industry, or a share in industrial decision-making; or both. There is everything to be said for the first definition and almost nothing for the second. It is desirable that workers should be given a stake in the financial success of the enterprises to which their labour contributes. But large organisations cannot be run on a committee basis. The decision-making must be left to those taking the risks, and is best handed over to those with the necessary managerial skills and training. This does not, however, exclude the constitution of advisory boards with worker participation.

But participation need not be limited to industry, and in recent years, especially in Britain and France, there has been much public advocacy of the need to extend the principle to politics, including local government, and to the schools and universities. The phrase 'participatory democracy' has enjoyed a vogue. Whether through ignorance or deliberate intent, little emphasis, or none, has been placed by the advocates of political participation upon the totalist implications of their schemes. That totalism would be the outcome, however, cannot be in doubt, for such examples as already exist in the world make it clear that 'participatory democracy' is in fact the most totalist form of polity ever devised. The largest and most important example is the Chinese People's Republic, where the entire population is required to 'participate' in all the processes of government at all levels except the top (where the real decisions are taken). The result is an *inescapable* tyranny. In a true participatory system (of which there are other examples, such as the Republic of Guinea in Africa) it is impossible to opt out of participation. All who value the liberties of pluralism should relentlessly resist the trend towards participation.

A suitable polity for the industrial and post-industrial societies has not been found, mainly because it has not been sought. The assumption that representative party democracy is the ultimate form of political evolution remains firmly established. It underlay the drafting of the post-colonial constitutions which enabled Britain, especially, to shed her dependent territories in Asia and Africa in the 1950s and 1960s, with mainly disastrous results. It underlay the drafting of the Preamble to the North Atlantic Treaty in 1949; although realism later permitted the inclusion of Portugal, an authoritarian State (while illogically excluding the very similar regime of Spain). Such was the force of these ideological assumptions that the Alliance was seriously weakened when the Greek colonels took over in 1967, and when the Turkish army intervened in May 1971. It apparently occurred to very few observers to blame the Greek situation on the venality and irresponsibility of the politicians, or to ask themselves how much longer the Turkish high command could stand idly by while terrorism tightened its grip on the country.

The first duty of a government is to maintain order and guarantee the physical safety of the citizens and then property. This is best done through due process of law. But if the law enforcement agencies fail to enforce the law, then the armed forces, where the ultimate physical power lies, must be the ultimate resort. To state this is not to advocate Caesarism but to remind politicians of the possible consequences of failure.

In 1974, the signs of failure were uncomfortably widespread. In Italy, the State was in a condition approaching paralysis and the party system had long ceased to show proof of viability. In France, the ruling Gaullist party was showing signs of strain in the difficult post-de Gaulle period; financial and property scandals involving leading members of the party had undermined public confidence; and the alternative to the Gaullists was a Communist–Socialist front that seemed to offer either a totalist system or a 'democratic Marxist experiment' that stood no greater chance of success than the similar experiment in distant Chile (where President Allende's rule had brought runaway inflation, polarised the country's politics and ended in a military coup d'état and the death of the President in September 1973). In the German Federal Republic, the ruling Social Democratic party was deeply penetrated by Marxists, and the infiltration of left-wing extremists in various institutions had created a feeling of fragility in a country without long-standing democratic roots.

In the United States, the irresponsibility of officials in leaking information or stealing it, and of journalists in publishing it, had gravely weakened the capacity of the executive to govern; a trend which the inquisitorial conduct of congressional committees and the obsession of the media with the right to total freedom of the unelected powerfully accentuated. In Britain, the Irish troubles and the success of Marxist extremists in identifying themselves with normal trade union interests threatened respect for the law, social harmony and the economic foundations of the State; in the prevailing climate of permissiveness, the public watched with apathy and disillusion the mutually imitative performance of the political parties.

In the face of this general situation, complacency—the satisfaction with things as they were—was surprisingly tenacious, though quite unjustified. The plain fact was that the party system, in its various forms, was proving insufficiently adaptable to deal with the stresses of the time. There are really two aspects to this problem: the fundamental one of the nature of the system and its limitations; and the auxiliary one of the behaviour of politicians. The two are, however, closely linked, since in my contention the imperfections of the system exert a continuously harmful influence upon the behaviour of the men who work within it.

The fundamental defect of the party system is that it encourages—indeed makes inevitable—competitive appeals to the lowest common electoral denominator. Politicians standing for election make promises which more often than not they are not going to be able to implement. They make these promises because they fear that if they do not, their rivals will be elected. Rival promises are made in deference to the same fear (one hesitates to call it a principle). When a party is in power, the politicians of the opposition expend much of their time not in constructive criticism but in systematic attacks upon the ruling party for failing to carry out its promises (while aware that if electoral fortunes had favoured them, the situation would be reversed).

Moreover, the competition for the spoils of office, including patronage, is so fierce that politicians are under strong temptation to offer bribes of one kind or another (that is, either political or financial, or both), or even (if in office) to misuse or misappropriate public funds. In a parliamentary system (such as Britain's), problems of public policy are only rarely considered on their merits: if they were, the delicate balance of parliamentary arithmetic would be frequently upset and governments would be short-lived. Party discipline therefore prevails, as a rule (though not as an invariable one).

I have rarely found myself in agreement with the political philosophy of the late General de Gaulle, but on one point I believe he was entirely right: on the nefarious consequences of the 'regime of parties'. It was a constructive aspect of his unsatisfactory legacy that he reduced the number of political groupings in electoral competition and the power of parliament to frustrate the exercise of government. His criticism was, of course, particularly applicable to multi-party parliamentary democracy as practised in France during the Third and Fourth Republics. But it applies with still greater force to systems based on proportional representational, as in Holland, which foster prolonged ministerial crises and force parliamentary parties into artificial and unworkable governing coalitions.

In Presidential systems (such as the American or French), the executive is not at the mercy of parliamentary numbers; and in the American Congress, especially, voting on important issues is much freer than in the Parliament at Westminster. These lines were written at a time when the principle of 'executive privilege' was under strong congressional challenge as a result of the abuses of the Watergate affair. My own view is that the presidential system offers distinct advantages over the parliamentary, but over limited periods: mid-term elections and the four-yearly presidential race tend to paralyse executive action, while the problems that require attention do not stay suspended or disappear. Between times, the frustrations of a partly impotent House and Senate encourage inquisitorial committee meetings the effect of which is to make government impossible without any corresponding benefit to the public.

In *The Masters of Power* (London and New York, 1969), I outlined in some detail proposals for an alternative representational system that would avoid the disadvantages of existing systems while preserving the essentials of democracy and pluralism. My proposals were, not unexpectedly, ignored by the politicians, whose personal interests might well be adversely affected by the Crozier system if it were ever introduced. They were criticised in the press on grounds of alleged impractibility, and one of the critics invited me to stand for Parliament on a platform based upon my proposals and see what happened.

The critics, however, had missed the point. The vested interests involved in existing systems are clearly overwhelming, and the systems are consequently self-perpetuating. It would be absurd to expect politicians to espouse proposals designed to remove existing abuses; and there would be no point in standing for election on a platform designed to destroy the existing system, even if I had political aspirations (which I have not).

The point of putting forward alternative proposals was to invite the public to think about the remediable imperfections of existing systems in the light of my view that these systems are doomed anyway, so that when the collapse comes, we shall avoid the painful alternatives of totalism and authoritarian rule. My proposals (or similar alternatives) would clearly stand no chance of serious consideration until either a grave national emergency forced existing parties to bury their differences—perhaps to the extent of consenting to a loss of identity; or in the event of a total breakdown of the system and a military or dictatorial take-over. *The Crozier system might well commend itself to a military or authoritarian government wishing to return to democracy under conditions offering a greater chance of success than the system that had collapsed.*

All that has happened in the world during the past few years has deepened my conviction that my proposals, or variants on the same principles, offer the only viable alternative to existing democratic polities in the industrial and post-industrial societies.

Since a fuller discussion of the issues is available in the work I have mentioned, I confine myself here to a bare restatement of the principles. The Crozier system is based on the concept of the No-Party State, existing political parties to be replaced by a profession of politics, which would sponsor two candidates for each constituency in a general election. The losing candidate would enter Parliament or Congress or National Assembly, as well as the winner. The losing candidates would form the opposition, and the winners would take office. At each election, candidates would be shuffled around, so that they would not stand twice running for the same constituency.

This system, which lends itself to infinite local or national variations, would preserve the essential benefits of pluralist and representational democracy: freedom of choice; the right to change the government peacefully at the polls; freedom of dissent; and government with the consent of the governed.

Since I have conceded that no such system is remotely likely to be introduced except at a time of grave national emergency or collapse, we are left with the question whether the behaviour of politicians is subject to improvement within existing systems. The question is overwhelmingly a moral one, especially in view of the temptations and pressures inherent in the democratic processes. It was considered at length and dispassionately by Walter Lippmann in his interesting book, *The Public Philosophy* (London and Boston, 1955 and later editions), which ought to be required reading for all men and women in public life. Essentially, his thesis, which he expressed felicitously, was that 'free institutions and democracy were conceived and established by men who adhered to a public philosophy'; that modern democracies have abandoned it; and that they cannot hope to survive against the totalist counter-revolution until it is regained. Essentially, what Lippmann was writing about was a philosophy of civility, the notion that the public good transcends individual or sectarian interests.

Writing today, eighteen years after his book appeared, I am struck afresh by the truth of its message, and also by the distance travelled, in the wrong direction, since it was written. We shall not reverse the trend towards self-destruction until political leaders learn afresh the need, in their own enlightened self-interest, for a public philosophy. And we shall not produce public men imbued with the necessary spirit until we succeed in reversing the Jacobin and Marxist dominance of certain schools and certain faculties and the absence of a coherent public philosophy in those that are not so dominated.

I have described some of the moral dilemmas of our time. It is bound to be difficult to agree upon moral precepts when there is no consensual recognition of a higher source of morality. But on one point there is still a consensus, even if it is an eroding one: that representative democracy is a good thing. This in itself is not a bad basis for a fresh educational start; for it can be shown that representative democracies work only when those engaged in them observe the spirit in which free institutions were created in the first place. To recognise this spirit is the public philosophy.

Paradoxically, as Professor Stanislav Andreski has pointed out, this is a matter on which the democracies can learn from the Soviet Union. Though denying any authority higher than the Communist Party, the Soviet system inculcates in the young 'simple civic virtues such as honesty, respect for work and a sense of duty towards the community'.[2]

One was inclined, in the prevailing situation, to agree with Andreski's pessimistic conclusion that the communist side was bound to win in its deadly struggle with the democracies, however grim life may continue to be under communism, because the Communists understand the need for moral training (even if we do not share their concept of 'morality'), while the democracies increasingly fail to provide any guidance beyond the false liberation of 'nature'. But the remedy, as in so many things, is in our hands: that is, in the hands of leaders in all walks of life. May they act before it is too late.

[2] In a stimulating article, 'Life is What you Learn' in the *Daily Telegraph* magazine, 29 Sept. 1972.

INDEX